Wide Angle

JENNIFER CARLSON

NANCY JORDAN

OXFORD
UNIVERSITY PRESS

OXFORD
UNIVERSITY PRESS

198 Madison Avenue
New York, NY 10016 USA

Great Clarendon Street, Oxford, OX2 6DP,
United Kingdom

Oxford University Press is a department of the University of Oxford. It furthers the University's objective of excellence in research, scholarship, and education by publishing worldwide. Oxford is a registered trade mark of Oxford University Press in the UK and in certain other countries

© Oxford University Press 2019

The moral rights of the author have been asserted

First published in 2019

2023 2022 2021 2020 2019

10 9 8 7 6 5 4 3 2 1

No unauthorized photocopying

ISBN: 978 0 19 452855 9   2 Wide Angle American 2 SB W/OP Pack
ISBN: 978 0 19 452831 3   2 Wide Angle American 2 SB
ISBN: 978 0 19 454664 5   2 Wide Angle American 2 OP

Printed in China

This book is printed on paper from certified and well-managed sources

ACKNOWLEDGEMENTS

Back cover photograph: Oxford University Press building/David Fisher

Illustrations by: A. Richard Allen/Morgan Gaynin Inc pp. 6; Ricardo Bessa/Folio Illustration Agency pp. 26; Mark Duffin pp. 62; Shaw Nielsen pp. 13, 25, 37, 49, 61, 73, 85, 97, 109, 121, 133, 145.

Video Stills: Mannic Productions: pp. 12, 24, 36, 48, 60, 72, 84, 96, 108, 120, 132, 144. Oxford University Press: pp. 4, 38, People's Television: pp. 40.

The Publishers would like to thank the following for their kind permission to reproduce photographs and other copyright material: **123rf:** pp. 4 (4/daisydaisy), 7 (Miranda/Daniel Ernst), 28 (roomba or cleaning robot/Pashkov Andrey), 64 (5/Iakov Filimonov), 113 (speaker/kasto), 118 (concert/Melinda Nagy), 143 (airplane/Vereshchagin Dmitry), 148 (family/Iakov Filimonov); **Alamy:** pp. 16 (4/Everett Collection Inc), 28 (1/Blend Images), (6/philipimage), (7/Greatstock), (9/Ian Allenden), (UV sanitiser/Ian Shaw), 41 (coffee and bagel/Fudio), 53 (Maker Faire demonstration/Xinhua), 55 (fashion design class/Cultura Creative (RF)), 64 (1/Ian Allenden), (3/ JeffG), 66 (6/ Alan Wilson), 67 (hotel view/Dinodia Photos), 69 (Monaco street/Riccardo Sala), 78 (photography exhibition/Derek Hudson), 89 (stars/Blend Images), 90 (1/ Lev Dolgachov), (3/Rob potter), (hikinh/Colby Lysne), 94 (fallen off bike/Alvey & Towers Picture Library), 97 (Mount Kilimanjaro climbers/imageBROKER), 100 (chimneys/ BIOSPHOTO), 114 (Johnny Hayes/Trinity Mirror/MirrorpixRM), 117 (actors on stage/ Paul Doyle), (ballerinas/theatrepix), 125 (tour bus/Design Pics Inc), 127 (languages/ Elizabeth Leyden), 129 (students/Cathy Topping), 130 (whitewater rafting/SB Photography), 142 (1/Vicki Beaver), (3/Rawpixel Ltd); **BLINK:** Cover, Edu Bayer, pp. 3 (dancing/Krisanne Johnson), 9 (selfie/Edu Bayer), 15 (erderly women/Gianni Cipriano), 21 (women laughing/Krisanne Johnson), 27 (doctors and baby/Nadia Shira Cohen), 31 (NGO workers/Krisanne Johnson), 39 (sand dune/Quinn Ryan Mattingly), 41 (lunch time/Gianni Cipriano), 51 (visitor looks at Marco Tirelli's "Senza Titolo" (2013)/Gianni Cipriano), 52 (ceramic artist/Gianni Cipriano), 63 (window view/Gianni Cipriano), 71 (Halong Bay/Quinn Ryan Mattingly), 75 (selling goods/Krisanne Johnson), 77 (ice skating/Gianni Cipriano), 87 (man with puppets/Gianni Cipriano), 95 (storm/Gianni Cipriano), 99 (boys on rusty boat/ Nadia Shira Cohen), 105 (woman on land rover/Krisanne Johnson), 111 (backstage make-up/Gianni Cipriano), 123 (boat/Nadia Shira Cohen), 126 (Angkor Wat/Quinn Ryan Mattingly), 135 (fisherman/Quinn Ryan Mattingly), 136 (cramped escalators/ Quinn Ryan Mattingly); **Bridgeman:** p. 58 (Van Gogh Dr Gachet/Portrait of Dr Paul Gachet (oil on canvas), Gogh, Vincent van (1853-90)/Private Collection); **Dexas:** p. 28 (Mudbuster/Dexas International Ltd); **Getty:** pp. 4 (1/Lane Oatey/ Blue Jean Images), (2/Peter Cade), (3/Don Smetzer), 7 (Takeshi/Purestock), (Zaid/ Dimitri Otis), 10 (Sergio/Lisa Peardon), 16 (1/Morsa Images), (2/Jeff Greenough), (3/ Thomas Barwick), (5/W2 Photography), 18 (family/Ariel Skelley), 28 (4/SolStock), (8/Jordan Siemens), 49 (customers café/Peathegee Inc), 55 (cake decorating class/ AleksandarNakic), 58 (Cezanne card players/Paul Cezanne), (Monet haystack/ Heritage Images), 61 (shopping/Anouk de Maar), 64 (4/Daniel Grill), (6/Juanmonino), (8/BJI/Blue Jean Images), 66 (2/Rob Brimson), 68 (girl reading/Kosamtu), 76 (Brandon Stanton/STAN HONDA/Staff), 79 (2/Gary D Ercole), (4/National Geographic/Babak Tafreshi), (6/Caiaimage/Paul Bradbury), 80 (Ada Lovelace portrait/Science & Society Picture Library), 85 (car rain/Andy Sotiriou), 86 (boys/Kinzie Riehm), 90 (2/George Doyle), (4/Mark Wilson/Staff), (5/AleksandarNakic), (6/Joss Joss), 98 (trying on coat/ images by Tang Ming Tung), 100 (factory robot/RicAguiar), 101 (man running/ Westend61), (solar farm Sahara/FADEL SENNA/StringerRM), 103 (make a movie/ollo), 103 (tv contestants/Eric McCandless/Contributor), 106 (RoboThespian and human/ Laura Lezza/Contributor), 109 (friends in kitchen/Westend61), 110 (cycling to work/ Jasper Cole), (eating breakfast/BJI/Blue Jean Images), (eating breakfast in a cafe/Oscar Wong), (jogging in the park/Blend Images - Terry Vine), 117 (receiving an academy award/Kevin Winter/Staff), 118 (woman/JGI), 121 (people at beach/Hero Images), 124 (Machu Picchu/Markus Daniel), 130 (cycling/Saro17), 131 (autograph/Caiaimage/ Tom Merton), 134 (woman writing/RUNSTUDIO), 137 (orangutan/BAY ISMOYO/Staff), 139 (female graduate/DAMIEN MEYER/Staff), 140 (Maria Montessori in a classroom with children/Kurt Hutton/Stringer), 142 (2/CraigRJD), (4/Vesnaandjic), 146 (friends/ Hinterhaus Productions); **iStock:** p. xvi, (phone/lvcandy), (tablet/RekaReka); **Matthew & Michael Youlden:** p. 128 (Matthew and Michael Youlden/Matthew & Michael Youlden); **Newscom:** p. 46 (house on top of apartment/Compass/Cover Images), (skateboard house/CB2/ZOB/WENN.com); **OUP:** pp. 4 (5/Evdokimov Maxim/ Shutterstock), 79 (1/Brand X/Getty Images); **REX:** p. 115 (Eliud Kipchoge/Sergei Ilnitsky/Epa); **Shutterstock:** pp. 4 (6/ sirtravelalot), 7 (hong kong/ Sean Pavone), 10 (bedroom/ Photographee.eu), (boys/Syda Productions), 13 (business women/ Rob Marmion), 14 (friends talking/ Goran Bogicevic), 16 (6/ wavebreakmedia), 28 (2/ Andrey_Popov), (3/ wavebreakmedia), (5/ antoniodiaz), 29 (man with mop/ Air Images), 41 (chilli pepper/ Superheang168), 43 (aquarium/ Phattranit Wk), 44 (boat/ Dennis van de Water), 47 (expensive house/ Artazum), 64 (2/ Andrey Arkusha), (7/ gracethang2), 66 (1/ PR Image Factory), (3/ Rawpixel.com), (4/ Alexandra Lande), (5/ Olga Gavrilova), 73 (tent/nampix), 74 (Hong Kong harbor and skyline/ By), 79 (3/ Antonio Guillem), (5/ IVASHstudio), 82 (window washer / Immaginario75), 88 (little girls/ Zabavna), 91 (tree shelter/peter jeffreys), 93 (stormy house/ Ersler Dmitry), 100 (computer chips/ RAGMA IMAGES), (solar panels/ elxeneize), 103 (view/ Roman Shatkhin), 107 (computer programmer / ESB Professional), 110 (commuting to work by bus/ szefei), (gym/ UfaBizPhoto), 116 (cyclists/ Radu Razvan), 117 (live singer/ hurricanehank), (models/ Jade ThaiCatwalk), (musicians/Asia Images), 130 (ice swimming/ Khrushchev Georgy), (parachuting/ Thipawan kongkamsri), 133 (friends/371922811), 138 (insomnia/ amenic181), 142 (5/ motive56), (6/ voy ager), 148 (flower/ Krieng Meemano).

Authentic Content Provided by Oxford Reference

The author and publisher are grateful to those who have given permission to reproduce the following extracts and adaptations or copyright material:

p.7 adapted from "Jung, Carl Gustav." In *Who's Who in the Twentieth Century*.: Oxford University Press, 1999. http://www.oxfordreference.com/view/10.1093/acref/9780192800916.001.0001/acref-9780192800916-e-885?rskey=e0Y8Vt&result=14

p.18 adapted from "extended family." In *A Dictionary of Public Health*, edited by Last, John M.: Oxford University Press, 2007. http://www.oxfordreference.com/view/10.1093/acref/9780195160901.001.0001/acref-9780195160901-e-1437

p.31 adapted from "community." In *A Dictionary of Human Geography*. by Castree, Noel, Kitchin, Rob, and Rogers, Alisdair.: Oxford University Press, 2013. http://www.oxfordreference.com/view/10.1093/acref/9780199599868.001.0001/acref-9780199599868-e-253

p.58 adapted from "Painting." In *Oxford Encyclopedia of the Modern World* edited by Stearns, Peter N.: Oxford University Press, 2008. http://www.oxfordreference.com/view/10.1093/acref/9780195176322.001.0001/acref-9780195176322-e-1191

p.69 adapted from "Monaco." In *A Guide to Countries of the World* edited by Riches, Christopher, and Stalker, Peter.: Oxford University Press, http://www.oxfordreference.com/view/10.1093/acref/9780191803000.001.0001/acref-9780191803000-e-0141

p.80 adapted from "Byron, Augusta Ada." In *A Dictionary of Scientists*.: Oxford University Press, 1999. http://www.oxfordreference.com/view/10.1093/acref/9780192800862.001.0001/acref-9780192800862-e-239

p.88 adapted from "folktale." In *The Oxford Dictionary of Literary Terms* by Baldick, Chris.: Oxford University Press, 2015. http://www.oxfordreference.com/view/10.1093/acref/9780198715443.001.0001/acref-9780198715443-e-472

p.124 adapted from "Machu Picchu." In *The Oxford Companion To Archaeology* edited by Silberman, Neil Asher.: Oxford University Press, 2012. http://www.oxfordreference.com/view/10.1093/acref/9780199735785.001.0001/acref-9780199735785-e-0259

p.140 adapted from "Montessori, Maria." In *Who's Who in the Twentieth Century*.: Oxford University Press, 1999. http://www.oxfordreference.com/view/10.1093/acref/9780192800916.001.0001/acref-9780192800916-e-1156

p.147 "Mark Zuckerberg." In *Oxford Essential Quotations*, edited by Ratcliffe, Susan.: Oxford University Press, http://www.oxfordreference.com/view/10.1093/acref/9780191843730.001.0001/q-oro-ed5-00017121

p.148 "Sallust." In *Oxford Essential Quotations*, edited by Ratcliffe, Susan.: Oxford University Press, http://www.oxfordreference.com/view/10.1093/acref/9780191843730.001.0001/q-oro-ed5-00009096

p.149 "Lyndon B. Johnson." In *The Oxford Dictionary of American Quotations*, edited by Rawson, Hugh, and Miner, Margaret.: Oxford University Press, 2006. http://www.oxfordreference.com/view/10.1093/acref/9780195168235.001.0001/q-author-00008-00000855

p.150 adapted from "extreme candy." In *The Oxford Companion to Sugar and Sweets* edited by Goldstein, Darra.: Oxford University Press, 2015. http://www.oxfordreference.com/view/10.1093/acref/9780199313396.001.0001/acref-9780199313396-e-183

p.150 "William Cowper." In *Oxford Dictionary of Quotations*, edited by Knowles, Elizabeth.: Oxford University Press, 2014. http://www.oxfordreference.com/view/10.1093/acref/9780199668700.001.0001/q-author-00010-00000830

p.151 "Maya Angelou." In *Oxford Essential Quotations*, edited by Ratcliffe, Susan.: Oxford University Press, http://www.oxfordreference.com/view/10.1093/acref/9780191843730.001.0001/q-oro-ed5-00000286

p.152 "Ralph Waldo Emerson." In *The Oxford Dictionary of American Quotations*, edited by Rawson, Hugh, and Miner, Margaret.: Oxford University Press, 2006. http://www.oxfordreference.com/view/10.1093/acref/9780195168235.001.0001/q-author-00008-00000517

p.153 "Apple Computer, Inc.." In *The Oxford Dictionary of American Quotations*, edited by Rawson, Hugh, and Miner, Margaret.: Oxford University Press, 2006. http://www.oxfordreference.com/view/10.1093/acref/9780195168235.001.0001/q-author-00008-00000055

p.154 "Charles A. Dana." In *The Oxford Dictionary of American Quotations*, edited by Rawson, Hugh, and Miner, Margaret.: Oxford University Press, 2006. http://www.oxfordreference.com/view/10.1093/acref/9780195168235.001.0001/q-author-00008-00000406

p.155 adapted from "Robotic instruments." In The Grove Dictionary of Musical Instruments edited by Libin, Laurence.: Oxford University Press, 2014. http://www.oxfordreference.com/view/10.1093/acref/9780199743391.001.0001/acref-9780199743391-e-6371

p.155 "Alan Kay." In *Oxford Essential Quotations*, edited by Ratcliffe, Susan.: Oxford University Press, http://www.oxfordreference.com/view/10.1093/acref/9780191843730.001.0001/q-oro-ed5-00006158

p.156 adapted from Reed, Eric. "Cycling." In *Oxford Encyclopedia of the Modern World* edited by Stearns, Peter N.: Oxford University Press, 2008. http://www.oxfordreference.com/view/10.1093/acref/9780195176322.001.0001/acref-9780195176322-e-398

p.156 "Michael Eisner." In *The Oxford Dictionary of American Quotations*, edited by Rawson, Hugh, and Miner, Margaret.: Oxford University Press, 2006. http://www.oxfordreference.com/view/10.1093/acref/9780195168235.001.0001/q-author-00008-00000506

p.157 "Andy Rooney." In *The Oxford Dictionary of American Quotations*, edited by Rawson, Hugh, and Miner, Margaret.: Oxford University Press, 2006. http://www.oxfordreference.com/view/10.1093/acref/9780195168235.001.0001/q-author-00008-00001393

p.158 "Perfection." In *Oxford Essential Quotations*, edited by Ratcliffe, Susan.: Oxford University Press, http://www.oxfordreference.com/view/10.1093/acref/9780191843730.001.0001/q-oro-ed5-00008264

The publisher and authors would like to thank the following for their time and assistance:

Matthew and Michael Youlden, the Super Polyglot Brothers at https://www.superpolyglotbros.com/

With special thanks to:

Linda Lee

Alice Savage

Colin Ward

Cover photo by Edu Bayer.
Chicago, Illinois, USA, March 2016.
Tourists take selfies at the sculpture Cloud Gate (also known as "The Bean") by British artist Anish Kapoor, located in Millennium Park in the Loop community area of Chicago.

Contents

UNIT	READING	LISTENING	SPEAKING	WRITING
1 Identity **3**	Recognizing adjectives *Do you think with your head or your heart?*	Understanding positive and negative contractions	Making introductions	Linking ideas with *and*, *also*, and *too*
2 Relationships **15**	Identifying audience and purpose *Why do you live with your family?*	Recognizing the end of a sentence	Describing people	Opening and closing an email
3 Responsibilities **27**	Recognizing and understanding contrast linking words: *But* and *however* *Good, clean fun!*	Recognizing linkers for addition	Talking about habits and routines ▶ Stay-at-Home Dad	Checking your work: Accuracy in word choice
4 Extremes **39**	Recognizing parts of speech and using them to figure out meaning from context *Extreme foods*	Understanding incomplete speech	Describe a room	Describing something with the adverbs *quite*, *very*, and *really*
5 Creativity **51**	Recognizing and understanding cause and effect linking words: *Because, as, so* *Why DIY?*	Recognizing weak sounds	Describe a hobby	Using appropriate register
6 Places **63**	Scanning for specific information *Everyday adventures*	Listening for details	Giving advice in a presentation	Writing an interesting introduction

ENGLISH FOR REAL	GRAMMAR	VOCABULARY	PRONUNCIATION	REVIEW
▶ Meeting people	*Have* *Be* Questions with *be*	Personality adjectives ▶ What's your best friend like? Adverbs of degree	Intonation with *yes/no* and *wh-* questions	see page 147
▶ Asking someone to repeat something	Possessive adjectives Nouns: Countable, uncountable, and plural Possessive *'s* and possessive pronouns	Words to describe relationships Family Verb + preposition	Sentence stress	see page 148
▶ Requesting by phone	Simple present: Positive, negative, and *yes/no* questions The simple present and adverbs of frequency Subject and object questions in the simple present	Household chores Time expressions Work-related words	*Do* and *does* in *yes/no* questions and short answers	see page 149
▶ Ordering food and drink; complaining about service	*How much / How many* with countable and uncountable nouns Quantifiers: *a few / a little / a lot / lots* *There is… / There are…*	Describing food ▶ Waffle truck Prepositions of place	Linking with *there's / there are*	see page 150
▶ Asking for and giving opinions	Present continuous Verbs + *to* infinitive Simple present and present continuous	Hobbies Skills Time expressions	Contractions: *be* and *do*	see page 151
▶ Giving, accepting, and rejecting advice	*Have to* and *don't have to* *Can* for possibility *Should / Shouldn't*: Advice	Places ▶ Allison's neighborhood Vacation Adverbs of manner	Chunking	see page 152

UNIT	READING	LISTENING	SPEAKING	WRITING
7 People 75	Finding main ideas *Biography of Ada Lovelace*	Understanding contrast linkers	Talking about a childhood friend	Writing dates
8 Stories 87	Recognizing and understanding references: Subject and object pronouns *Missing 11-year-old girl found safe in woods*	Understanding the speaker's purpose	Using adjectives in a story	Choosing a title
9 Future 99	Using context clues *Four predictions for 2050*	Focusing on key words	Describing plans	Checking your work: Spelling and grammar
10 Performance 111	Previewing *Forty-seven minutes faster*	Listening for gist	Talking about likes and dislikes; giving preferences	Checking your work: Spelling rules
11 Experiences 123	Identifying opinions *Super Polyglot Brothers*	Listening for specific information	Talk about goals	Using pronouns to avoid repetition
12 Change 135	Using visuals and data *Effects of population growth*	Identifying levels of formality	Describe a change	Using *because* and *so* to talk about reasons and results

GRAMMAR FOCUS 159–170

ENGLISH FOR REAL	GRAMMAR	VOCABULARY	PRONUNCIATION	REVIEW
▶ Thanking and responding	Simple past: *Be* Simple past: Regular and irregular verbs Simple past questions	Time expressions Verbs	*Did you* and *did he*	see page 153
▶ Listening and showing interest	*Must* and *must not / can't* Past continuous Simple past and past continuous	Verbs Verbs Time expressions in stories	Silent letters	see page 154
▶ Giving encouragement	*Going to* and *will* for predictions *Be going to* and *will* for future plans and decisions *A / an*, *the*, and no article	Verbs for predictions Future time expressions	Contractions with *will*	see page 155
▶ Making, accepting, and refusing invitations	*-ing* forms Review of comparative and superlative adjectives; comparative adverbs Comparative adjectives; negative comparatives and superlatives	Adjective + preposition Performers and performances	Weak sounds	see page 156
▶ Making, accepting, and refusing offers	Present perfect with *for* and *since* Present perfect with *just*, *already*, and *yet* Present perfect with *ever* and *never*	Collocations with *for* and *since* Language learning	Contractions of *have / has*	see page 157
▶ Agreeing and disagreeing with opinions	Zero conditional First conditional	Climate change Noun suffixes: *-tion*, *-ment* Airplane travel	Suffixes and syllable stress	see page 158

Acknowledgments

AUTHOR

Jennifer Carlson holds a BA in Comparative Literature in English, German, and Spanish from the University of Massachusetts at Amherst. As a VISTA volunteer, she coordinated an ESL program for immigrants and refugees, and she has taught ESL/EFL in the United States and Mexico. She has been working in academic publishing for nearly two decades, more than half of which has been spent developing and writing content for Spanish and English language learning.

Nancy Jordan has written and edited numerous student books and workbooks in the area of academic ESL/EFL. She has taught general and academic English to adults and young adults in Portugal and in the Boston area. Currently, she is a writing tutor in the ELL program at Southern Maine Community College in South Portland, Maine.

SERIES CONSULTANTS

PRAGMATICS Carsten Roever is Associate Professor in Applied Linguistics at the University of Melbourne, Australia. He was trained as a TESOL teacher and holds a PhD in Second Language Acquisition from the University of Hawai'i at Manoa. His research interests include interlanguage pragmatics, language testing, and conversation analysis.

Naoko Taguchi is an Associate Professor of Japanese and Second Language Acquisition at the Dietrich College of Modern Languages at Carnegie Mellon University. She holds a PhD from Northern Arizona University. Her primary research interests include pragmatics in Second Language Acquisition, second language education, and classroom-based research.

PRONUNCIATION Tamara Jones is an instructor at the English Language Center at Howard Community College in Columbia, Maryland.

INCLUSIVITY & CRITICAL THINKING Lara Ravitch is a senior instructor and the Intensive English Program Coordinator of the American English Institute at the University of Oregon.

ENGLISH FOR REAL VIDEOS Pamela Vittorio acquired a BA in English/Theater from SUNY Geneseo and is an ABD PhD in Middle Eastern Studies with an MA in Middle Eastern Literature and Languages from NYU. She also designs ESL curriculum, materials, and English language assessment tools for publishing companies and academic institutions.

MIDDLE EAST ADVISORY BOARD Amina Saif Al Hashami, Nizwa College of Applied Sciences, Oman; **Karen Caldwell,** Higher Colleges of Technology, Ras Al Khaimah, UAE; **Chaker Ali Mhamdi,** Buraimi University College, Oman.

LATIN AMERICA ADVISORY BOARD Reinaldo Hernández, Duoc, Chile; **Mauricio Miraglia,** Universidad Tecnológica de Chile INACAP, Chile; **Aideé Damián Rodríguez,** Tecnológico de Monterrey, Mexico; **Adriana Recke Duhart,** Universidad Anáhuac, Mexico; **Inés Campos,** Centro de Idiomas, Cesar Vallejo University, Peru.

SPAIN ADVISORY BOARD Alison Alonso, EOI Luarca, Spain; **Juan Ramón Bautista Liébana,** EOI Rivas, Spain; **Ruth Pattison,** EOI, Spain; **David Silles McLaney,** EOI Majadahonda, Spain.

We would like to acknowledge the educators from around the world who participated in the development and review of this series:

ASIA Ralph Baker, Chuo University, Japan; **Elizabeth Belcour**, Chongshin University, South Korea; **Mark Benton**, Kobe Shoin Women's University, Japan; **Jon Berry**, Kyonggi University, South Korea; **Stephen Lyall Clarke**, Vietnam-US English Training Service Centers, Vietnam; **Edo Forsythe**, Hirosaki Gakuin University, Japan; **Clifford Gibson**, Dokkyo University, Japan; **Michelle Johnson**, Nihon University, Japan; **Stephan Johnson**, Rikkyo University, Japan; **Nicholas Kemp**, Kyushu International University, Japan; **Brendyn Lane**, Core Language School, Japan; **Annaliese Mackintosh**, Kyonggi University, South Korea; **Keith Milling**, Yonsei University, Korea; **Chau Ngoc Minh Nguyen**, Vietnam - USA Society English Training Service Center, Vietnam; **Yongjun Park**, Sangi University, South Korea; **Scott Schafer**, Inha University, South Korea; **Dennis Schumacher**, Cheongju University, South Korea; **Jenay Seymour**, Hongik University, South Korea; **Joseph Staples**, Shinshu University, Japan; **Greg Stapleton**, YBM Education Inc. - Adult Academies Division, South Korea; **Le Tuam Vu**, Tan True High School, Vietnam; **Ben Underwood**, Kugenuma High School, Japan; **Quyen Vuong**, VUS English Center, Vietnam

EUROPE Marta Alonso Jerez, Mainfor Formación, Spain; **Pilar Álvarez Polvorinos**, EOI San Blas, Spain; **Peter Anderson**, Anderson House, Italy; **Ana Anglés Esquinas**, First Class Idiomes i Formació, Spain; **Keith Appleby**, CET Services, Spain; **Isabel Arranz**, CULM Universidad de Zaragoza, Spain; **Jesus Baena**, EOI Alcalá de Guadaira, Spain; **José Gabriel Barbero Férnández**, EOI de Burgos, Spain; **Carlos Bibi Fernandez**, EIO de Madrid-Ciudad Lineal, Spain; **Alex Bishop**, IH Madrid, Spain; **Nathan Leopold Blackshaw**, CCI, Italy; **Olga Bel Blesa**, EOI, Spain; **Antoinette Breutel**, Academia Language School, Switzerland; **Angel Francisco Briones Barco**, EOI Fuenlabrada, Spain; **Ida Brucciani**, Pisa University, Italy; **Julie Bystrytska**, Profi-Lingua, Poland; **Raul Cabezali**, EOI Alcala de Guadaira, Spain; **Milena Cacko-Kozera**, Profi-Lingua, Poland; **Elena Calviño**, EOI Pontevedra, Spain; **Alex Cameron**, The English House, Spain; **Rosa Cano Vallese**, EOI Prat Llobregate, Spain; **Montse Cañada**, EOI Barcelona, Spain; **Elisabetta Carraro**, We.Co Translate, Italy; **Joaquim Andres Casamiquela**, Escola Oficial d'Idiomes – Guinardó, Spain; **Lara Ros Castillo**, Aula Campus, Spain; **Patricia Cervera Cottrell**, Centro de Idiomas White, Spain; **Sally Christopher**, Parkway S.I., Spain; **Marianne Clark**, The English Oak Tree Academy, Spain; **Helen Collins**, ELI, Spain; **María José Conde Torrado**, EOI Ferrol, Spain; **Ana Maria Costachi**, Centro de Estudios Ana Costachi S.I., Spain; **Michael Cotton**, Modern English Study Centre, Italy; **Pedro Cunado Placer**, English World, Spain; **Sarah Dague**, Universidad Carlos III, Spain; **María Pilar Delgado**, Big Ben School, Spain; **Ashley Renee Dentremont Matthäus**, Carl-Schurz Haus, Deutch-Amerikanisches-Institut Freiburg e.V., Germany; **Mary Dewhirst**, Cambridge English Systems, Spain; **Hanna Dobrzycka**, Advantage, Poland; **Laura Dolla**, E.F.E. Laura Dolla, Spain; **Paul Doncaster**, Taliesin Idiomes, Spain; **Marek Doskocz**, Lingwista Sp. z o.o., Poland; **Fiona Dunbar**, ELI Málaga, Spain; **Anna Dunin-Bzdak**, Military University of Technology, Poland; **Robin Evers**, l'Università di Modena e Reggio Emilia, Italy; **Yolanda Fernandez**, EOI, Spain; **Dolores Fernández Gavela**, EOI Gijón, Spain; **Mgr. Tomáš Fišer**, English Academy, Czech Republic; **Juan Fondón**, EOI de Langreo, Spain; **Carmen Forns**, Centro Universitario de Lenguas Modernas, Spain; **Ángela Fraga**, EOI de Ferrol, Spain; **Beatriz Freire**, Servicio de Idiomas FGULL, Spain; **Alena Fridrichova**, Palacky University in Olomouc, Faculty of Science, Department of Foreign Languages, Czech Republic, **Elena Friedrich**, Palacky University, **JM Galarza**, Iruñanko Hizkuntz Eskola, Spain; **Nancie Gantenbein**, TLC-IH, Switzerland; **Gema García**, FOI, Spain; **Maria Jose Garcia Ferrer**, EOI Moratalaz, Spain; **Josefa García González**, EOI Málaga, Spain; **Maria García Hermosa**, EOI, Spain; **Jane Gelder**, The British Institute of Florence, Italy; **Aleksandra Gelner**, ELC Katowice, Bankowa 14, Poland; **Marga Gesto**, EOI Ferrol, Spain; **Juan Gil**, EOI Maria Moliner, Spain; **Eva Gil Cepero**, EOI La Laguna, Spain; **Alan Giverin**, Today School, Spain; **Tomas Gomez**, EOI Segovia, Spain; **Mónica González**, EOI Carlos V, Spain; **Elena González Diaz**, EOI, Spain; **Steve Goodman**, Language Campus, Spain; **Katy Gorman**, Study Sulmona, Italy; **Edmund Green**, The British Institute of Florence, Italy; **Elvira Guerrero**, GO! English Granada, Spain; **Lauren Hale**, The British Institute of Florence, Italy; **Maria Jose Hernandez**, EOI de Salou, Spain; **Chris Hermann**, Hermann Brown English Language Centre, Spain; **Robert Holmes**, Holmes English, Czech Republic; **José Ramón Horrillo**, EOI de Aracena, Spain; **Laura Izquierdo**, Univeristy of Zaragoza, Spain; **Marcin Jaśkiewicz**, British School Żoliborz, Poland; **Mojmír Jurák**, Albi - jazyková škola, Czech Republic; **Eva Kejdová**, BLC, Czech Republic; **Turlough Kelleher**, British Council, Callaghan School of English, Spain; **Janina Knight**, Advantage Learners, Spain; **Ewa Kowalik**, English Point Radom, Poland; **Monika Krawczuk**, Wyższa Szkoła Finansów i Zarządzania, Poland; **Milica Krisan**, Agentura Parole, Czech Republic; **Jędrzej Kucharski**, Profi-lingua, Poland; **V. Lagunilla**, EOI San Blas, Spain; **Antonio Lara Davila**, EOI La Laguna, Spain; **Ana Lecubarri**, EOI Aviles, Spain; **Lesley Lee**, Exit Language Center, Spain; **Jessica Lewis**, Lewis Academy, Spain; **Alice Llopas**, EOI Estepa, Spain; **Angela Lloyd**, SRH Hochschule Berlin, Germany; **Helena Lohrová**, University of South Bohemia, Faculty of Philosophy, Czech Republic; **Elena López Luengo**, EOI Alcalá de Henares, Spain; **Karen Lord**, Cambridge House, Spain; **Carmen Loriente Duran**, EOI Rio Vero, Spain; **Alfonso Luengo**, EOI Jesús Maestro Madrid, Spain; **Virginia Lyons**, VLEC, Spain; **Anna Łętowska-Mickiewicz**, University of Warsaw, Poland; **Ewa Malesa**, Uniwersytet SWPS, Poland; **Klara Małowiecka**, University of Warsaw, Poland; **Dott. Ssa Kim Manzi**, Università degli Studi della Tuscia - DISTU – Viterbo, Italy; **James Martin**, St. James Language Center, Spain; **Ana Martin Arista**, EOI Tarazona, Spain; **Irene Martín Gago**, NEC, Spain; **Marga Martínez**, ESIC Idiomas Valencia, Spain; **Kenny McDonnell**, McDonnell English Services S.I., Spain; **Anne Mellon**, EEOI Motilla del Palacar, Spain; **Miguel Ángel Meroño**, EOI Cartagena, Spain; **Joanna Merta**, Lingua Nova, Poland; **Victoria Mollejo**, EOI San Blas-Madrid, Spain; **Rebecca Moon**, La Janda Language Services, Spain; **Anna Morales Puigicerver**, EOI TERRASSA, Spain; **Jesús Moreno**, Centro de Lenguas Modernas, Universidad de Zaragoza, Spain; **Emilio Moreno Prieto**, EOI

Universidad Cesar Vallejo Centro de Idiomas, Peru; **Jim Osorio**, Instituto Guatemalteco Americano, Guatemala; **Erika del Carmen Partida Velasco**, Univam, Mexico; **Mrs. Katterine Pavez**, Universidad de Atacama, Chile; **Sergio Peña**, Universidad de La Frontera, Chile; **Leonor Cristina Peñafort Camacho**, Universidad Autónoma de Occidente, Colombia; **Tom Rickman**, British Council, Colombia; **Olga Lucia Rivera**, Universidad Externado de Colombia, Colombia; **Maria-Eugenia Ruiz Brand**, DUOC UC, Chile; **Gabriela S. Eguiarte**, London School, Mexico; **Majid Safadaran**, Instituto Cultural Peruano Norteamericano, Peru; **María Ines Salinas**, UCASAL, Argentina; **Ruth Salomon-Barkmeyer**, UNILINGUAS – UNISINOS, Brazil; **Mario Castillo Sanchez Hidalgo**, Universidad Panamericana, Mexico; **Katrina J. Schmidt**, Universidad de Los Andes, Colombia; **Jacqueline Sedore**, The Language Company, Chile; **Lourdes Angelica Serrano Herrera**, Adler Schule, Mexico; **Antonio Diego Sousa de Oliveira**, Federal University of Amazonas, Brazil; **Padraig Sweeney**, Universidad Sergio Arboleda, Colombia; **Edith Urquiza Parra**, Centro Universitario México, Mexico; **Eduardo Vásquez**, Instituto Chileno Britanico de Cultura, Chile; **Patricia Villasante**, Idiomas Católica, Peru; **Malaika Wilson**, The Language Company, Chile; **Alejandra Zegpi-Pons**, Universidad Católica de Temuco, Chile; **Boris Zevallos**, Universidad Cesar Vallejo Centro de Idiomas, Peru; **Wilma Zurita Beltran**, Universidad Central del Ecuador, Ecuador

THE MIDDLE EAST Chaker Ali Mhamdi, Buraimi University College, Oman; **Salama Kamal Shohayb**, Al-Faisal International Academy, Saudi Arabia

TURKEY M. Mine Bağ, Sabanci University, School of Languages; **Suzanne Campion**, Istanbul University; **Daniel Chavez**, Istanbul University Language Center; **Asuman Cincioğlu**, Istanbul University; **Hatice Çelikkanat**, Istanbul Esenyurt University; **Güneş Yurdasiper Dal**, Maltepe University; **Angeliki Douri**, Istanbul University Language Center; **Zia Foley**, Istanbul University; **Frank Foroutan**, Istanbul University Language Center; **Nicola Frampton**, Istanbul University; **Merve Güler**, Istanbul University; **H. Ibrahim Karabulut**, Dumlupınar University; **Catherine McKimm**, Istanbul University; **Merve Oflaz**, Dogus University; **Burcu Özgül**, Istanbul University; **Yusuf Özmenekşe**, Istanbul University Language Center; **Lanlo Pinter**, Istanbul University Language Center; **Ahmet Rasim**, Amasya University; **Diana Maria Rios Hoyos**, Istanbul University Language Center; **Jose Rodrigues**, Istanbul University; **Dilek Eryılmaz Salkı**, Ozyegin University; **Merve Selcuk**, Istanbul Kemerburgaz University; **Mehdi Solhi Andarab**, Istanbul Medipol University; **Jennifer Stephens**, Istanbul University; **Özgür Şahan**, Bursa Technical University; **Fatih Yücel**, Beykent University

UNITED KINGDOM Sarah Ali, Nottingham Trent International College, Nottingham; **Rolf Donald**, Eastbourne School of English, Eastbourne, East Sussex; **Nadine Early**, ATC Language Schools, Dublin, Ireland; **Dr. Sarah Ekdawi**, Oxford School of English, Oxford; **Glynis Ferrer**, LAL Torbay, Paignton Devon; **Diarmuid Fogarty**, INTO Manchester, Manchester; **Ryan Hannan**, Hampstead School of English, London; **Neil Harris**, ELTS, Swansea University, Swansea; **Claire Hunter**, Edinburgh School of English, Edinburgh, Scotland; **Becky Ilk**, LAL Torbay, Paignton; **Kirsty Matthews**, Ealing, Hammersmith & West London's college, London; **Amanda Mollaghan**, British Study Centres London, London; **Shila Nadar**, Twin ECL, London; **Sue Owens**, Cambridge Academy of English, Girton, Cambridge; **Caroline Preston**, International House Newcastle, Newcastle upon Tyne; **Ruby Rennie**, University of Edinburgh, Edinburgh, Scotland; **Howard Smith**, Oxford House College, London; **Yijie Wang**, The University of Edinburgh, Scotland; **Alex Warren**, Eurotraining, Bournemouth

UNITED STATES Christina H. Appel, ELS Educational Services, Manhattan, NY; **Nicole Bollhalder**, Stafford House, Chicago, IL; **Rachel Bricker**, Arizona State University, Tempe, AZ; **Kristen Brown**, Massachusetts International Academy, Marlborough, MA; **Tracey Brown**, Parkland College, Champaign, IL; **Peter Campisi**, ELS Educational Services, Manhattan, NY; **Teresa Cheung**, North Shore Community College, Lynn, MA; **Tyler Clancy**, ASC English, Boston, MA; **Rachael David**, Talk International, Miami, FL; **Danielle De Koker**, ELS Educational Services, New York, NY; **Diana Djaboury**, Mesa Community College, Mesa, AZ; **Mark Elman**, Talk International, Miami, FL; **Dan Gauran**, EC English, Boston, MA; **Kerry Gilman**, ASC English, Boston, MA; **Heidi Guenther**, ELS Educational Services, Manhattan, NY; **Emily Herrick**, University of Nebraska-Lincoln, Lincoln, NE; **Kristin Homuth**, Language Center International, Southfield, MI; **Alexander Ingle**, ALPS Language School, Seattle, WA; **Eugenio Jimenez**, Lingua Language Center at Broward College, Miami, FL; **Mahalia Joeseph**, Lingua Language Center at Broward College, Miami, FL; **Melissa Kaufman**, ELS Educational Services, Manhattan, NY; **Kristin Kradolfer Espinar**, MILA, Miami, FL; **Larissa Long**, TALK International, Fort Lauderdale, FL; **Mercedes Martinez**, Global Language Institute, Minneapolis, MN; **Ann McCrory**, San Diego Continuing Education, San Diego, CA; **Simon McDonough**, ASC English, Boston, MA; **Dr. June Ohrnberger**, Suffolk County Community College, Brentwood, NY; **Fernanda Ortiz**, Center for English as a Second Language at the University of Arizona, Tuscon, AZ; **Roberto S. Quintans**, Talk International, Miami, FL; **Terri J. Rapoport**, ELS, Princeton, NJ; **Alex Sanchez Silva**, Talk International, Miami, FL; **Cary B. Sands**, Talk International, Miami, FL; **Joseph Santaella Vidal**, EC English, Boston, MA; **Angel Serrano**, Lingua Language Center at Broward College, Miami, FL; **Timothy Alan Shaw**, New England School of English, Boston, MA; **Devinder Singh**, The University of Tulsa, Tulsa, OK; **Daniel Stein**, Lingua Language Center at Broward College, Miami, FL; **Christine R. Stesau**, Lingua Language Center at Broward College, Miami, FL; **David Stock**, ELS Educational Services, Manhattan, NY; **Joshua Stone**, Approach International Student Center, Allston, MA; **Maria-Virginia Tanash**, EC English, Boston, MA; **Noraina Vazquez Huyke**, Talk International, Miami, FL

Overview

A REAL-WORLD VIEWPOINT

Whatever your goals and aspirations, *Wide Angle* helps you use English to connect with the world around you. It empowers you to join any conversation and say the right thing at the right time, with confidence.

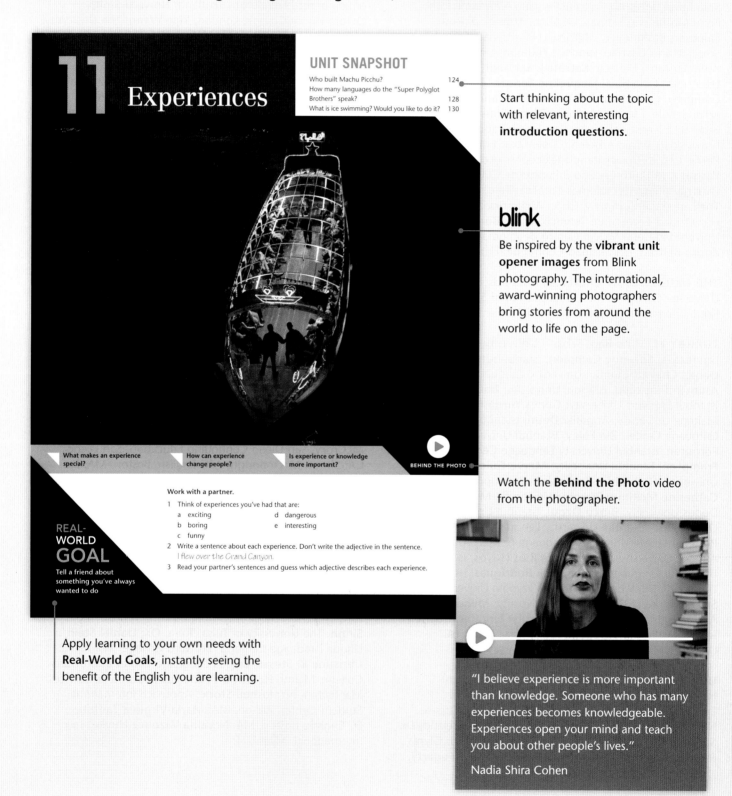

11 Experiences

UNIT SNAPSHOT

Who built Machu Picchu? 124
How many languages do the "Super Polyglot Brothers" speak? 128
What is ice swimming? Would you like to do it? 130

Start thinking about the topic with relevant, interesting **introduction questions**.

blink

Be inspired by the **vibrant unit opener images** from Blink photography. The international, award-winning photographers bring stories from around the world to life on the page.

BEHIND THE PHOTO

Watch the **Behind the Photo** video from the photographer.

What makes an experience special?

How can experience change people?

Is experience or knowledge more important?

Work with a partner.

1 Think of experiences you've had that are:
   a exciting   d dangerous
   b boring   e interesting
   c funny
2 Write a sentence about each experience. Don't write the adjective in the sentence.
   I flew over the Grand Canyon.
3 Read your partner's sentences and guess which adjective describes each experience.

REAL-WORLD GOAL

Tell a friend about something you've always wanted to do

Apply learning to your own needs with **Real-World Goals**, instantly seeing the benefit of the English you are learning.

"I believe experience is more important than knowledge. Someone who has many experiences becomes knowledgeable. Experiences open your mind and teach you about other people's lives."

Nadia Shira Cohen

Enjoy learning with the huge variety of **up-to-date, inventive and engaging audio and video**.

Understand what to say and how to say it with **English For Real**.

These lessons equip you to choose and adapt appropriate language to communicate effectively in any situation.

ENGLISH FOR REAL

1 ACTIVATE Discuss the questions with a partner.

1 When was the last time you offered something to someone? Did the person accept (say yes to) or refuse (say no to) the offer? Why?

2 When was the last time someone offered something to you? Did you accept or refuse the offer? Why?

2 ▶ IDENTIFY Watch the video. What offers does Andy make? Does Max accept or refuse the offers?

What is the offer?	Does Max accept or refuse the offer?

3 ▶ ANALYZE Watch the video again. What words does Max use to accept or refuse the offers? Why do you think he chose those words?

REAL-WORLD ENGLISH Making, accepting, and refusing offers

To make offers, we can say:
You can use my phone.
Would you like a cup of coffee?
Would you like me to open a window?

To accept offers, we can say:
Great, thanks. (for smaller offers)
That's very / really nice of you, thanks. (for bigger offers)
That would be great. (for bigger offers)

To refuse offers, we can say:
That's all right, thanks. (for smaller offers)
That's OK, I can just… (for smaller offers)
That's very / really nice of you, thanks. But… (for bigger offers)

4 ANALYZE Work with a partner, and read the situations language could you use for offering, refusing, and accep

1 Someone forgets their pen in class, and another stude

2 A group of friends are in a restaurant. One of them re with them, and someone offers to buy them dinner.

3 A group of colleagues are having an informal meeting decides to join them. One of the group offers to get t

5 PREPARE Work with a partner. Write a short conversat Exercise 4. Use the language from the Real-World English acceptance or a refusal.

132

6 INTERACT Practice reading the conversations from Exe

7 ANALYZE Work with another pair. Watch their role plays. How did they make an offer in each conversation? Did they accept or refuse the offer? Was their language appropriate?

GO ONLINE
to create your own version of the
English For Real video.

133

Step into the course with **English For Real videos** that mimic real-life interactions. You can record your voice and respond in real time for out-of-class practice that is relevant to your life.

COMPREHENSIVE SYLLABUS

Ensure progress in all skills with a pedagogically consistent and appropriately leveled syllabus.

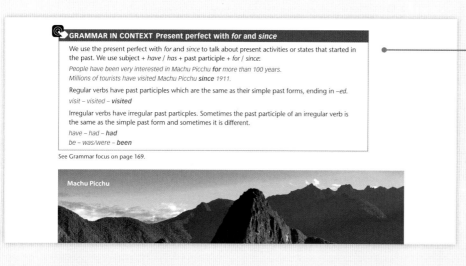

2 VOCABULARY Complete the sentences with words from the box.

method	meaning	translate	progress
memory	communicate	culture	goal

♀ Oxford 3000™

1 Robert can read Spanish, but he can't _____ in Spanish very well.
2 Lily has an excellent _____. She never forgets a name.
3 Kadir is studying Turkish. His _____ is to speak Turkish to his grandparents when he visits Istanbul next summer.
4 My favorite _____ of learning a language is to listen to songs while reading the lyrics (words).
5 Our Arabic teacher gives us a test every week to measure our _____.
6 I don't speak Portuguese. Can you please _____ this into English for me?
7 I'm really interested in Chinese _____. I like learning about Chinese food, holidays, and beliefs.
8 You can often guess the _____ of a word by looking at the words near it.

3 WHAT'S YOUR ANGLE? Discuss the questions with a partner.

1 Do you have a good memory? What is easy for you to remember? What is difficult for you to remember?
2 What is your favorite method of learning a language?
3 What cultures do you know a lot about? Which cultures would you like to learn

▼ VOCABULARY

The ♀Oxford 3000™ is a word list containing the most important words to learn in English. The words are chosen based on frequency in the Oxford English Corpus and relevance to learners of English. Every word is aligned to the CEFR, guiding you on the words you should know at each level.

⊚ GRAMMAR IN CONTEXT Present perfect with *for* and *since*

We use the present perfect with *for* and *since* to talk about present activities or states that started in the past. We use subject + *have / has* + past participle + *for / since*:

*People have been very interested in Machu Picchu **for** more than 100 years.*
*Millions of tourists have visited Machu Picchu **since** 1911.*

Regular verbs have past participles which are the same as their simple past forms, ending in –*ed*.

*visit – visited – **visited***

Irregular verbs have irregular past particples. Sometimes the past participle of an irregular verb is the same as the simple past form and sometimes it is different.

*have – had – **had***
*be – was/were – **been***

See Grammar focus on page 169.

Machu Picchu

▼ GRAMMAR

The carefully graded grammar syllabus ensures you encounter the most relevant language at the right point in your learning.

11.1 A Wonder of the World

1 ACTIVATE What do you know about Machu Picchu? Discuss these questions with a group.

1 Where is Machu Picchu?   3 How old is it?
2 Why is it famous?   4 Who lived there?

2 IDENTIFY Read the report about Machu Picchu. Does it mention any of the things you talked about in Exercise 1?

Machu Picchu is the site of an ancient city high in the mountains of southern Peru. The Incas lived in Machu Picchu in the 1400s and 1500s. They made buildings, walls, streets, and steps from stones. They left the city before they completed it, probably because of a war. After that, no one knew about the city for many years.

People have been very interested in Machu Picchu for more than 100 years. Millions of tourists have visited Machu Picchu since 1911. In that year, the American explorer Hiram Bingham "discovered" it. Now, hundreds of thousands of people visit Machu Picchu every year. In 2007, people chose it as one of the New Seven Wonders of the World. The Peruvian government has tried to protect Machu Picchu and prevent damage to the mountainside.

—adapted from "Machu Picchu," in *The Oxford Companion to Archaeology*, 2nd ed., edited by Neil Asher Silberman

Oxford Reference is a trusted source of over two million authentic academic texts.

Free access to the Oxford Reference site is included with Student Books 4, 5, and 6.

Explicit reading and listening skills focus on helping you access and assimilate information confidently in this age of rapid information.

READING SKILL Identifying opinions

When you read, it is important to know when someone is giving their opinion (saying what they think). To identify opinions, look for expressions like the following:

I think (that)…
I feel (that)…
I believe (that)…
In my opinion,…

4 IDENTIFY Read the article. Find four opinions.

Super Polyglot Brothers

Matthew and Michael Youlden are twin brothers. They're also polyglots—they speak many languages. The brothers have studied languages together since they were eight years old. They've already learned eleven languages, and they plan to learn more! Michael says, "I haven't learned to speak Dutch yet, but I really want to."

The "Super Polyglot Brothers" believe that anyone can learn a lot of languages. It isn't necessary to have an excellent memory or a special study method. Matthew feels that the most important thing is to have a goal. Michael thinks that you should study a language if you are interested in a country's culture. Both brothers believe that having a partner helps them learn languages. Matthew says, "We're lucky. We've always had someone to practice communicating with." But competition between the brothers also helps. They each want to know more languages (and speak them better) than their brother!

Matthew   Michael

5 WHAT'S YOUR ANGLE? Do you agree with Matthew and Michael's opinions? Discuss your opinions with a partner.

Opinion	Do you agree or disagree?	Does your partner agree or disagree?
1		
2		
3		
4		

128

Build confidence with the **activation-presentation-practice-production** method, with activities moving from controlled to less controlled, with an increasing level of challenge.

GRAMMAR IN CONTEXT Present perfect with *just*, *already*, and *yet*

We can use *just*, *already*, and *yet* in present perfect sentences.

We use *just* in positive sentences to talk about very recent events and actions.
*He **has just started** learning Korean.*

We use *yet* in questions and negative sentences to talk about events and actions up to now.
*Have you **learned** the present perfect tense **yet**?   Yes, I have.   No, I haven't.*
*I **haven't studied** Dutch yet.*

We use *already* in positive sentences to talk about events that happened before now or earlier than expected.
*They**'ve already learned** eleven languages.*

We usually use the short forms (*I've, you've, we've, he's, she's, it's, they've*) in speaking.

See Grammar focus on page 169.

6 APPLY Complete the sentences with *just*, *already*, or *yet*. Sometimes more than one answer is possible.
1   Taylor hasn't cut the grass _____. He'll do it tomorrow.
2   Have you visited Machu Picchu _____?
3   Ben has _____ graduated from college, and he _____ has a job!
4   I've _____ bought his birthday present.
5   They've _____ arrived at the airport.

7 INTEGRATE Complete the sentences with the present perfect and *just*, *already*, or *yet*.
1   _____ you _____ (do) the Portuguese homework *just / already / yet*?
2   Sam is only ten years old, and he _____ *just / already / yet* _____ (learn) three languages!
3   Lina _____ *just / already / yet* _____ (start) learning English. She only knows a few words.
4   I don't want to watch that movie. I _____ *just / already / yet* _____ (see) it.
5   They _____ (not study) for the French test *just / already / yet*. They're going to study tonight.

8 WHAT'S YOUR ANGLE? Work with a small group. Discuss your experiences learning a language.
1   What helped you the most?
2   What was most difficult for you?
3   How well do you speak the language? Do you want to improve? How do you plan to do that?

129

Personalize the lesson topics and see how the language can work for you with **What's Your Angle** activities.

WRITING SKILL Using pronouns to avoid repetition

When we write, we use subject pronouns (*I, you, we, he, she, it, they*) and object pronouns (*me, you, us, him, her, it, them*) to avoid repeating the noun.

In this sentence, *it* refers to *Machu Picchu*.
*People have been very interested in **Machu Picchu** since 1911. In that year, the American explorer Hiram Bingham "discovered" **it**.*

6 APPLY Rewrite the second sentence in each set. Replace the repeated nouns with pronouns.
1   My mother called last night. My mother wanted to talk about our trip to Peru.
2   The Incas built a beautiful city. The Incas made the city from stone.
3   My cousins visited last month. I gave my cousins a tour of my city.
4   Henry is leaving for vacation tomorrow. I'm going to give Henry a ride to the airport.
5   Many people visit Machu Picchu. People travel from all over the world to see Machu Picchu.

◥ WRITING

The writing syllabus focuses on the writing styles needed for today, using a **process writing approach** of **prepare-plan-draft-review-correct** to produce the best possible writing.

3 ◀) EXPAND Listen again. What do the people need to do next? Take notes.

PRONUNCIATION SKILL Contractions of *have / has*

◀) In speaking, we usually contract the subject pronoun and *have* or *has*.

Listen to the pronunciation of these contractions. Notice that the *s* sounds like /s/ in *it's*, but it sounds like /z/ in *he's* and *she's*.

you've	we've	she's
they've	he's	it's

4 ◀) NOTICE Listen to the sentences. What sound do you hear at the end of the contractions?
1   /s/   /z/   /v/   4   /s/   /z/   /v/
2   /s/   /z/   /v/   5   /s/   /z/   /v/
3   /s/   /z/   /v/

5 APPLY Work with a partner. Take turns reading the sentences aloud. Give your partner feedback on their pronunciation of the contractions.

◥ SPEAKING

Speaking and **pronunciation skills** build the functional language you need outside of class.

A BLENDED LEARNING APPROACH

Make the most of *Wide Angle* with opportunities for relevant, personalized learning outside of class.

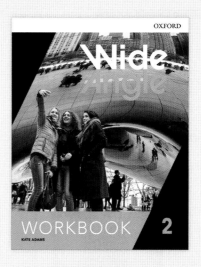

ONLINE PRACTICE

When you see this icon in your Student Book, go online to extend your learning.

With Online Practice you can:

- Review the skills taught in every lesson and get **instant feedback**.

- Practice grammar and vocabulary through **fun games**.

- Access **all audio and video** material. Use the Access Code in the front of this Student Book to log in for the first time at wideangle.oxfordonlinepractice.com.

WORKBOOK

Your Workbook provides additional practice for every unit of the Student Book.

Each unit includes:

- An entirely new reading with skill practice linked to **Oxford Reference**.

- Support for the **Discussion Board**, helping students to master online writing.

- Listening comprehension and skill practice using the **Unit Review Podcast**.

- Real-life English practice linked to the **English For Real** videos.

- **Grammar** and **vocabulary** exercises related to the unit topic.

Use your Workbook for homework or self-study.

FOCUS ON THE TEACHER

The Teacher's Resource Center at wideangle.oxfordonlinepractice.com saves teachers time by integrating and streamlining access to the following support:

- **Teacher's Guide,** including fun **More to Say** pronunciation activities, and **professional development** materials.

- **Easy-to-use** learning management system for the student Online Practice, **answer keys**, **audio**, lots of **extra activities**, **videos**, and so much more.

The **Classroom Presentation Tool** brings the Student Book to life for heads-up lessons. Class audio, video, and answer keys, as well as teaching notes, are available online or offline and are updated across your devices.

1 Identity

UNIT SNAPSHOT

What are "head" and "heart" personalities?   5
Why join a meetup group?   7
What makes a good roommate?   10

Talk about the person in the photo.

What can an image tell you about someone's identity?

What does identity mean to you?

▶ BEHIND THE PHOTO

REAL-WORLD GOAL

Introduce a classmate to a friend or relative

1 Answer the questions. Then discuss your answers with a partner.

1 Imagine your identity is a type of food. What food are you? Why?
I think I am a vegetable curry. It has lots of different ingredients, and I have lots of different parts to my personality.

2 Are you similar to or different from people in your family?

3 What can we learn from people who are different from us?

2 Discuss your answers with a partner.

1 ▶ **ACTIVATE** Watch the video. Choose the correct answer.

1 Antonia's best friend is: ☐ shy. ☐ friendly.
2 Jess's best friend is: ☐ quiet. ☐ loud.
3 Antonia and Jess are: ☐ outgoing. ☐ shy.

2 VOCABULARY Match the phrases to the pictures.

fun to be around	serious at work	shy around people
a calm person	always honest	sometimes lazy

🔑 Oxford 3000™

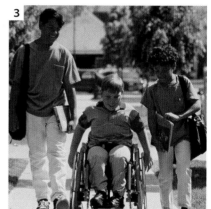

_____   _____   _____

_____   _____   _____

3 WHAT'S YOUR ANGLE? Work with a partner. What words describe you and your family and friends? Use the adjectives from Exercises 1 and 2 and your own ideas.

I think I'm…	My parents are…
I'm not really…	My brother/sister is…
My family says I'm…	My best friend is…

READING SKILL Recognizing adjectives

We use adjectives to describe people, places, and things. Recognizing adjectives helps you understand the details in a text. Adjectives come before a noun or after a form of *be*.
*Our **new** neighbors are **polite**.*

4 IDENTIFY Find the adjectives in the sentences.

1 My best friend is fun to be around. She has a nice personality.
2 My friends say I'm shy, but that's not always true. Sometimes I'm very friendly.
3 My parents are caring, and they are happy together.
4 Her brother is a smart person, and he's a good student.
5 I think I'm outgoing. I like to try new things.

5 ASSESS Find the adjectives that describe these words in the quiz. Do they have a positive (+) or negative (–) meaning?

1 _famous_ Swiss doctor _positive_   4 _____ clothing store _____
2 _____ friend _____   5 _____ bird _____
3 _____ haircut _____   6 _____ person _____

6 INTEGRATE Take the quiz.

Do you think with your head or your heart?

 Carl Jung (1875–1961) was a famous Swiss doctor. According to Jung, the mind has four functions or jobs. Two of these functions are thinking and feeling. Some people are thinking types. Other people are feeling types. Which one are you? Take the quiz to find out!

1 Your good friend has a terrible haircut. What do you say?
A "Umm, I have to be honest…"
B "You got a new cut? It's great!"

2 Your co-worker plays computer games in the office. What do you do?
A I tell my boss. That's not right.
B Nothing. I play games, too.

3 There's a cake in the fridge at work. It's not yours, but no one sees you. What do you do?
A I don't eat any.
B I have a little piece and run.

4 Your favorite clothing store has a one-day sale. What do you think?
A I have a lot of clothes already. Do I really need more?
B I'm ready to go shopping!

5 Your neighbor has a very noisy bird. What do you do?
A I talk to my neighbor about it.
B I'm quiet about it, and I don't sleep.

Count your As and Bs. Then read about your personality below.

More As: You're a thinking type. You think with your head. You're serious at work, and you're always honest. You want to do the right thing—and the smart thing!
More Bs: You're a feeling type. You think with your heart. You're fun to be around, and you do things that make you happy. You're also a kind person.

—adapted from "Carl Gustav Jung" in *Who's Who in the Twentieth Century*

 7 WHAT'S YOUR ANGLE? Do you agree with your quiz result? Tell your partner. Are you the same or different?

We can use *have* to talk about our family, friends, pets, and things we own. We can also use *have* to describe people.

*I **have** a lot of clothes.*
*My neighbor **has** a very noisy bird.*
*I don't **have** shy friends.*
*Does he **have** a nice personality?*
Yes, he does. / No, he doesn't.

See Grammar focus on page 159.

8 **APPLY** Complete the descriptions with the correct form of *have*. Then choose the person's personality type. Compare your answers with a partner.

I _____ a good friend. His name is Alan. He _____ a fun and outgoing personality, but he also _____ a shoe problem! Alan says he _____ enough shoes, but he _____ more than 100 pairs! When the stores _____ sales, he's always the first one there! Do you _____ any friends like him?

Alan is a *thinking / feeling* type.

My best friend Cleo is a good person to be around. She _____ a shy, calm personality. When I _____ a decision to make, I often talk to Cleo. She _____ good ideas because she thinks about what's right and wrong. We _____ similar personalities—we're very different!—but I'm really glad I _____ her as a friend.

Cleo is a *thinking / feeling* type.

9 🔊 **IDENTIFY** Listen to each conversation. Complete the sentences with the correct form of *have*.

1 Cynthia _____ good people skills.
2 They _____ class on Friday.
3 Kendra _____ a job.
4 Paul _____ a lot of free time.
5 Andy _____ a big family.
6 They _____ a new place to live.

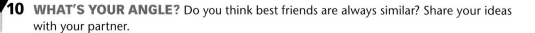

10 **WHAT'S YOUR ANGLE?** Do you think best friends are always similar? Share your ideas with your partner.

1.2 Let's Meet Up!

1 ACTIVATE Do you practice English with other people? Do you practice English online? What other things do you do online?

2 IDENTIFY Read about the meetup group. Answer the questions.

1 What is the name of the meetup group? Why do they meet together?
2 When is their next meeting? Where is it?
3 Why is the group good for Zaid, Miranda, and Takeshi?

International Friends of Hong Kong

Next meeting: Friday, June 6, 6–8 p.m. @ The Cafe Common

Are you a fun, friendly person? Do you like meeting people from different countries? Try our group! Every month we talk and share stories, and we practice our English, too! Take a few minutes to introduce yourself below. See you at the next meeting!

Are You Going?

Yes   No

(114 members)

Zaid

Hi, there. I'm Zaid, and I'm from Jordan. I'm a young, busy guy. My life isn't boring! I'm a college student, and I have a part-time job, too. I like going to the movies and meeting people. I'm excited to meet you all!

Miranda

Hello! I'm Miranda. I'm 22 years old, and I'm from Spain. I have a friendly personality, and I like to have fun. I really like listening to music. I also play the guitar. I'm here to study business, and I have family here, too. Ciao!

Takeshi

Hey, everyone. My name is Takeshi. I'm from Tokyo, and now I'm here in Hong Kong. I'm kind, and I'm also kind of funny. 😂 I play games online, and I really like soccer, too! I have a few friends here now. Can they come, too?

3 INTEGRATE Read the people's comments again. Find other phrases that follow each verb. Then brainstorm other phrases you know.

I am	I have	I like
a college student	a part-time job	going to the movies

We use the verb *be* (*is, am, are*) when we describe people or things. We also use *be* to talk about age. Contracted forms are common in speaking and informal writing.

I'm (not) 22 years old.
We're (not) from Hong Kong.
Our city isn't boring.

See Grammar focus on page 159.

4 APPLY Complete the sentences with nouns and the correct form of *be*. Use contractions.

1 Zaid's life is fun. _____ boring.
2 Takeshi is from Tokyo. _____ from Hong Kong.
3 Miranda is 22. _____ a business student and a musician.
4 Miranda and Zaid are both young. _____ also both students.
5 International Friends of Hong Kong is a meetup group. _____ for people who want to practice their English.
6 I like meeting new people and sharing stories. _____ shy!

5 WHAT'S YOUR ANGLE? Make three sentences with *be* to describe yourself to your partner.

@ **WRITING SKILL Linking ideas with *and*, *also*, and *too***

We can link ideas using the addition words *and*, *also*, and *too*. Linking ideas makes your writing more interesting. We use *and*, *also*, and *too* when we add new or similar ideas or facts. Notice the position of the words in these sentences.

*Every month we talk **and** share stories.*
*I'm Zaid, **and** I'm from Jordan.*
*I really like listening to music. I **also** play the guitar.*
*I play games online, **and** I really like soccer, **too**!*

6 INTEGRATE Find the addition words. Then replace the underlined words with your own ideas and write the sentences.

1 I'm <u>Miguel</u>, and I'm from <u>Colombia</u>.
   I'm Christophe, and I'm from France.
2 I like <u>watching</u> movies. I also like <u>playing video games</u>.
3 My friend <u>Alex</u> speaks <u>English</u>. He speaks <u>German</u>, too.
4 I'm a <u>quiet</u> person, and I like <u>reading</u>.
5 My classmates are <u>friendly</u>. They're <u>fun</u>, too.
6 My friends and I talk a lot about <u>sports</u> and <u>movies</u>.

7 PREPARE You are going to write your personal profile for a discussion board. Write notes below.

Your name: _____

Where you're from: _____

Your age: _____

Your personality: _____

What you do for fun (list three things): _____ _____ _____

8 WRITE Write one paragraph (60 words) about yourself for your online profile. Use phrases from Exercise 3. Use *and*, *too*, and *also* to link your ideas.

9 **IMPROVE** Read your draft, and correct any grammar and spelling mistakes. Check for examples of what you have learned.

☐ Information about who you are

☐ Information about what you like

☐ Sentences with *and*, *also*, and *too*

10 **INTERACT** Swap profiles with a partner. Give your partner feedback on:

- Spelling
- Grammar
- Sentences with *and*, *too*, *also*
- Essential information (name, age, nationality)
- Interesting information (personality, fun activities)

11 **DEVELOP** Use your partner's feedback to rewrite your profile.

12 **SHARE** Put your finished profile on the class discussion board.

13 **WHAT'S YOUR ANGLE?** Respond to a classmate on the discussion board who is similar to you. Use *too* and *also* to discuss how you are similar.

Tourists take selfies with Anish Kapoor's sculpture *Cloud Gate* in Chicago

1.3 Are You an Early Riser?

1 ACTIVATE What is important in a roommate? Take the survey and share answers as a class.

Good roommates have similar...	Important	Not important
schedules and routines		
feelings about housework		
personalities		
taste in music and TV shows		

2 IDENTIFY Read Jason's post for a roommate. Eric and Sergio are interested in the room. How are they similar to or different from Jason?

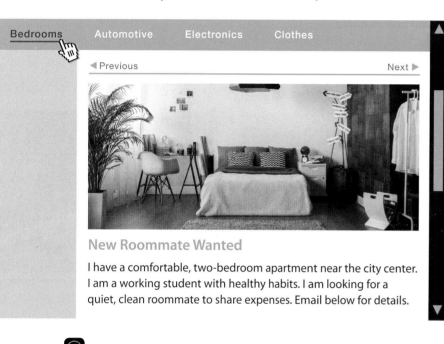

Bedrooms   Automotive   Electronics   Clothes

◀ Previous   Next ▶

New Roommate Wanted

I have a comfortable, two-bedroom apartment near the city center. I am a working student with healthy habits. I am looking for a quiet, clean roommate to share expenses. Email below for details.

Eric

Sergio

VOCABULARY DEVELOPMENT Adverbs of degree

Adverbs of degree show how weak or strong an adjective is. They come after the verb *be* and before the adjective.
*Your roommate is **really** funny!*

Some adverbs of degree make adjectives weaker. These are useful when you want to be polite.
*He's cool, but he's **kind of** young. I want to live with someone my age.*

The words *fairly* and *pretty* are in between weak and strong.
*My apartment is **fairly** clean.*

(It's more than a little clean, but it's not 100 percent clean.)
*The rent here is **pretty** expensive, but it's cheaper than most other apartments in this neighborhood.*

Weaker ◀━━━━━━━━━━━━━━━━━━━━━━━━━━▶ Stronger
    a bit / a little / kind of / sort of   fairly   pretty   very / really

3 INTERACT Use adverbs of degree with adjectives to write notes about Eric and Sergio. Then work in groups. Which one is a good roommate for Jason?

4 WHAT'S YOUR ANGLE? What kind of roommate are you? What kind of roommate is right for you? Discuss your ideal roommate in groups.

I'm fairly clean, and I'm pretty fun. My ideal roommate is interesting but also kind of clean.

Contractions with *be* are very common in spoken English. It's important to hear and understand the difference between the positive and negative forms of *be* because they change the meaning of a sentence. In positive statements, *be* is not stressed. In negative statements, we stress *not*, *isn't*, and *aren't*.

I**'m** happy. / I**'m** not happy.
We**'re** roommates. / We **aren't** roommates.
It**'s** nice. / It **isn't** nice.

5 🔊 **IDENTIFY** Listen to the sentences with contractions. Choose the one you hear. Then practice with a partner. Partner A says a sentence from 1 or 2. Partner B listens and says *1* or *2*. Switch.

	1	2
1	☐ They're cheap.	☐ They're not cheap.
2	☐ We're busy.	☐ We aren't busy.
3	☐ I'm excited about it.	☐ I'm not excited about it.
4	☐ He's a student.	☐ He isn't a student.
5	☐ She's tall.	☐ She's not tall.

6 🔊 **INTEGRATE** Rasheed comes to see the apartment and meet Jason. Listen to the conversation, and discuss your answers to the questions.

1 What is Rasheed like?
2 Why is Rasheed a good roommate for Jason?
3 Why isn't Rasheed a good roommate for Jason?

7 🔊 **EXPAND** What does Jason think about Rasheed? Choose the statement you think Jason will say. Then listen to Jason talk about Rasheed, and check your answers.

	A	B
1	☐ He's a nice guy.	☐ He isn't a nice guy.
2	☐ We're both pretty busy.	☐ We're not very busy.
3	☐ He's interesting.	☐ He's not very interesting.
4	☐ We're on the same schedule.	☐ We're not on the same schedule.
5	☐ He's not home a lot, and that's a problem.	☐ He's not home a lot, so that's good.

We form *yes/no* questions with *be* with *Am / Are / Is* + subject…

Are you an early riser?   Yes, I am. / No, I'm not.   **Is** tomorrow OK?   Sure, I'll call you.

We form *wh-* questions with *be* with question word + *be* + subject…

What is the rent?   It's $1,500 a month.
Where is your apartment?   It's near here.

See Grammar focus on page 159.

8 **IDENTIFY** Match the questions with the answers. Then practice the questions with a partner. Give information about yourself.

1 Who are your roommates?	a Oh, I live with my family.
2 Are they early risers?	b Yes, I am.
3 Are you usually very busy?	c For work.
4 Is your best friend similar to you?	d Yes, we're fairly similar.
5 Why are you learning English?	e No, they aren't.

9 **INTERACT** Take a whole class vote. Are Jason and Rasheed a good roommate match? Why or why not? Discuss your answers.

1.4 How's it Going?

1 ACTIVATE Look at the pictures and the greetings. Which greeting fits each picture?

☐ It's nice to meet you all.

☐ Hey, how's it going?

2 ▶ IDENTIFY Watch the video. Are the people formal or informal with each other? Watch again, and choose *Formal* or *Informal* for each expression you hear.

	Formal	Informal
1 Hey, how's it going?		
2 How are you?		
3 My name is…		
4 Nice to meet you.		
5 Good morning, everyone.		
6 It's nice to meet you all.		
7 Hey, I'm…		
8 How do you do?		

3 ANALYZE Which expressions from Exercise 2 would you use when meeting each of the following people? Why? Discuss your answers in groups.

1 a new colleague at work
2 an older neighbor
3 your younger sister's friend
4 a server in a restaurant
5 a friend of a friend

REAL-WORLD ENGLISH Meeting people

When you meet new people, you use formal or informal language depending on the situation. You usually use formal language when meeting people older than you, people in authority, and people in a work or professional context. In a formal situation, people usually say complete sentences and do not make a joke or comment about the other person.

We can use informal language when meeting people in a social situation and with family and friends. In informal situations, people often use shorter phrases and joke or comment about other people and things.

4 **INTEGRATE** Read the conversations. Are the second speaker's expressions acceptable for the situation? Why or why not? How would you change them?

1 at a university

Professor: Good morning, I'm Professor Brown.

Student: Hi teacher, what's up?

Professor: Hmm.

2 at a friend's house

Teenager 1: Hi, I'm Duc. How's it going?

Teenager 2: Good morning, Duc. My name is Eric Caldwell. It's nice to meet you.

Teenager 1: Uh…nice to meet you, too.

Teenager 2: How are you today?

3 at an office

New colleague: Good morning, I'm Alex. I work upstairs.

Colleague: Oh, that's good.

New colleague: Uh, OK, you're busy…

Colleague: Yeah, I am.

4 at a meeting

Presenter: Hello everyone, and thank you for coming. My name is Tony Garcia. I'm the new sales manager. First I'd like to learn all of your names, and then we can talk about our business plan for the year.

Colleague: Hi, Tony, are you tired? You look tired.

Presenter: Really? Uh, I don't feel tired.

Colleague: Ha ha, it's just a joke.

5 at a coffee shop

Server: Hi, I'm Morgan—I'm your server.

Customer: Good morning, Morgan. It's nice to meet you.

Server: Uh, you too.

5 **INTERACT** Work with a partner. Choose a situation from Exercise 4, and write a new conversation. Use appropriate language for the situation. Role-play the conversation.

6 **EXPAND** Watch another pair's role play. Is it formal or informal? How can you tell?

GO ONLINE
to create your own version
of the English For Real video.

1.5 Hello!

1 ACTIVATE Choose three good and three bad topics to discuss with someone new. Share with the class. Which topics are popular?

your problem(s)	your neighborhood	your class(es)/job	politics
your friends	your family	weather	traffic
TV shows	sports	money	

 PRONUNCIATION SKILL
Intonation with *yes/no* and *wh-* questions

🔊 When you ask someone a *yes/no* question, use rising intonation. When you ask a *wh-* question, use falling intonation. Listen to the examples of people getting to know each other.

Are you busy?　　　　　　　　　Am I right?

Do you like your job?　　　　　Does your apartment have a view?

What's your best friend like?　　What do you like about her?

How are you?

2 🔊 **INTERACT** Listen to the questions and select rising or falling intonation. Then practice asking and answering the questions with a partner.

		Rising	Falling
1	Are you busy?		
2	Do you have everything you need?		
3	Where is your office?		
4	Is she upstairs?		
5	How is it going so far?		
6	Do you work together?		

3 🔊 **IDENTIFY** Listen to the conversation between Molly, Chaz, and Ari. Choose the correct answers.

1 Ari is the new *IT manager* / *sales manager*.
2 Chaz works in *tech support* / *sales*.

4 🔊 **INTEGRATE** Listen to the conversation again. Write three questions you hear. Then write the answers. Work with a partner, and practice the questions and answers. Use the correct intonation.

 SPEAKING Making introductions

When you introduce someone, give details about the person. When you meet someone new, ask a question about the details to continue the conversation.

This is Ari. **She's our new IT manager.**　　　*Hello, Ari.* **How's it going so far?**

This is Eva. **Eva is an international student.**　*Hi Eva,* **where are you from?**　　*I'm from…*

5 WHAT'S YOUR ANGLE? What interesting fact about yourself would you tell someone you meet?

Now go to page 147 for the Unit 1 Review.

2 Relationships

UNIT SNAPSHOT

What is an "online friend"?   16
What is an extended family?   18
What's the correct way to begin a
formal email?   22

What relationships can you see in the picture?

What makes a good friend?

Why are relationships important?

BEHIND THE PHOTO

REAL-WORLD GOAL

Tell someone about your oldest friend

1 **How do you communicate with your friends and family? Choose *True* or *False* for each statement.**

1	I text my family.	True	False
2	I text my friends.	True	False
3	I talk to my friends five hours or more each week.	True	False
4	I talk to my family five hours or more each week.	True	False
5	I talk to my family about everything.	True	False

2 **Discuss your answers with a partner.**

2.1 Friends in the Digital Age

1 ACTIVATE Match the words with the pictures.

a classmate	an opposite	a close friend
a friendly colleague	a good neighbor	an online friend

2 WHAT'S YOUR ANGLE? Look at the pictures in Exercise 1. What is good about each type of friend? Do you have each type of friend? Talk to a partner.

A friendly colleague can give you advice about situations at work.

LISTENING SKILL Recognizing the end of a sentence

If you can recognize the end of a sentence, your listening comprehension will improve. At the end of a sentence, the speaker's voice usually goes up or down. Speakers also often pause between sentences.

3 IDENTIFY Listen to the pairs of sentences. Choose the last word in the first sentence.

1 thanks / listening / today
2 have / call / hello
3 colleagues / work / phones
4 great / world / Internet
5 life / problems / see
6 school / online / groups

4 ASSESS Now listen to the radio show. Which caller has a more positive opinion of social media?

5 INTEGRATE Listen again, and put the numbers of the descriptions in the correct places in the chart.

1 uses social media
2 has online friends around the world
3 goes out with friends in real life
4 has grandchildren
5 her friends are always looking at their phones
6 goes out after work with younger colleagues
7 meets people in online groups
8 shares photos with friends in China and California
9 thinks social media sites are not the real world

Caller 1	Caller 2	Caller 1 and Caller 2

6 **WHAT'S YOUR ANGLE?** Which caller do you agree with more—or do you have a different opinion about social media and friendship? Talk to a partner.

A: I agree with Caller 1. People look at their phones a lot now and don't talk to their friends.

B: I agree that people look at their phones a lot, but I don't think it's a big problem.

GRAMMAR IN CONTEXT Possessive adjectives

We use possessive adjectives with a noun to talk about things and people that belong to someone. They are *my, your, his, her, our,* and *their.*

I think it's cool that **my** *friends in California or China can see* **my** *pictures and I can see* **their** *pictures.*

See Grammar focus on page 160.

7 **APPLY** Complete the sentences with the correct possessive adjectives.

1 The second caller on the radio show often uses social media, but she also goes out with _____ friends in real life.

2 My friends are always looking at _____ phones.

3 With social media, you can talk or send messages to _____ friends anywhere in the world at any time.

4 I have some online friends who are also _____ close friends.

5 My friends and I post photos and chat about _____ pets in a special Facebook group.

8 **INTERACT** Talk with a group. Discuss this question: Can online friends (friends you meet online and don't see in real life) be real friends? Can they be close friends?

PRONUNCIATION SKILL Sentence stress

When we speak, we usually stress content words. That means that we say these words louder and longer. Content words are important words that give meaning to a sentence, such as nouns, main verbs, adjectives, and adverbs. We don't stress structure words, like prepositions (*to, at, in*), articles (*the, a, an*), or conjunctions (*and, but, or*). Giving stress to content words will improve your speaking skills and make you easier to listen to.

My **sister's name** *is* **Matilda**.
My **brother** *is* **shy** *around* **new people**, *but he has* **fun** *with his* **friends**.

9 **◆》 NOTICE** Listen and choose the stressed words in each sentence. Then listen again and repeat.

1 My friend Alex is serious at work.

2 Our friend Kim is always honest.

3 I met a new friend online. His name is Luke.

4 My friends and I go to the movies on Friday nights.

5 My friend Carol is about 70 years old. I learn a lot from her.

10 **INTERACT** Who are your friends? Complete the sentences. Discuss your answers with a partner.

1 I always have fun with _____.

2 I tell _____ my secrets.

3 Online, I talk to _____ a lot.

4 _____ watches my house for me when I'm on vacation.

5 _____ teaches me new things.

2.2 A Full House

1 ACTIVATE Describe the family in the photo. How is your family similar or different?

2 🔊 VOCABULARY Read the text. Choose the word or phrase that can replace the underlined phrase in the text. Then listen and check.

aunts **and** uncles	cousins	grandparents	grandchildren
take care of	nieces	nephews	

 Oxford 3000™

An extended family is a group of related people, often including a married couple, their children, and their (1) <u>children's children</u>. There are often other relatives, too. Children who grow up with their extended family may live with their (2) <u>parents' brothers and sisters</u> and (3) <u>children of their parents' brothers and sisters</u>.

Living with extended families was common in farm communities in the past. Today, people move around more, so nuclear families (one married couple and their children) are more common. However, extended families are still important. (4) <u>Parents' parents</u> teach the family about traditions. Aunts and uncles can (5) <u>stay with, watch, and help</u> their (6) <u>brothers' and sisters' daughters</u> and (7) <u>brothers' and sisters' sons</u>. Having extended family can be positive and healthy.

—adapted from *A Dictionary of Public Health* edited by John M. Last

3 WHAT'S YOUR ANGLE? Does your mother's family or your father's family have more people? What are two ways that their families are different? Tell a partner.

4 ASSESS Read the blog post. In the author's opinion, is it good or bad to live with extended family?

| Home | About | | Search | 🔍 |

Why do you live with your family?

I get that question a lot. Most of my college friends live in the dorms because they like being around people their own age.

A few of my friends live with their parents. Like me, they want to save money. We don't have to pay for our room or buy furniture. Also, we eat home-cooked food!

But for me, it's not just about saving money.

Our house has two apartments. My parents, my younger sister, my mother's parents, and I live on the first floor. My aunt, uncle, and three cousins live on the second floor. Some people say, "There are too many people in your house!" But I don't agree.

First of all, it's fun. We often have parties. I know what you're thinking: *parties* with your *parents* and *grandparents*? Yes—and believe me, they are funnier and dance better than most college students! 😄

Also, we help each other. I take care of my younger cousins. Everybody does cooking and cleaning. If I have a problem, my older family members give me advice. It's great to be around people that care about me!

5 IDENTIFY Read the blog post again, and complete the sentences.

1 Most of the blogger's college friends live _____.
2 The blogger saves _____ by living at home.
3 He doesn't have to pay for _____.
4 He takes care of his _____.
5 He gets _____ from his older family members.

@ READING SKILL Identifying audience and purpose

You can understand a text better if you know who a writer is writing for (audience) and why they are writing (purpose). Language style and content can tell us this.

Informal language such as contractions, opinion phrases and personal words (*I think*, *for me*, *we / us*, etc.), exclamation marks, and emojis show us that the text is personal and for people the writer knows or feels comfortable with. Formal language is for essays and factual texts such as news articles and encyclopedias.

Look for opinions, facts, and examples to understand the purpose of a text. The purpose of a personal text is often to share opinions, tell a story, or make people laugh. The purpose of a factual text is usually to share information.

6 INTEGRATE Choose the correct answers.

1 A _____ wrote the blog post.
   student   professional author
2 The author wrote the text for _____.
   young children   other people his age
3 The text is _____.
   formal   informal
4 The blog post is an example of a _____.
   personal text   factual text
5 The writer's purpose is to _____.
   give information to students who are starting college   tell his story and give his opinion

7 WHAT'S YOUR ANGLE? Do you live alone, with family, or with roommates? What are three good things about the way you live? Tell a partner.

> ## GRAMMAR IN CONTEXT
> ### Nouns: Countable, uncountable, and plural
>
> There are two types of nouns in English: countable and uncountable nouns. Countable nouns are things that we can count. They can be singular or plural. We can use *a* or *an* with them.
>
> *a* **sister** → *two* **sisters**
>
> Uncountable nouns are things we usually can't count. We don't use *a* or *an* with them, and they are never plural.
>
> *information, some information (NOT ~~an information~~ or ~~a lot of informations~~)*

See Grammar focus on page 160.

8 IDENTIFY Complete the chart with nouns from the blog post.

Singular countable	Plural countable	Uncountable
question		

9 APPLY Choose the correct word or phrase to complete the statements.

1 I have a large extended *family / families* with many *cousin / cousins*.
2 I have *a lot of / a* fun with my family members.
3 I can't spend a lot of *time / times* with my grandparents.
4 I don't cook *a / any* food at my house.
5 I live in *a / some* dorm, so I don't save *a / much* money.
6 *A / Some* people say there are *lot of / a lot of* people in our house.

10 INTEGRATE Complete the sentences about the blog post.

1 A few of his friends live with their _____.
2 Their _____ has two apartments.
3 The writer's _____ and uncle live on the second floor.
4 There are too many _____ in the house.
5 The writer takes care of his younger _____.

11 INTERACT Talk with a partner. Are the sentences from Exercise 9 true for you?

12 WHAT'S YOUR ANGLE? What kind of blogs, websites, or magazines do you like to read? What is the purpose, and who is the audience?

2.3 A New Friend

1 ACTIVATE What are some different ways that you meet new people?

2 WHAT'S YOUR ANGLE? Complete the chart with information about two of your friends.

Name	How we met	Interesting details
Maria	We went to school together.	We have the same birthday!

VOCABULARY DEVELOPMENT Verb + preposition

Some prepositions are commonly used with certain verbs.

agree with someone	**talk to** someone	**ask for** something	**wait for** someone
spend time with someone	**talk about** something	**work on** something	**write** an email **to** someone
We **talk about** sports.	Jack **asked** Alex **for** the recipe.	He **spends** a lot of **time with** his family.	

Some verbs use more than one preposition. The preposition depends on what follows.

*I **talked to my sister** this morning. We **talked about our vacation plans**.*

3 VOCABULARY Complete each phrase with *to, with, for, about,* or *on.*

1 I talk _____ my new colleague about our project.
2 We work _____ a lot of projects together.
3 I spend time _____ my best friend every weekend.
4 My friends and I never talk _____ work.
5 You can always ask _____ help if something is too difficult for you.
6 My friend and I have similar opinions, but I don't always agree _____ her about everything.
7 She writes emails _____ her friends in Australia.
8 We always wait _____ our manager at meetings.
9 Bob talks _____ soccer a lot. It's his favorite sport.
10 Maria spends time _____ her family on holidays.

Young women in Cape Town, South Africa

4 APPLY Complete the sentences with the correct prepositions plus your own information.

1 When I have a big problem, I usually talk _____ my _____.

2 When I chat with a stranger in line or at a bus stop, I usually talk _____ things like _____.

3 I agree _____ most of my friends that _____ is very important.

4 I often have to wait _____ my friend _____ because she is always late.

5 I like to spend time _____ my _____. We have a lot of fun.

5 IDENTIFY Read the email. Who are Jack's two new friends? Where did he meet them?

✉

From: jack@mailinator.com

To: erik@mailinator.com

Subject: New friends!

Today at 12:10

Hey Erik,

I love Chicago. It's great! I already have two new friends.

Colin is my new friend at work. His desk is next to mine. We talk about sports, especially soccer because it's Colin's favorite sport.

My other new friend is Alex. He's a great neighbor. His apartment is on the third floor, and mine is on the fourth floor. I go to Alex's apartment for dinner sometimes. He's a great cook—his pasta is really good. I asked for the recipe!

I'll talk to you soon,

Jack

6 INTEGRATE Complete the sentences.

1 Jack wrote this email to _____.

2 _____ loves Chicago.

3 Colin's favorite sport is _____.

4 Alex likes to _____, and he makes good _____.

5 Jack and Colin talk about _____.

6 Jack goes to Alex's apartment for _____.

WRITING SKILL Opening and closing an email

We use different phrases to open and close informal and formal emails. The readers of your email will feel more comfortable if you use appropriate phrases.

Informal (to a friend or family member)

Opening: Hi [name], Hey [name], Hello [name],

Closing: See you soon, I'll talk to you soon, Take care, Love,* Thanks,**

*only for good friends or family members

**only when you asked for something in your email

Formal (to a teacher, a boss, or someone you don't know)

Opening: Dear Sir / Madam: Dear Mr. / Mrs. / Ms. [name]:

Closing: Best regards, Best wishes, Sincerely,

7 IDENTIFY Find the opening and closing in the email in Exercise 5. Is it a formal or informal email?

8 EXPAND Write a new opening and closing for the email in Exercise 5.

We use possessive 's to say that something or someone belongs to a person, place, or thing. The possessive 's always comes after a noun.

I go to Alex's apartment for dinner.

We use possessive pronouns instead of a possessive adjective + noun to talk about things we possess.

my = mine	*his = his*	*her = hers*
your = yours	*our = ours*	*their = theirs*

His apartment is on the third floor, and mine is on the fourth floor.

See Grammar focus on page 160.

9 ◀) **IDENTIFY** Complete the conversation between Jack and Colin. Then listen and check your answers.

Jack: Hi, my name is Jack.

Colin: Hi, _____ is Colin.

Jack: It's nice to meet you, Colin. Are you on Tim_____ team?

Colin: No, I think I'm on _____.

Jack: Oh, that's great. I need someone new on my team.

Colin: Is that a picture of your son_____ soccer team?

Jack: Yes, it is.

Colin: How funny! I have that picture on my desk. My son is on the same team.

Jack: Wow, that's amazing.

Colin: This is my son right here. Where's _____?

Jack: He's right there next to _____!

10 **WHAT'S YOUR ANGLE?** How often do you write emails? Who do you usually write to? When do you write formal emails? Share with a partner.

11 **WRITE** Choose one of the friends you described in Exercise 2. Write an email (one paragraph of 80–100 words) to someone in your family, and tell that family member about your friend. Include information about:

- how and where you met your friend
- your friend's personality
- how you spend time with your friend and what you talk about
- your feelings about your friend

✉
From:
To:
Subject:

12 **IMPROVE** Read your email again. Did you…

- ☐ include interesting details about your friend, how you met, and what you do together?
- ☐ open and close your email with the correct phrases?
- ☐ use correct prepositions with your verbs?
- ☐ use possessive 's and possessive pronouns correctly?

13 **INTERACT** "Send" your email to a partner. Read your partner's email. What other information would you like to know about your partner's friend? Ask questions.

2.4 What Did You Say?

1 ACTIVATE What do you think the people in the pictures are talking about? What do you think one speaker is asking the other speaker to repeat? When is it hard for you to understand people?

2 ▶ IDENTIFY Watch the video. Match the quotes from the video to the speaker.

a I didn't catch that.

b Have a seat! We were just talking about our summers.

c Sorry. Say that again.

d Yeah, I was chuffed!

1 Andy _____

2 Max _____

3 Phil _____

REAL-WORLD ENGLISH Asking someone to repeat something

When you don't understand what someone says, you can ask them to repeat it. There are different phrases you can use to do this.

Less formal

What? / What did you say? / What was that?   *Sorry, I didn't catch that.*
Say that again.

More formal

I'm sorry, I didn't hear that.   *Excuse me, could you please repeat that?*

If you just want to confirm one detail, you can ask a more specific question.

A: *The movie starts at 7:15.*

B: *Sorry. What time does it start? / Did you say it starts at 7:15?*

When someone repeats information for you, they don't always say the same sentence. Sometimes they give the same information using different words, or they just repeat the important information.

A: *He and I are taking a history class together.*

B: *I'm sorry, what did you say?*

A: *I said we're in the same history class.*

3 ▶ ANALYZE Watch the video again. Answer the questions.

1 Why is it hard for Phil to understand Max?

2 Which expressions from the box do the speakers use?

3 When they repeat information, do they say the same sentences or do they say the information differently?

ENGLISH FOR REAL

4 IDENTIFY Read and complete each conversation. What do you notice about the way speaker A repeats information? Who is talking in each conversation?

1 A: Sam's office is down the hall and on the right.
   B: Could you please say that _____?
   A: Sure, his office is down the hall and on the right side.

2 A: Marta's brother is here this weekend.
   B: Sorry, _____ was that?
   A: Marta's brother Jose is here.

3 A: How about Thursday, June 5, at 1:30?
   B: Excuse me, could you _____ that?
   A: Does June 5 at 1:30 work for you?

4 A: Can you help me with this homework assignment?
   B: _____?
   A: I'm having trouble with my homework. Can you help me?

5 A: Can you tell Dr. Simms that Leah James is here?
   B: I'm sorry, I didn't _____ that.
   A: Leah James is here to see Dr. Simms.

5 APPLY Complete the conversations with an expression from the box. You may change an expression to match the situation.

1 A: Don't forget, we have a meeting about our new project at 2:30.
   B: _____
   A: 2:30.

2 A: Yeah, I'd like two large cheese pizzas, please. The address is 275 Washington Street.
   B: _____
   A: Sure—it's 275 Washington Street in Salem.

3 A: For homework, please read pages 100–130 of your textbook, and do exercises A, B, and C in your workbook.
   B: _____
   A: Of course. The homework is to read pages 100–130 and to do exercises A to C.

6 EXPAND Work in pairs. Read each situation. Prepare what you will say.

1 A: You ask your friend, speaker B, for the time. You can't hear what speaker B says.
   B: Respond to speaker A.

2 A: You work at a doctor's office. You're on the phone with a patient, speaker B. You ask speaker B to spell their name. You can't hear what speaker B says.
   B: Respond to speaker A.

3 A: You are at a family dinner. You ask a family member, speaker B, what they did today. You can't hear what speaker B says.
   B: Respond to speaker A.

4 A: You ask your boss, speaker B, when your project is due. You can't hear what speaker B says.
   B: Respond to speaker A.

5 A: You ask a salesperson, speaker B, how much a shirt costs. You can't hear what speaker B says.
   B: Respond to speaker A.

7 INTERACT Now work together, and role-play each situation from Exercise 6. Be sure to alternate who is speaker A and who is speaker B.

GO ONLINE
to create your own version
of the English For Real video.

2.5 She's Smart and Fun

1 🔊 **ACTIVATE** Split into two teams. Listen to the descriptions. The first team to say the letter of the correct picture gets a point.

1 ___   2 ___   3 ___   4 ___   5 ___   6 ___

2 **INTERACT** Talk with a group. Take turns describing students in the class. Guess who each person is describing.

A: She's tall and has short black hair.   B: Is it Aïsha?

3 **WHAT'S YOUR ANGLE?** Think of three of your family members or friends. Complete the chart.

Name	Relationship	Physical description	Personality	Likes / is good at
Lana	sister	black hair, brown eyes	smart, fun	reading, sports

SPEAKING Describing people

When you describe people, you can talk about what they look like and give information about their personality or what they are good at.

Use *be* + adjective for personality and some physical descriptions.

*He's **sociable**.   He's **not shy**.   He's **tall**.*

Use *have* for other physical descriptions.

*He **has curly** brown hair and blue eyes.*

Use *be* + *good at* and *like / love* + *-ing* verb to talk about talents and interests.

*He **loves playing** tennis, and he's really **good at** soccer.*

4 **INTEGRATE** Work with a partner. Describe three people you know, including interesting details. Use your notes from Exercise 3.

Now go to page 148 for the Unit 2 Review.

3 Responsibilities

UNIT SNAPSHOT

How can you make housework fun? 29

What is a community? 31

What phrase can you use before you make a difficult request? 36

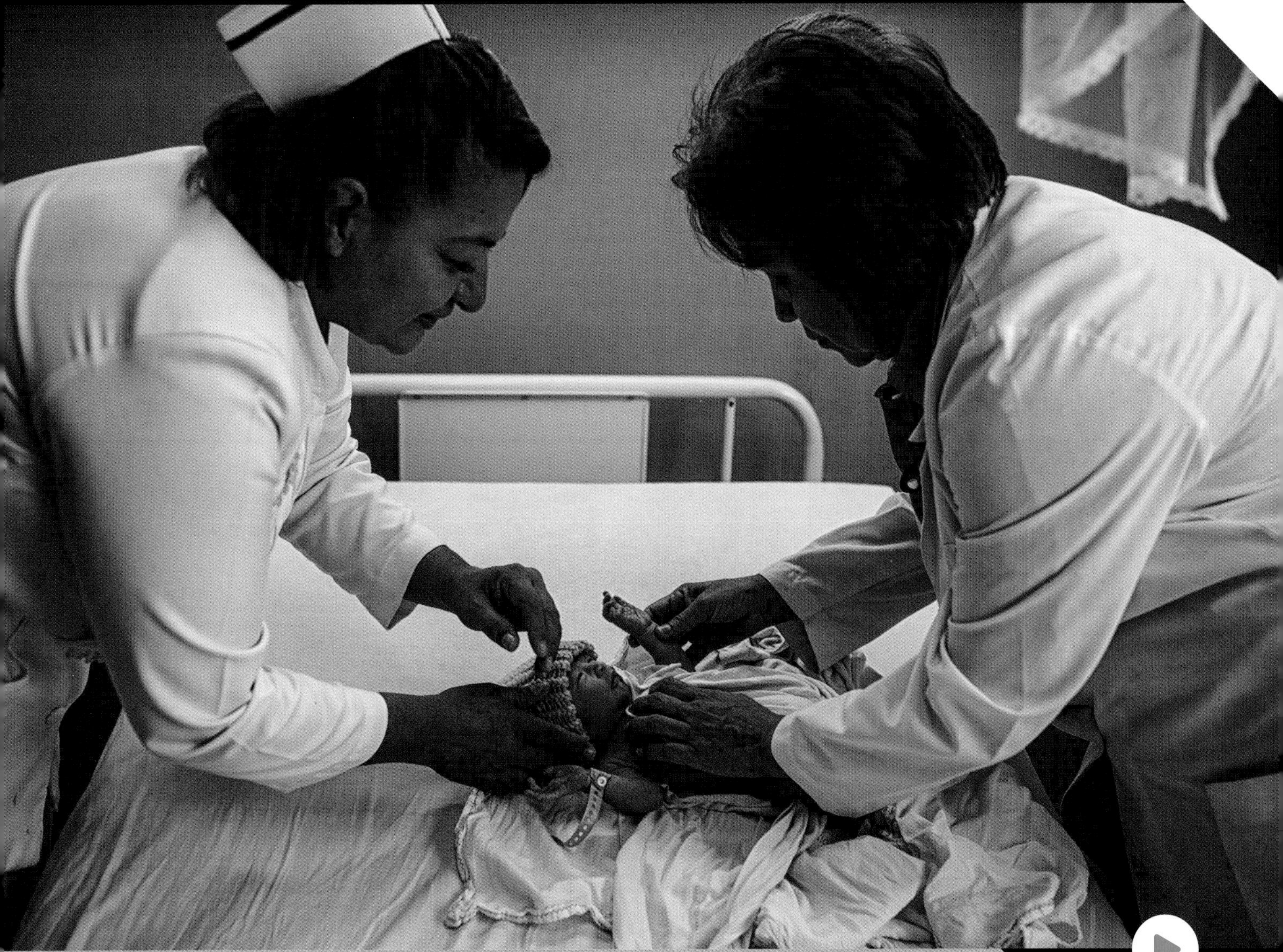

What jobs have the most responsibility?

What responsibilities do parents have?

What are your responsibilities?

BEHIND THE PHOTO

1 Brainstorm four things you love doing because they're fun and four things you do because they are necessary.

Fun	Necessary

REAL-WORLD GOAL

Call a local business and request their hours

2 How much time do you spend doing each thing? Number them from 1–8, 1 being the thing you spend the most time doing. Share with a partner.

3.1 Crazy Clean

1 ACTIVATE Look at the pictures. Do you know (or can you guess) what the objects are for?

2 VOCABULARY Match the phrases to the images.

cut the **grass**	wash the **dishes**	**prepare** meals	change the **sheets**	pay **bills**
clean the **carpets**	**fold** clean clothes	empty the **garbage**	go **grocery** shopping	

Oxford 3000™

1 _____ 2 _____ 3 _____

4 _____ 5 _____ 6 _____

7 _____ 8 _____ 9 _____

3 IDENTIFY Look at the chores in Exercise 2. Which ones are about…

1 food?   2 cleaning?   3 spending money?

4 WHAT'S YOUR ANGLE? Is being neat and clean important to you? How important? Do you do a lot of work around the house? Does someone else? Is it equal?

5 **INTERACT** Before you read, look at the photo and title of the article. Work with a partner.

1 What do you think the article is about?

2 What advice do you think the article gives?

READING Recognizing and understanding contrast linking words:
But and *however*

When reading a text, it's important to understand how ideas are connected.

Linking words connect ideas. Contrast words show that two ideas are different.

The contrast word *but* usually goes in the middle of a sentence. The word *however* usually goes at the beginning.

*I always wash my dishes, **but** my roommate leaves his dirty dishes in the kitchen.*
*I enjoy washing the clothes. **However**, I hate folding them!*

6 **ASSESS** Match the contrasting ideas. Then read the article to check your answers.

1 ___ People don't enjoy housework.

2 ___ You don't have children.

3 ___ A clean house is great.

4 ___ You have a busy schedule.

5 ___ When you're alone at home, it's easy to be lazy.

a You don't need a lot of time to clean.

b When people are coming to your house, you want it to be neat.

c Chocolate cake is better.

d There are ways to make housework fun.

e You can play games, too.

Good, clean fun!

Most people don't enjoy housework. However, there are ways to make it more fun.

1 Nobody likes cleaning the floors, but everyone loves a dance party! Play your favorite music, and sing while you work.

2 Do you have children? They love games and contests. Give everyone a small chore, and the first person to finish wins a prize.

4 Maybe you don't have children, but you can play games, too! Imagine you have a plane ticket to an amazing place. You aren't just folding clean clothes—you're packing your suitcase!

4 Do you have a busy schedule? You probably have a lot to do, but you don't need a lot of time to clean! Set a timer for 15 minutes once or twice a day, and see how much you can do in that time.

5 A clean house is great, but chocolate cake is better! Choose a treat to help you celebrate after your hard work.

6 It's easy to be lazy at home. However, when people are coming, you want your house to look neat. Invite your friends over for a dinner party, and start cleaning! Then you can celebrate with them.

7 **WHAT'S YOUR ANGLE?** What do you usually do to make chores less boring? Do you do any of the things in the article?

We use the simple present to talk about routines, habits, and facts.

*Most people **don't enjoy** housework.*

Remember to add *Do* or *Does* to form *yes/no* questions.

***Do** you have a busy schedule?*   *Yes, I do. / No, I don't.*

See Grammar focus on page 161.

8 **INTEGRATE** Complete the sentences about the article. Use the correct positive or negative form of the verb.

1   The article _____ (say) that housework can be fun.

2   Most people _____ (like) cleaning the floors.

3   Children _____ (love) playing games.

4   In the game, each person _____ (get) a chore, and the fastest person _____ (win) a prize.

5   A person _____ (need) much time to clean—just 15 minutes!

6   You probably _____ (want) a neat and clean house for your dinner party.

PRONUNCIATION SKILL *Do* and *does* in *yes/no* questions and short answers

🔊 In *yes/no* questions in the simple present, we often shorten the word *do.*

***Do you** do a lot of work around the house?*   ***Do your** kids help you?*
(dyə)   (dəyər)

Notice how *does* blends with *he* and *she.*

***Does he** wash the dishes?*   ***Does she** like listening to music?*
(dəzi)   (dəzʃi)

In short answers, *do(n't)* and *does(n't)* are pronounced fully.

*Yes, I **do.***   *No, he **doesn't.***

9 🔊 **NOTICE** Listen. Choose the phrase you hear. Then listen again and repeat.

1   _____ pay bills on time?

    Does your roommate   Do your roommates

2   _____ usually make a mess?

    Does he   Does she

3   Yes, _____!

    he does   she does

4   _____ invite friends over for dinner?

    Do you   Does he

5   _____ usually help prepare the food?

    Do you   Do they

6   No, _____.

    I don't   they don't

10 **INTERACT** Get together in a group of four. Have a conversation. Pair A begins the conversation, and Pair B responds.

Pair A: You think cleaning every day is a waste of time.

Pair B: You think *not* being neat and clean is a waste of time.

1 ACTIVATE Read the description of a community. What communities are you a part of?

Community

A community is a group of people who share interests or live in the same area. For example, people living in a town or neighborhood form a community. Other types of communities can be related to common interests or experiences: for example, religion, nationality, hobbies, etc. These communities can be place-based or online. Being part of a community means helping and supporting other members and sharing time and activities.

—adapted from *A Dictionary of Human Geography* by Noel Castree, Rob Kitchin, and Alisdair Rogers

Women in Swaziland receive certificates for completing a free business training course

VOCABULARY DEVELOPMENT Time expressions

To say how often you do something, you can use time expressions. Some time expressions are:

once a (day / week / month / year)
twice a (day / week / month / year)
three / a few / several times a (day / week / month / year)
every (day / week / weekday / weekend / month / year)

every (four, few) years
on (Saturdays)
once in a while

We usually use these time expressions at the end of a sentence.
*I do volunteer work **twice a week**.*

They can also go at the beginning of a sentence followed by a comma (,).
***Once in a while**, I give money to a charity.*

2 USE Choose five of the events or activities. Choose a time expression, and write a true sentence about you or people you know.

read or watch local news	use social media	go to a community party or meeting
talk to neighbors	help someone with a problem	eat at local restaurants
shop at a local store	give money to a charity	visit a local park

I go to the local park several times a week.   Every weekday, I take the bus to work.

3 WHAT'S YOUR ANGLE? Describe one fun activity you do with people in your community.

I am in a running club in my town. We run together on Thursdays.

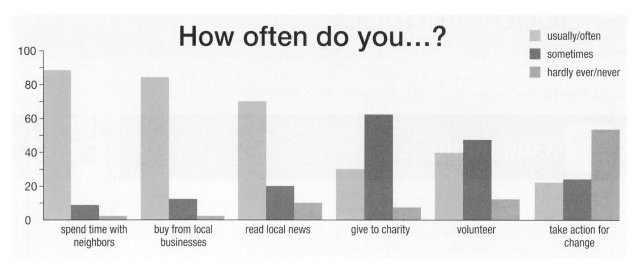

How often do you...?

Legend:
- usually/often
- sometimes
- hardly ever/never

4 ASSESS Look at the bar graph.

1 What do the bars in the graph mean?
2 How many people answered the survey?
3 What activity is the most popular?
4 What activity is the least popular?
5 Which activity do 20 people sometimes do?

5 INTEGRATE Read the explanation of the information in the bar graph from a community blog. Find an example or explanation in the text for each of the six activities from the graph.

1 spend time with neighbors: _____
2 buy from local businesses: _____
3 read local news: _____
4 give to charity: _____
5 volunteer: _____
6 take action for change: _____

We surveyed 100 local people to see what they do to make our community strong.

Most people here are friendly with their neighbors. They often talk to them or invite them to their house. Also, many people go to local stores and restaurants more than once or twice a week.

A lot of people read newspapers or information online about events in our town. Many people do this every day or every week.

The other activities are harder. Most people don't give to charity more than once in a while. However, 62 percent say they sometimes give. This includes giving food to hungry people or running in a race for medical research.

Volunteering—like cleaning the park or helping older people with chores—takes time. So, it's no surprise that only 40 percent usually or often do this.

Finally, there is "taking action for change"— for example, going to town meetings, writing on social media, or calling the mayor about a problem. Most people never or hardly ever do these things.

How about you—what do you do to make the community a better place?

GRAMMAR IN CONTEXT The simple present and adverbs of frequency

We use adverbs of frequency with the simple present to say how often we do something. Notice the word order.

They often talk to their neighbors.   *Our streets are always clean.*

Notice the difference in meaning and use in the negative.

I don't usually give to charity. (= I hardly ever do.)
Some people never do these things. NOT Some people don't never…

See Grammar focus on page 161.

6 **APPLY** Read the clues from the bar graph and blog post. Write a sentence using an adverb of frequency.

22 people / take action for change

1 _Twenty-two people often take action for change._

2 three people / buy from local businesses   _____

3 nine people / spend time with neighbors   _____

4 30 people / give to charity   _____

5 48 people / do volunteer work   _____

6 54 people / take action   _____

7 20 people / read local news   _____

7 **WHAT'S YOUR ANGLE?** Which of the activities from the blog do you do in your community? How often?

I volunteer once a year to clean the streets. I sometimes spend time with my neighbors.

8 **PREPARE** Work with a group. First, choose a topic and brainstorm five related activities. Then write a question for each activity. Some ideas are below, but you can use others.

friends and family	health	chores at home	social media use

9 **INTERACT** Interview 4–6 classmates about your topic. Each member of your group should ask 1–2 of the questions you wrote. Take notes; then work together as a group to put your results into a bar graph. Use the one from this lesson as a model.

10 **WRITE** Write 2–3 paragraphs (120 words) to explain the information from your bar graph. Give more details about the people and their habits.

WRITING SKILL Checking your work: Accuracy in word choice

Readers will understand your writing better if you choose the best word for each situation. Some words have similar meanings, but they are not quite the same.

For example, imagine one person checks her email almost every night:
She usually checks her email at night. NOT ~~She sometimes checks her email at night.~~

Check a dictionary if you aren't sure about a word's meaning.

---

11 **APPLY** Choose the correct word.

1 I have class _two / twice_ a week, on Monday and Wednesday.

2 He hardly _ever / never_ travels because it's expensive.

3 I don't have a lot of time, so I _clean / wash_ the house once a month.

4 How often do you _give / spend_ money to charity?

5 I _do / make_ my homework every night.

12 **IMPROVE** Check your description. Did you…

☐ choose the most accurate words?

☐ put adverbs of frequency and time expressions in the correct places?

☐ use the correct simple present forms of your verbs?

13 **SHARE** Share your graph and your explanation with the class.

3.3 What Can You Do?

1 ACTIVATE Work with a partner. Complete the sentences with words from the box.

lead	manage	experience	decisions	serve	projects
develop	customers	responsibilities	research	programs	

 Oxford 3000™

1 I'm applying for a job. I need to tell them about my past work _____.
2 Nurses have a lot of _____, like taking care of people, giving medicine, and writing reports.
3 Managers do a lot. They _____ large groups of people, _____ meetings, and make important _____.
4 My brother works with computers. He writes software _____.
5 My mother is a scientist. She works at a lab and does important cancer _____.
6 I work at a fast-food restaurant. I help _____ and _____ them their food.
7 In art class, we work on some cool _____. We _____ our ideas into interesting paintings.

2 WHAT'S YOUR ANGLE? Choose three expressions from Exercise 1. Write sentences about your job or responsibilities or about someone you know.

My friend has three children, so she has a lot of responsibilities.

3 ASSESS Look at the job ads. What responsibilities does each job have?

Angelina's: cook, serve, or deliver food

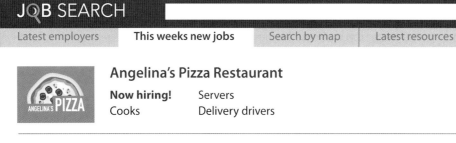

JOB SEARCH

| Latest employers | **This weeks new jobs** | Search by map | Latest resources |

Angelina's Pizza Restaurant

Now hiring! Servers
Cooks Delivery drivers

House Cleaners Wanted!

Royal House Cleaning Service
We pay excellent rates!

UPTOWN FURNITURE

Store manager needed Lead a large team of hard workers
Must have experience Develop ideas to grow our business

Helios Labs

Looking for scientists, part-time assistants for important medical research project
Call now! Training on 5/15

Wayside Farm

Help your local community!
Work with animals or vegetables **Must have car; workday starts at 5 a.m.**

🔊 Linkers are words or phrases that connect ideas. When someone is giving information and wants to add a related idea, they use expressions like:

Also,...   *In addition,...*   *...and...*   *...as well as...*

Also and *In addition* often begin a sentence, and there is a comma after them. When you're listening, you'll hear a pause before and after the expression.

I'm studying business at college. [pause] **In addition,** *[pause] I work part time in an office.*

In fast speech, the expressions *and* and *as well as* are shortened.

I studied English and French.	*I have experience teaching children as well as adults.*
Sounds like: English /n/ French	*Sounds like: children /əzwɛləz/ adults*

4 🔊 **ASSESS** Listen. Complete the sentences with the correct linker.

1   I majored in computer science. _____, I worked at the university computer lab for two years.

2   I helped students _____ teachers with their computer problems.

3   I'm a scientist _____ a professor. _____, I do research and develop robots.

4   I have ten years of experience cleaning homes _____ office buildings.

5   I work quickly, _____ I always do excellent work.

5 🔊 **IDENTIFY** Listen to the phone conversations. Brian needs a job. Which two ads does he respond to?

6 🔊 **INTEGRATE** Listen again to the phone calls. Choose all of the correct answers.

1   What does Brian do at the soup kitchen?
   ☐ gives money   ☐ serves meals
   ☐ prepares meals   ☐ cleans the kitchen

2   What job responsibilities does the woman describe?
   ☐ prepare food   ☐ buy food
   ☐ serve food   ☐ keep customers happy

3   Why does Brian think he's qualified for the first job?
   ☐ He's a good manager.   ☐ He's good with people.
   ☐ He learns fast.   ☐ He has restaurant experience.

4   What experience does Brian have related to the second job?
   ☐ He's a science student.   ☐ He takes lab classes.
   ☐ He wants to be a doctor.   ☐ He reads a lot about medical research.

In subject questions, the question word is the subject. We don't use *do / does*.

Subject + main verb + object? → *Who makes the decisions?*

In object questions, the question word is the object. We use *do / does* in the simple present.

Object + auxiliary verb + subject + main verb? → *What job experience do you have?*

See Grammar focus on page 161.

7 **APPLY** Look at the question word. Write *subject* or *object*.

1   Who is the director of your language school?

2   Who do you practice your English with?

3   What makes a job interesting?

4   What kind of work do you like doing?

5   What is your biggest responsibility right now?

8 **INTERACT** Work with a partner. Ask and answer the questions from Exercise 7.

3.4 A Few Requests

1 ACTIVATE How do you ask for something politely? Think of phrases you might use to ask for something in a store and phrases to use at home with family.

2 ▶ IDENTIFY Watch the video. Read the statements. Choose *True* or *False*.

1	The professor doesn't know Max.	True	False
2	The professor is Max's advisor.	True	False
3	Max wants to meet with the professor to talk about a campus job.	True	False
4	Max is going to meet the professor at his office tomorrow.	True	False
5	Andy forgot two important things in the apartment.	True	False
6	Max arranges to meet Andy at the main building.	True	False

REAL-WORLD ENGLISH Requesting by phone

There are many ways to ask for something. When we feel confident and we don't think we're asking for too much, we use polite, direct phrases:

I'd like to (meet with you).
Could you (tell me what your office hours are), please?
Do you have time to…?

If we're worried that our request is not convenient for the other person, we use less direct phrases:

I'm wondering if you could (bring me my book).
Would you mind (giving me a ride home)?
Is it possible for you / me to…?

Sometimes we add an extra phrase to show that we know we are asking a lot:

Can I ask you a favor?   Sorry to bother you…   …if you have time / if possible.

It helps to add an explanation, so the person understands your situation.

My car broke down. Could you give me a ride?

If the person says *yes*, thank them. If they say *no*, it's good to make sure they don't feel bad about it.

Request accepted

A: *Could I borrow your car today?*
B: *Sure, no problem.*
A: *Great! Thank you so much!*

Request rejected

A: *Do you have time to pick me up at the train station?*
B: *I'm sorry, I don't. I'm visiting my grandmother.*
A: *Oh, that's OK. Thanks anyway!*

3 ▶ **ANALYZE** Watch the video again. Answer the questions.

1   Write one of the phrases that Max uses when making a request to his professor.

2   Write one phrase that Max uses when making a request to Andy.

3   How are Max's phrases, tone, and attitude different in each situation? Why do you think so?

4 **INTEGRATE** Read each situation. Rate each one from 1–5, 1 being a comfortable request and 5 being a difficult request. Compare your answers with a partner.

1   You're outside your friend's house. Your friend is waiting for you. You want your friend to come downstairs and open the door.

   1   2   3   4   5

2   You invited a classmate to your apartment in an hour for dinner. You are shopping for the food. You want your roommate to clean the kitchen and the living room before you arrive. (Your roommate hardly ever cleans.)

   1   2   3   4   5

3   You have an early flight tomorrow—6 a.m.! The problem is you just learned that there is no bus to the airport before 5:30, and you want to be there at 5:00. Taxis are too expensive. Your close friends don't have cars, but your neighbor has one. You want to ask your neighbor to give you a ride.

   1   2   3   4   5

4   It's 10 p.m., and you have an important job interview in the morning. However, your neighbor has some friends over, and they are very loud. You can't sleep. Your neighbor is a nice person, so you don't want to sound very angry. You call your neighbor to ask them to keep the noise down.

   1   2   3   4   5

5   The local library's website is not very helpful. It has old information. You want to know if the library has a new book you are interested in. Also, you need to know its hours. You call the library and ask.

   1   2   3   4   5

6   You went running (or for a walk) and lost your keys. The door is locked. You have an important appointment, but you are wearing exercise clothes. You need to get inside! You call your roommate (or someone who lives with you) to see if they can open the door.

   1   2   3   4   5

5 **APPLY** For each scenario from Exercise 4, choose a phrase or phrases from the box, and write a request. Include extra explanation if you think it's needed.

6 **INTERACT** Work with a partner. Follow the instructions for a role play.

1   Choose two scenarios from Exercise 4.

2   Write a complete conversation for each scenario. Student A calls Student B and makes the request (see Exercise 5), and Student B responds to the request. Take at least two turns each in the conversation.

3   Role-play both conversations. Switch roles, so each of you makes a request and responds to a request.

4   Share your favorite role play with the class.

GO ONLINE
to create your own version
of the English For Real video.

3.5 Stay-at-Home Dad

1 ▶ **ACTIVATE** Watch the video. How does Brian feel about being a stay-at-home dad? What does he like and what doesn't he like about it?

2 **ASSESS** Watch the video again. Choose the correct answer.

1 *Brian / Brian's wife* wakes up at 6:00 a.m.
2 Brian drives *the girls to school / his wife to work* in the morning.
3 *Brian and his oldest daughter / The twins* like doing homework.
4 The girls *like / don't like* doing chores.
5 *Brian / Brian's wife* reads stories to the girls at night.
6 Brian's wife *likes / doesn't like* going to work every day.
7 Before he was a stay-at-home dad, Brian was a *schoolteacher / manager at an office*.
8 Brian *would like / wouldn't like* to go back to his old job.

3 **PREPARE** Imagine you have your dream life. Make a list of 8–10 things you do every day at home and at work.

wake up at 9:00   take a walk on the beach   paint in my art studio

 SPEAKING Talking about habits and routines

Use the simple present to talk about your routines.

I get up at seven and take the train to work.

Use adverbs of frequency to say how often you do things.

I always buy a coffee before I get on the train. I never eat breakfast because it's too early.

Use *when* and *how often* to ask about people's routines.

When do you study?   *How often do you go to the gym?*

4 **DEVELOP** Use your notes to write sentences about your dream routine. Add information about how you feel about the activities you do.

I get up at 9:00 because I love sleeping late. I'm an artist, so I enjoy spending all day painting in my studio. My favorite part of the day is…

5 **INTERACT** Work with a partner. Describe a typical day in your dream life. Talk about your favorite and least favorite parts of the day. Then listen to your partner describe their day. Ask questions to get more information.

A: So, what do you do on a typical day?
B: Well, in the morning, I usually take a walk on the beach. I love walking on the beach!

Now go to page 149 for the Unit 3 Review.

4 Extremes

UNIT SNAPSHOT

What is the world record for the most
kinds of cheese on a pizza? 41

What is unusual about the Goodfysh Restaurant? 43

Would you like to live on a roof? 46

| ◤ Where do you think this photo was taken? | ◤ What places in the world have extreme conditions? | ◤ Why do people enjoy extreme sports? | ▶ BEHIND THE PHOTO |

REAL-WORLD GOAL

Write an online restaurant review

1 *Extreme* means "not usual" or "very." Complete the chart with examples of the "extremes" listed.

an extremely cold place	
an extremely loud song	
an extremely unusual food	
an extremely dangerous sport	
an extremely tall building	

2 Share your ideas with a partner.

1 ▶ **ACTIVATE** Watch the video. Then answer the questions.

1 Do you ever eat waffles? Do you like them? Which kind of waffle in the video would you like most?

2 Do you like to eat "street food" from vendors or trucks on the street? Why or why not? What kind of street food do you like to eat?

2 VOCABULARY Complete the sentences with words from the box.

perfect	typical	cook	cream
sugar	energy	sweet	frozen

♟ Oxford 3000™

1 _____ foods, like cake and candy, have a lot of _____.
2 I don't like _____ vegetables. Fresh vegetables taste better.
3 Many people like to drink coffee because it gives them _____.
4 On a _____ day, I have two cups of coffee. But I have more if I'm really tired.
5 This meal was great! You're an excellent _____.
6 A lot of people like _____ in their coffee, but I like milk.
7 Thanksgiving dinner was _____. Everything tasted great.

3 APPLY Are the vocabulary words in Exercise 2 nouns or adjectives?

1 noun / adjective, noun / adjective
2 noun / adjective
3 noun / adjective
4 noun / adjective
5 noun / adjective
6 noun / adjective
7 noun / adjective

4 WHAT'S YOUR ANGLE? Discuss the questions with a partner.

1 Tell about a typical dinner for you.
2 What is your perfect breakfast?
3 What are some of your favorite sweet foods?
4 What foods or drinks give you energy?

5 IDENTIFY Read the article. Are the statements true or false? Correct the false statements.

	True	False
1 The Espresso Buzz Bagel has more caffeine than a cup of coffee.	☐	☐
2 The Espresso Buzz Bagel can give you energy.	☐	☐
3 Most pizzas have about five kinds of cheese on them.	☐	☐
4 Scottie's Pizza Parlor only served the 101-cheese pizza for one day.	☐	☐
5 Scottie's broke a record for the largest pizza.	☐	☐
6 A farmer in the UK grew a very hot chili pepper.	☐	☐
7 The farmer ate the pepper, and it killed him.	☐	☐
8 The farmer grew the pepper because he likes hot food.	☐	☐

Extreme foods

Here is this month's "Extreme Foods" news!

How much cheese can you fit on a pizza? Well, a typical pizza has one to four kinds of cheese. But the Centuono Formaggio Pizza at Scottie's Pizza Parlor in Portland, Oregon, was not typical. For one day only, Scottie's made pizza with 101 different kinds of cheese! Scottie's broke the world record for the most kinds of cheese on one pizza.

Read more >

How many people love coffee and bagels? Well, now you can have both together! Einstein Brothers Bagels has a new bagel on its menu. The Espresso Buzz Bagel has 32 milligrams of caffeine. That's about a third of the caffeine in a small cup of coffee. If you need something to give you energy, but you don't want to drink coffee, this new bagel is perfect for you!

Read more >

A British farmer has grown an extremely fiery chili pepper—the hottest pepper in the world. If you eat a bite of the pepper, it can kill you. Why did he grow a pepper that can kill people? Even the farmer can't answer that question. It's a mystery!

Read more >

 READING SKILL Recognizing parts of speech, and using them to figure out meaning from context

If we know the parts of speech of words in a sentence (verb, noun, adjective), it's easier to understand the meaning of the sentence.

***Einstein Brothers Bagels** has a **new bagel** on its **menu**.*

After you know the parts of speech, think about their position in the sentence. This is a subject-verb-object sentence with three different nouns.

***Einstein Brothers Bagels** has a new **bagel** on its **menu**.*

6 INTEGRATE In the text below, identify the part of speech of each bold word.

A British farmer has grown an extremely **fiery** (1) chili pepper—the hottest pepper in the world. if you eat a **bite** (2) of the pepper, it can **kill** (3) you. Why did he **grow** (4) a pepper that can kill people? Even the farmer can't answer that question. It's a **mystery** (5)!

7 WHAT'S YOUR ANGLE? Discuss the questions with a small group.

1 What is your favorite kind of pizza?
2 Name some foods with chili peppers in them. Do you like them?
3 Name some "extreme foods." Which ones do you like? Which ones do you dislike?

GRAMMAR IN CONTEXT
How much / How many with countable and uncountable nouns

We use *How much* to ask about uncountable nouns and *How many* to ask about countable nouns.

How much cheese can you fit on a pizza? (***Cheese*** *is an uncountable noun.*)
How many people love coffee and bagels? (***People*** *is the plural of the countable noun* ***person***.)

See Grammar focus on page 162.

8 IDENTIFY Look at the article in Exercise 4. Find three uncountable nouns.

9 APPLY Write questions with *How much* or *How many*.

1 coffee / you drink / every day?
   How much coffee do you drink every day?
2 time / you spend studying / every day?
3 hours/ you sleep / every night?
4 money / you have in your pockets or bag / right now?
5 movies / watch / every month?

10 EXPAND Complete each question with *How much* or *How many*.

1 _____ pizza do you eat every month?
2 _____ days do you go to school each week?
3 _____ students are in your class?
4 _____ sugar do you use in coffee?
5 _____ cheese is on a typical pizza?

11 WHAT'S YOUR ANGLE? Work with a partner. Ask and answer the questions in Exercise 9.

Lunchtime
in Rome, Italy

1 ACTIVATE Do you read restaurant reviews before you go to a restaurant? Where do you find the reviews? What information do they usually give?

2 IDENTIFY Read the restaurant review. What is "extreme" about the restaurant?

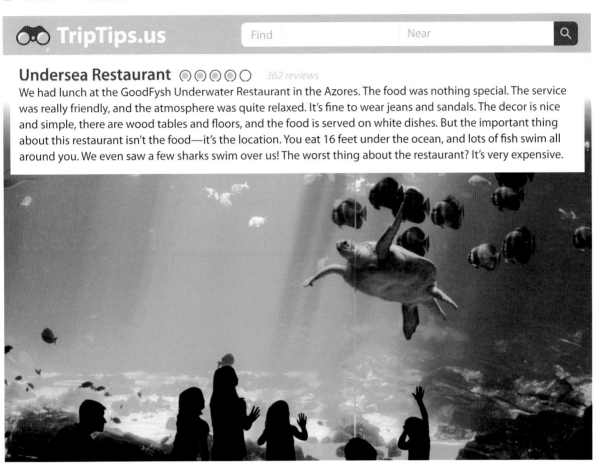

TripTips.us   Find   Near   🔍

Undersea Restaurant ◉◉◉◉◯   *362 reviews*

We had lunch at the GoodFysh Underwater Restaurant in the Azores. The food was nothing special. The service was really friendly, and the atmosphere was quite relaxed. It's fine to wear jeans and sandals. The decor is nice and simple, there are wood tables and floors, and the food is served on white dishes. But the important thing about this restaurant isn't the food—it's the location. You eat 16 feet under the ocean, and lots of fish swim all around you. We even saw a few sharks swim over us! The worst thing about the restaurant? It's very expensive.

3 INTEGRATE Read the review again, and answer the questions.

1 Where is the restaurant?

_____

2 How was the food?

_____

3 How was the service?

_____

4 How was the atmosphere?

_____

5 Is the restaurant expensive?

_____

4 WHAT'S YOUR ANGLE? When you choose a restaurant, how important is each thing to you? Rate each thing from 1 (not important) to 6 (very important). Compare your answers with a partner.

____ How expensive is it?   ____ How is the atmosphere?

____ What kind of food do they have?   ____ How is the service?

____ How is the food?   ____ Where is it?

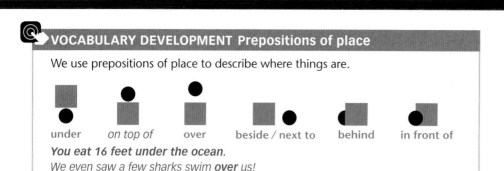

VOCABULARY DEVELOPMENT Prepositions of place

We use prepositions of place to describe where things are.

under   *on top of*   over   beside / next to   behind   in front of

You eat 16 feet under the ocean.
*We even saw a few sharks swim **over** us!*

🔑 Oxford 3000™

5 APPLY Complete the sentences with the correct prepositions.

1   At our company dinner, I sat *beside / in front of / behind* the company president.
    We had an interesting conversation.
2   That restaurant is noisy. Lots of planes fly *over / on top of / under* it.
3   The San Francisco Fairmont Hotel is *over / on top of / in front of* Nob Hill. You can see for
    miles from its roof.
4   The boat went *under / behind / over* the bridge.
5   You can't park your car *in front of / under / on top of* the restaurant. But there's a parking
    lot behind it.
6   Please stand *under / behind / over* your desk. Don't stand in front of it.
7   There is a gym *next to / over / on top of* my apartment—it's very convenient.

6 INTERACT Follow the instructions.

1   Pick five prepositions from the box above.
2   Write a sentence with each preposition.
3   Show your sentences to a partner.
4   Look at your partner's sentences. Identify the preposition in each sentence.
    Can you replace it with another preposition?

GRAMMAR IN CONTEXT Quantifiers: *a few / a little / a lot / lots*

See Grammar focus on page 162.

We use *a few* with countable nouns in positive sentences to talk about a small
number of people or things.
*I went to the restaurant with **a few** friends.*

We use *a little* with uncountable nouns in positive sentences to talk about a
small amount of something.
*Let's eat somewhere with fast service. I only have **a little** time.*

We use *lots of / a lot of* with countable or uncountable nouns to talk about a
big amount of something.
*There were **lots of / a lot of** fish swimming around us as we ate lunch.*

7 APPLY Choose the correct quantifier.

1   Could I please have *a few / a little* milk in my coffee?
2   If you want to eat at the GoodFysh Underwater Restaurant, you need *a lot of / a few* money!
3   Ben is going to take *a few / a little* days off from work.
4   There were *lots of / a little* people at the restaurant. We had to wait an hour to get a table.
5   I need *a few / a little* more time to think about that.
6   Scottie's Pizza Parlor used *a lot of / a little* different kinds of cheese on its pizza.
7   The Espresso Buzz Bagel has *a few / lots of* caffeine in it.
8   I can't stay long. I only have *lots of / a few* minutes before I have to go to work.

WRITING SKILL
Describing something with the adverbs *quite*, *very*, and *really*

We use the adverbs *quite*, *very*, and *really* before adjectives to make our writing more interesting.

Very and *really* make an adjective stronger.
*That restaurant is **very / really** expensive. We'll spend hundreds of dollars if we eat there!*

Quite makes an adjective less strong.
*The atmosphere was **quite** relaxed.*

---

8 IDENTIFY Read the restaurant review again. Find examples of adverbs in the review.

9 WHAT'S YOUR ANGLE? Make true sentences. Read them to a partner. Does your partner agree?

1   _____ is quite beautiful.
2   The food is really good at _____.
3   _____ is quite interesting.
4   _____ is very difficult.
5   _____ is really expensive.
6   _____ is a very tall building.

10 PREPARE You are going to write an online restaurant review. Think of a restaurant. What do you like and dislike about it? Make notes. Use the ideas in the box and your own ideas.

| food | service | atmosphere | price | location (where it is) |

11 WRITE Write a draft of your review. Use some of these words: *a few / a little / a lot / lots / quite / very / really*. Your review should be about 100 words and two paragraphs.

12 IMPROVE Read your restaurant review, and correct any grammar and spelling mistakes.

13 SHARE Swap reviews with a partner. Give your partner feedback on:
- Ideas: Did they say what they like and dislike about the restaurant?
- Grammar: Did they use *a few, a little, a lot,* and *lots* correctly?
- Writing skill: Did they use *quite, very,* and *really* correctly?
- Spelling: Did they spell the adverbs correctly?

14 DEVELOP Use your partner's feedback to rewrite your review.

1 ACTIVATE Work in a group. Look at the photos. What is "extreme" about each house?

House 1   House 2

2 INTERACT You are going to hear a conversation about the two houses in Exercise 1. Do you think the words will be about House 1 or House 2?

___ apartment building   ___ walls   ___ windows

___ skateboard   ___ corners   ___ fun

___ city   ___ trees   ___ roof

3 ◀)) ASSESS Listen to the conversation. Check your answers to Exercise 2.

LISTENING SKILL Understanding incomplete speech

When we speak, we often use sentences or phrases that are incomplete (not complete) or that are not grammatically complete. You can often guess what the person means or didn't say by the context.

In this conversation, speaker B says *Skateboarding* instead of *He's skateboarding*. But speaker A understands the meaning.

A: *What is he doing?*
B: *Skateboarding on the wall!*

In this conversation, speaker A understands that speaker B means *I'm still reading it, so you can't look at it now.*

A: *Can I look at that magazine?*
B: *Well, I'm still reading it, so…*

---

4 **INTEGRATE** Listen to excerpts from the conversation. What does the second speaker mean?

1 a I'm reading an article about extreme houses.
  b I'm going to read an article about extreme houses.
2 a That's a skateboard house.
  b They built a skateboard house.
3 a You can skateboard in every room.
  b There are a lot of rooms.
4 a It's just a house.
  b It's just a plan.
5 a I like the windows.
  b There are lots of windows.

5 WHAT'S YOUR ANGLE? Would you like to live in these houses? Why or why not?
Do you know someone who would like to live in them? Discuss your ideas with a partner.

GRAMMAR IN CONTEXT *There is... / There are...*

We use *There is / There are* to talk about things that are in a place. We use *There is* with singular nouns and *There are* with plural nouns. We often use the short form *There's* for *There is*.

There's a curved wall in every room.
There are trees on the roof.
Is there a curved wall in every room?
Are there any corners in the house?

There isn't a corner in the whole house!
There aren't any corners in the house.
Yes, **there is**. / No, **there isn't**.
Yes, **there are**. / No, **there aren't**.

See Grammar focus on page 162.

6 **INTEGRATE** Complete the conversations with the correct form of *There is / There are*. Then listen to check your answers.

1 A: _____ eight bedrooms in that house. It's really big!
  B: Wow! _____ a bathroom for every bedroom?
  A: No, _____. _____ four bathrooms.
2 A: _____ a garden on the roof?
  B: Yes, _____. _____ a vegetable garden.
3 A: _____ a lot of light in my house.
  B: Really? _____ a lot of windows?
  A: Yes, _____.
4 A: _____ some really expensive homes in that neighborhood.
  B: Oh? _____ some less expensive ones, too?
  A: No, _____. They're all expensive.

7 WHAT'S YOUR ANGLE? Think of an unusual home that you know of. Tell a partner about it. Your partner will ask and answer questions about it.

4.4 My Food Is Cold!

1 ACTIVATE What do you do when you don't like your food at a restaurant?

2 ▶ **IDENTIFY** Watch the video, and answer the questions.

1 Who has a problem with their food?
2 What does the person do?
3 How does the server respond?

REAL-WORLD ENGLISH Ordering food and drink, complaining about service

Ordering food

Server: Hello. What can I get for you today?
Customer: Can I have… / I'll have… / I'd like…, please.
Server: Sure.

Asking about food

What's in the coleslaw?
Is the burrito really/very spicy?
Are there nuts in the salad?

To complain about food, first say *Excuse me* to get the server's attention. Then explain the problem.

Excuse me. My food is cold.

3 ▶ **NOTICE** Watch the video again. What does the customer say?

1 Sarah: Hello. What can I get for you today?
   Kevin: Uh, _____ the mac and cheese, please. And a lemonade.
2 Sarah: OK. For you?
   Andy: Um, _____ a salad? And a medium coffee? Thanks.
   Max: And I'll have the burrito, please. Uh, _____ spicy?
   Sarah: No. Mild to medium.
   Max: OK. _____ the burrito, please.
3 Sarah: Hi! Oh,… your food. Is everything OK?
   Kevin: Uh,… no. My mac and cheese is _____!

4 **ANALYZE** Read the conversations. Do you think the customer is polite? Why or why not? Work in pairs. Revise the conversations to make the customer more polite.

1 Customer: Hey, server!
    Server: Yes, how can I help you?
    Customer: Well, I ordered my steak medium. But this is well done.

2 Server: What can I get for you today?
    Customer: A hamburger.

3 Customer: Excuse me. Uh, this isn't what I ordered. I wanted the fish. Why did you bring me this?
    Server: I'm so sorry. Let me take that. I'll bring you the fish as quickly as possible.

4 Server: Can I take your order?
    Customer: Give me a piece of chocolate cake with ice cream.

5 **INTERACT** Work with two other students. Think of three things to complain about at a restaurant. Then create role plays with two customers and a server. Do the following:

Server: Take the customers' orders.

Customers: Order your food and drinks.

Server: Bring the food and drinks.

Customers: Talk to each other about your food.

Customer: Get the server's attention, and then complain politely.

Server: Explain how you will fix the problem.

6 **ANALYZE** Work with another group, and watch their role play. Did they do the things in Exercise 5? Were they polite?

7 **WHAT'S YOUR ANGLE?** Think of a successful complaint you made. What kind of language did you use? What was the situation?

GO ONLINE
to create your own version
of the English For Real video.

49

4.5 An Extremely Messy Room

1 ACTIVATE Is your home messy or neat? Do you want it to be neater?

2 **IDENTIFY** Listen. A person is describing a room. What does she say?

1 ☐ His bed is in the middle of the room.
2 ☐ There are a lot of chairs.
3 ☐ There's a nice, soft rug on the floor.
4 ☐ There are also clothes all over the floor and the chair.
5 ☐ In the corner, there's a big trash can.
6 ☐ There are beautiful mirrors on the walls.
7 ☐ There are plates on the desk.
8 ☐ There's a glass on the table.

> **PRONUNCIATION SKILL Linking with *there's* / *there are***
>
> We usually link, or connect, the *s* in *there's* or the second *r* in *there are* to the first vowel in the next word. *There's a* sounds like *Thereza*. *There are only* sounds like *There aronly*.
>
> Listen to the linking of *there's* and *there are* and the vowels that follows them.
>
> *In the corner,* **there's a** *big trash can.*   **There are** *always clothes on it.*

3 APPLY Mark the links in these sentences. Then read the sentences aloud to a partner. Listen to your partner read the sentences. Did they link *there is* / *there are* to the vowel in the next word?

1 There are a lot of papers on the desk.
2 There's a bed in the middle of the room.
3 There are only two restaurants in my town.
4 There's a lot of light.
5 There are clothes on the bed.
6 There's a nice cafe near my office.

> **SPEAKING Describe a room**
>
> Here are some ways to describe a room:
>
> *It's a tiny / small / middle-sized / big / huge room.*
> *It's very neat / messy.*
> *There are a lot of windows / rugs / pillows / books.*
> *There's / There isn't a lot of furniture.*
> *It's light / dark.*

4 WHAT'S YOUR ANGLE? Think of an "extreme" room. It can be extremely messy, neat, or big. Or think of your own idea. Make notes on why the room is extreme and what is in it.

5 INTERACT Follow the instructions.

1 Tell a partner about the room from Exercise 4. Answer their questions.
2 Listen to your partner talk about their room. Ask questions and take notes.
3 Work with another pair. Tell them about your partner's room.
   Work together and decide whose room is the most extreme.

Now go to page 150 for the Unit 4 Review.

5 Creativity

UNIT SNAPSHOT

What do the letters *DIY* stand for?   53

Who were the Impressionists?   58

How can you give a negative opinion
without making someone feel bad?   60

Why do people look
at art?

What things are better
made at home?

What art is popular
in your country?

BEHIND THE PHOTO

REAL-WORLD GOAL

Learn how to make
something by reading or
watching a video online

Take the quiz about famous creative people. Compare your answers with a partner.

1 This ancient Greek poet is best known for writing the *Odyssey* and the *Iliad*.

   a Aeschylus   b Homer   c Socrates

2 This Chinese-born architect designed the pyramid at the Louvre Museum in
Paris, the Bank of China Tower in Hong Kong, and the Museum of Islamic
Art in Doha, Qatar.

   a I. M. Pei   b Maya Lin   c Ai Weiwei

3 Farmers in which country developed vallenato folk music as a form of
entertainment and communication?

   a Brazil   b Peru   c Colombia

5.1 Are You a Maker?

1 ACTIVATE Describe the picture. What are some special things that people make in your country or region? Discuss with the class.

A ceramic artist in Sciacca, Italy

2 VOCABULARY Match the creative hobbies to the descriptions.

build things with wood	**build machines**	**sell** things **online**	**bake** breads and cakes
make your **own** clothes	**grow** a garden	**make jewelry**	

 Oxford 3000™

1 I work with silver, gold, and stones to make pretty things to wear.
2 I plant flowers and vegetables behind my house.
3 I sometimes design, sew, and then wear new shirts and pants.
4 I'm putting an ad on the Internet, so people can buy my things.
5 I'm making a tree house for my kids to play in.
6 I love working in the kitchen to make something delicious.
7 I work with electronic parts to make things that move, like a robot or a toy car.

3 WHAT'S YOUR ANGLE? Think of people you know who do the activities from Exercise 2. Write sentences.

My uncle Richard grows a beautiful garden every year.

4 INTERACT Work with a partner. Ask if your partner does the activities, then switch roles. If you do one of the activities, add details.

READING SKILL Recognizing and understanding cause and effect linking words: *Because, as, so*

The words *because* and *as* show a reason or cause. They can be used at the beginning or in the middle of a sentence.

*A lot of people sell things online **because** it's easy.*
As nice jewelry is expensive, I don't buy much of it.

Because selling things online is easy, a lot of people do it.
*I don't buy much nice jewelry, **as** it is expensive.*

The phrase *because of* is followed by a noun or pronoun.

*Handmade items are often more expensive **because of** the time and skill it takes to make them.*

The word *so* shows an effect or result. It can be used in the middle of a sentence that links two ideas.

*I wanted to learn how to build birdhouses, **so** I watched some videos online.*

Knowing these words will help you understand how ideas or actions described in a text are connected.

5 **ASSESS** Read the sentences. Decide which part is the cause and which is the effect.

<u>cause</u>   <u>effect</u>
Original paintings are too expensive for me to buy. Because of this, I'm learning how to paint.

1   I often visit the Pinterest website because of the many great ideas people post there.

2   As I'm very good at making jewelry, I'm starting my own online store.

3   You need space outdoors to have a garden, so many people in cities can't grow their own vegetables.

4   I don't make my own clothes because it's difficult.

5   Cakes from the supermarket are usually terrible, so I always bake my own cakes.

6 **IDENTIFY** Read the article. Why did we stop making our own things? Why are many people starting to make their own things now?

Why DIY?

by Sarah Hill

Right now, I'm making a dress for my daughter and building a bookcase for our living room. Why is this special?

In today's world, so many things come from factories. We can buy them, so we don't need to make them. We also don't make things because we don't know how. As technology made life easier for us, we lost many skills that our grandparents had.

This is changing. Many of us want to relearn old skills, so we're starting to make our own things. Say hello to the DIY (do it yourself) movement! People all over the world are using websites such as Pinterest to share ideas about DIY projects like baking and making clothes. There are online videos about how to cook, build things, and grow gardens. People are making jewelry and other items and selling them on sites like Etsy. Because of this, we can have things that are special, not factory-made.

There are also international Maker Faires. There, people build machines and play with science and technology. Maker Faires were the idea of Dale Dougherty. He started them because he thinks everyone can make things.

It's true. We can all be makers. What are you making right now?

A Japanese robot at a Maker Faire in China

GRAMMAR IN CONTEXT Present continuous

We use the present continuous to talk about actions happening now or to talk about the situation around now.

We're starting to make our own things.

For *wh-* questions, use question word + *be* + *-ing*:

What are you making right now?   *I'm making a dress for my daughter.*

When we answer *yes/no* questions, we can use short forms with *be*:

Is your brother learning how to bake?   *Yes, he is. / No, he isn't.*

See Grammar focus on page 163.

7 **INTEGRATE** Answer the questions.

1   What two DIY projects is the author of the article doing now?
2   Name three other DIY activities that are popular now.
3   What is the person in the photo at the Maker Faire doing?
4   What are some people doing with the items they make?

8 ◀ッ **APPLY** Complete the conversation with the correct verbs in the present continuous. Then listen and check your answers.

have	visit	take	shop	make	stay	do

A: What _____ you _____?
B: I___ _____ dinner for my cousins. They ___ _____ this week from Mexico.
A: Oh. Where _____ they _____?
B: At a hotel downtown. My apartment is too small!
A: Where are they now?
B: My cousin Mario _____ _____ for gifts, and Lorena and my sister _____ _____ my niece to the zoo.
A: Sounds like fun.
B: We ___ _____ a lot of fun!

9 **APPLY** Write sentences in the present continuous. Then write *True* or *False* based on what's true for you.

1   I / take a class   _____ _____
2   my neighbors / grow a garden   _____ _____
3   my friends and I / work on an interesting project   _____ _____
4   I / read a good book   _____ _____
5   my friend / learn how to play an instrument   _____ _____
6   I / make jewelry   _____ _____

10 **WHAT'S YOUR ANGLE?** How often do you make things? What do you make? What would you like to learn how to make?

I like to bake cookies and cakes. I do this once or twice a month. I would like to learn how to make French pastries.

1 ACTIVATE Imagine you can take any kind of class you want. What would you like to take? Why?

2 VOCABULARY Look at the course catalog. What course should each person take?

1   I want to learn how to develop and write interesting stories and books.
2   I want to design and make clothes.
3   I need to organize my ideas better in my work emails.
4   I want to improve my language skills.
5   I'd like to organize weddings and other large events.
6   I'd like to learn how to write a computer program.
7   I like to bake, so I'd like to learn to decorate cakes so they look nice.

🔑 Oxford 3000™

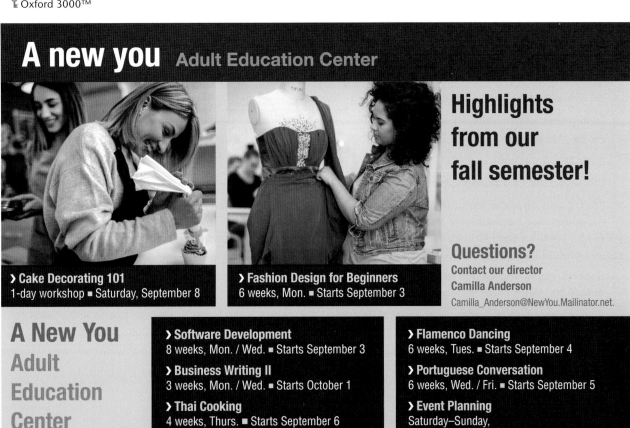

A new you Adult Education Center

Highlights from our fall semester!

Questions?
Contact our director
Camilla Anderson
Camilla_Anderson@NewYou.Mailinator.net.

❭ **Cake Decorating 101**
1-day workshop ▪ Saturday, September 8

❭ **Fashion Design for Beginners**
6 weeks, Mon. ▪ Starts September 3

A New You Adult Education Center

❭ **Software Development**
8 weeks, Mon. / Wed. ▪ Starts September 3

❭ **Business Writing II**
3 weeks, Mon. / Wed. ▪ Starts October 1

❭ **Thai Cooking**
4 weeks, Thurs. ▪ Starts September 6

❭ **Creative Writing I**
4 weeks, Tues./Thurs. ▪ Starts October 2

❭ **Flamenco Dancing**
6 weeks, Tues. ▪ Starts September 4

❭ **Portuguese Conversation**
6 weeks, Wed. / Fri. ▪ Starts September 5

❭ **Event Planning**
Saturday–Sunday,
September 8–9 or October 6–7

GRAMMAR IN CONTEXT Verbs + *to* infinitive

We sometimes use a second verb after a main verb.

Subject + verb + *to* infinitive

*I **would like to study** computer programming.*

The first verb changes according to the subject or the tense. The *to* infinitive never changes.

*He **wants to take** cooking classes.*   *We **needed to improve** our writing skills.*

Some verbs that are often followed by a *to* infinitive are:

| want | like | would like | need | plan | decide |

See Grammar focus on page 163.

3 APPLY Write the words in the correct order. Add punctuation.

1 don't classes take want online to I

    _____

2 need develop skills to you your writing

    _____

3 evening in would they to the like study

    _____

4 to like doesn't he have classes Saturday on

    _____

5 Japanese learn want we to

    _____

4 WHAT'S YOUR ANGLE? What do you usually like to do after class? What do you plan to do today? Tell a partner.

I usually like to…

5 EXPAND Write a statement using a verb + *to* infinitive to describe a class that you would find interesting.

6 IDENTIFY Read the email.

1 What class does Paul Mason want to take?

2 Is his email formal or informal? How can you tell?

✉

To: Camilla_Anderson@NewYou.Mailinator.net

From: paul.mason@mailinator.net

Re: Fall classes

Dear Ms. Anderson:

I received the fall catalog for your school, and I would like to ask you a few questions about the classes.

First, I want to know about the Software Development class. I am interested in writing computer programs, but I do not have much programming experience. Do you think I can do well in this class? Also, I want to learn how to design computer games as a hobby. Does the class teach this? If not, do you plan to have a game development class in the future?

Second, could you please tell me a little about the teacher? I like to know about the teacher before I decide to take a class. Is it possible for me to email him or her?

Also, I plan to go on vacation at the end of August and return September 6. I would like to know what to do about the first two classes. Can I take a private lesson, or can I pay for five weeks instead of six?

Finally, what do I need to bring with me to class? Do I need a laptop?

Thank you very much for your time.

Sincerely,

Paul Mason

---

7 INTEGRATE Read the email again. Choose *True* or *False*.

		True	False
1	Paul learned about the classes on the school's website.	True	False
2	Paul wants to study game design.	True	False
3	Paul works as a computer programmer.	True	False
4	Camilla Anderson is the Software Development teacher.	True	False
5	Paul is going to miss the first week of class.	True	False

8 PREPARE Choose a class that you would like to take from the catalog. What do you want to learn this skill for? What information do you need to know before you take the class? Make notes.

It's important to use appropriate language in an email. When writing to someone you don't know, use formal language. This way your message will sound polite and respectful.

Use a formal opening and closing.

Openings:	*Closings:*
Dear Mr./Ms./Dr. _____:	*Sincerely,*
(if you don't know the person's name) Dear Sir or Madam:	*Regards,*

Avoid contractions, exclamation marks, emojis, and very emotional language.

I am interested in your school's cooking classes. NOT ~~I'm really excited about the cooking classes!! ☺~~

Choose polite expressions.

Could you please send me...? NOT ~~Send me...~~

Look for more formal words.

excellent, interesting NOT ~~cool~~
receive NOT ~~get~~

9 DEVELOP Rewrite the underlined parts of the email using appropriate register.

✉

To: Marlon_Gibbs@NewYou.mailinator.net

Re: teaching job

(1) <u>Hey, Marlon!</u>

(2) <u>What's up?</u> (3) <u>I'm Sonia Ruiz.</u> I saw your ad for a Flamenco Dancing teacher. (4) <u>I'd like to do it!</u> I have 18 years of experience dancing flamenco. I started dance lessons when I was just four years old. (5) <u>My mom and dad are both musicians.</u>

I also have some experience as a teacher. I like to teach Spanish in my free time.

(6) <u>The job sounds soooo cool.</u> (7) <u>I really wanna teach at your school! :D</u>

(8) <u>Love,</u>

(9) <u>Sonia</u>

---

1 _____   4 _____   7 _____
2 _____   5 _____   8 _____
3 _____   6 _____   9 _____

10 WRITE Write an email of about 100 words (two paragraphs) to the director of the Adult Education Center. Use your notes from Exercise 8.

11 IMPROVE Read your email. Make sure that…

☐ you used formal and polite language.
☐ you used verbs + *to* infinitive correctly.
☐ the names of your courses are spelled correctly.

12 SHARE Share your email with a partner. Read your partner's email. Ask questions and give feedback.

13 WHAT'S YOUR ANGLE? Are there any adult education centers where you live? What is your opinion of the kinds of classes they offer? How are they different from colleges and universities?

5.3 Painting Millions

1 ACTIVATE What makes a painting good in your opinion? Choose the two most important things from the list, and discuss with the class.

- ☐ uses pretty colors
- ☐ is interesting or different
- ☐ is beautiful
- ☐ makes me feel a strong emotion

- ☐ people and things look real
- ☐ shows a scene from history
- ☐ shows a scene from daily life
- ☐ makes an important statement

2 WHAT'S YOUR ANGLE? Think of a famous artist from your country. What kind of work does the artist make?

LISTENING SKILL Recognizing weak sounds

When you are listening to someone talk, you usually notice the stressed words. These are usually content words (the important nouns, action verbs, adjectives, and adverbs). It's usually harder to hear the weak sounds of the unstressed, shorter words (*are, and, of, to*, etc.).

People often pay a lot of money for paintings by famous artists.

Focusing on hearing these words will improve your listening skills.

---

3 🔊 IDENTIFY Listen to the sentences and fill in the unstressed words.

1 Impressionism _____ _____ art movement _____ _____ mid- _____ late 1800s.

2 Do _____ notice _____ soft light _____ shapes?

3 _____ Post-Impressionists _____ interested _____ colors, like _____ Impressionists, _____ they want _____ do something bigger.

4 _____ work _____ very emotional, _____ _____ uses strong colors.

5 This painting sold _____ $82,500,000 _____ 1990, _____ _____ _____ time _____ was _____ most expensive painting _____ _____ world.

4 🔊 ⟦QR⟧ ASSESS Listen to the talk. Number the paintings in the order you hear about them, and label them with the name of the correct painter.

— adapted from *Oxford Encyclopedia of the Modern World*, edited by Peter N. Stearns

Van Gogh   Monet   Cézanne

___ _____   ___ _____   ___ _____

5 🔊 **INTEGRATE** Listen again. Put the numbers in the correct columns.

1 Impressionist	5 most famous Post-Impressionist	9 $81 million
2 soft light and shapes	6 interested in color and shapes	10 $300 million
3 emotional	7 haystack	11 playing cards
4 strong, bright colors	8 $82,500,000	12 famous Post-Impressionist

Monet's painting	Van Gogh's painting	Cézanne's painting

GRAMMAR IN CONTEXT Simple present and present continuous

We use the simple present to talk about general facts, habits or routines, and things that happen all the time.

*People often **pay** a lot of money for paintings by famous artists.*

We use the present continuous to talk about something happening now or around now.

*Today **we're talking** about some of the world's most expensive paintings.*

See Grammar focus on page 163.

6 **APPLY** Simple present or present continuous? Complete the sentences with the correct form of the verb.

Right now, we __are looking__ (look) at some famous paintings.

1 Many people these days _____ (love) Impressionist paintings.

2 Monet's painting _____ (show) a haystack on his farm.

3 Van Gogh _____ (be) one of the most famous Post-Impressionist painters.

4 In the painting, Dr. Gachet _____ (sit) and _____ (think) about something.

5 The men in Cézanne's painting _____ (not talk) to each other.

VOCABULARY DEVELOPMENT Time expressions

Time expressions tell you when something happens.

Here are some time expressions that can be used with the simple present or present continuous:

now   these days   today

These time expressions are most often used with the simple present:

always   usually   often   sometimes   never

These time expressions are most often used with the present continuous:

right now   at the moment

7 **VOCABULARY** Complete the sentences with a time expression that fits.

1 _____, most people use the Internet instead of the library for research.

2 I'm from Hong Kong, but _____ I'm living in London.

3 _____, I'm wearing a blue shirt and black pants.

4 I hated vegetables when I was a kid, but _____ I love them.

5 My friends and I _____ meet at a coffee shop after class on Fridays.

8 **INTERACT** Work with a partner. Rewrite the sentences from Exercise 7 so they are true for you.

5.4 In My Opinion

1 ACTIVATE When did you last share an opinion with someone? What was it about?

2 ▶ **IDENTIFY** Watch the video. Choose the correct answers.

1 _____ thinks Mary Cassatt's art is interesting.
   Max   Dave

2 Max _____ Impressionist paintings.
   likes   doesn't like

3 Dave _____ Professor Armstrong likes Impressionist painting.
   thinks   doesn't think

4 Professor Armstrong thinks the Impressionists are _____.
   boring   wonderful

5 Dave _____ with Max about the Impressionists.
   agrees   doesn't agree

REAL-WORLD ENGLISH Asking for and giving opinions

If you want to get someone's opinion, you can ask:

What do you think about / of…?   *How do you feel about…?*   *Do you like…?*
What's your opinion about / of…?   *In your opinion, …?*

When you have a negative opinion about something but you don't want to seem rude or to make someone feel bad, you can make your opinion softer. Compare the two sets of expressions below.

Very honest	Honest but softer
I don't like it.	*It's different, but it's not really my style.*
I hate it!	*It's OK, but to be honest, it's not my favorite.*
I think it's boring.	*In my opinion, / For me, / I think _____ is more interesting.*
I don't understand why it's popular.	*I know it's very popular, but I like _____ more.*

3 **APPLY** Complete the conversations with a phrase from the box.

1 A: _____ the new Thai restaurant?

   B: In my opinion, it's a little too expensive.

2 A: _____ classical music?

   B: Hmm, I guess it's OK. Why?

   A: I have tickets to see the London Symphony this weekend.

3 A: _____, what is the best place to go hiking near here?

   B: I think Shady Glen Forest is really nice.

4 A: What do you think about baseball?

   B: _____, it's fun to play but not to watch.

5 A: Do you like to draw or paint?

   B: _____

6 A: How do you feel about cooking?

   B: _____

4 ⏵ **ANALYZE** Watch the video again. How is Dave's reaction to Max's opinion different from his reaction to Professor Armstrong's? How does he give his opinions differently to each person? Why do you think he reacts differently?

5 **EXPAND** Discuss in groups. Is it important to always give an honest opinion? Think of an example of when you might not give an honest opinion.

6 **ASSESS** Read the scenarios. In each one, can you be very honest, or do you need to soften your opinion?

1 You see your good friend at a clothing store. Your friend is trying on some clothes, but you think they look terrible on your friend.

2 You're reading a book for a class. Your professor loves the book, but you think it's boring.

3 You and your friend watched the same movie last night. You thought it was OK.

4 You see your friend's parent at a local restaurant. They ask your opinion about the place. You have a positive opinion.

5 Your classmate shows you a painting they made. You think it's weird.

6 A classmate asks your opinion about a poem they are writing. You have a positive opinion.

7 **INTERACT** Work with a partner. Choose a scenario from Exercise 5. Write a complete conversation with a greeting and an ending. Use appropriate phrases for asking for and giving opinions.

8 **INTEGRATE** Present your role play for another pair. Then watch their role play, and give feedback.

 GO ONLINE
to create your own version
of the English For Real video.

5.5 A High-Flying Hobby

1 ACTIVATE Describe the image. What hobby do you think the people are going to talk about?

2 🔊 **IDENTIFY** Listen to the man's live video from a Maker's Faire. Choose the correct statements.

The woman at the Maker's Faire...

☐ makes drones out of recycled trash. ☐ is selling paintings.
☐ plans to study engineering at school. ☐ is an artist.
☐ wants to save the world. ☐ wants to travel the world.
☐ is working for a technology company. ☐ loves her job.

@▶ PRONUNCIATION SKILL Contractions: *be* and *do*

🔊 We usually use contractions when we talk. Using contractions will improve your listening and will make your speaking sound more natural. Contractions make words shorter and faster to say.

I am (2 syllables) → *I'm /aɪm/ (1 syllable)*

Sometimes the number of syllables in a contraction is the same, but the sounds are still shorter.

does not (2 syllables) → *doesn't /dʌz ən?/ (2 syllables)*

We don't clearly pronounce the *t* at the end of negative contractions.

aren't /ɑrn?/

Contractions with *be*   Contractions with *do*

I'm /aɪm/   we're /wɪr/   *don't /don?/   doesn't /dʌz ən?/*
you're /jʊr/   they're /ðer/
she's /ʃiz/   he's /hiz/
it's /ɪtz/
isn't /ɪz ən?/   aren't /ɑrn?/

---

3 🔊 **NOTICE** Choose the contraction you hear. Write the number of syllables. Then listen again and repeat.

1	We're	They're	You're	syllables: ___
2	doesn't	isn't	it's	syllables: ___
3	don't	doesn't	isn't	syllables: ___
4	He's	She's	aren't	syllables: ___
5	They're	You're	aren't	syllables: ___
6	I'm	don't	doesn't	syllables: ___

4 WHAT'S YOUR ANGLE? Choose a hobby that you enjoy. Make notes about what you do, why you enjoy it, and what project(s) you're working on now (or plans you're making).

@▶ SPEAKING Describe a hobby

You can use *I like / love / enjoy* + noun or *–ing* verb to introduce your hobby.
I really enjoy bike riding.

To say how often you do your hobby, use *once / twice / three times a week,* or *every day / week / month.*
In the summer, I go bike riding once a week.

---

5 INTERACT Describe your hobby to the class. Answer your classmates' questions. Then listen to your classmates' presentations, and ask them questions about their hobbies.

Now go to page 151 for the Unit 5 Review.

6 Places

UNIT SNAPSHOT

What is an "everyday adventure"? 66

What is one way to learn a language without traveling? 67

What country can you walk across in an hour? 69

What kind of place is this?

What makes some places popular with tourists?

Where do you like visiting?

BEHIND THE PHOTO

1 Answer the questions.

1 What is one of your favorite places? Why do you like it?
   I really like my local park. It has lots of trees and a lake. It's very peaceful but lots of people go there to walk and enjoy nature.

2 What place do you want to visit? Why?

3 Why do people like to visit different places?

2 Discuss your answers with a partner.

REAL-WORLD GOAL

Give someone advice about a place you know well

6.1 A Good Neighborhood

1 ACTIVATE What makes a good neighborhood? Discuss your ideas with a partner.

2 VOCABULARY Match the places to the pictures.

a bakery	a shopping mall
a department store	a farmers' market
a grocery store	a gym
an ATM	a hairdresser

Oxford 3000™

3 IDENTIFY Complete the sentences with a place from Exercise 2.

1 You buy bread at _____.
2 You exercise at _____.
3 You can buy clothes at _____ or _____.
4 You can buy vegetables at _____ or _____.

4 ▶ EXPAND Watch the video. What places does Allison visit? Make a list.

5 WHAT'S YOUR ANGLE? Ask and answer the questions with a partner.

1 How often do you go to the places in Exercise 2?
2 What is your favorite bakery? Park? Cafe?

You usually listen for details after you understand the main idea. Details are often places, numbers, or dates. Before you listen, know what details you need. This helps you understand the meaning. You can use these questions to help you find details: *Who? What? When? Where? How many?*

6 ▶ **ASSESS** Read the statements. What details do you need? Then watch the video again. Are the statements true (T) or false (F)? Correct the false statements.

___ 1 Allison works at a grocery store.

___ 2 Today is Saturday.

___ 3 Allison works on Saturdays.

___ 4 The muffin costs $1.15.

___ 5 Allison moved to this neighborhood in August.

___ 6 Allison pays $5.50 for the strawberries.

7 WHAT'S YOUR ANGLE? Discuss the questions with a group.

1 What do you like about Allison's neighborhood?

2 How is your neighborhood the same as Allison's neighborhood? How is it different?

GRAMMAR IN CONTEXT *Have to* and *don't have to*

We use *have to* to talk about rules, or when something is necessary.

*I **have to** go to the ATM.* *He **has to** work tonight.*

We use *don't have to* when there is a choice or when something isn't necessary.

*I **don't have to** work until later.* *She **doesn't have to** study tonight.*

We use *do / does* with *have to* to form questions.

***Do you have to** study tonight?* *Yes, I do.*
***Does she have to** work tonight?* *No, she doesn't.*

See Grammar focus on page 164.

8 IDENTIFY Complete the sentences. Use the correct form of *have to* or *don't have to*.

1 Isabel _____ work today. She's going to go to the beach.

2 Sorry, I can't go out for pizza tonight. I _____ study.

3 You _____ give me a ride home. I can take the bus.

4 Henry needs money. He _____ go to the ATM.

9 APPLY Complete the conversations. Use the correct form of *have to* or *don't have to*.

1 A: _____ she _____ go to the grocery store after work?

B: Yes, she _____.

2 A: _____ they _____ get up early tomorrow?

B: No, they _____.

3 A: _____ he _____ go to the doctor?

B: No, he _____.

4 A: _____ we _____ learn this grammar?

B: Yes, we _____.

10 WHAT'S YOUR ANGLE? Work with a partner. Take turns asking and answering questions with *Do you have to...?* You can use the verbs in the box and your own ideas.

study	work	go to the grocery store
go to another class	clean your home	go to the ATM

Do you have to _____ today?
Do you have to _____ this weekend?

1 **ACTIVATE** Where do you like to go on vacation? What do you like to do there? Share your ideas with a group.

2 🔊 **VOCABULARY** Match the sentences. Then listen and check your answers.

1   I like to go **abroad**. ___

2   I can't **afford** expensive vacations. ___

3   I like to **relax**. ___

4   I want **adventure**. ___

5   I like to stay in a place with a great **view**. ___

6   I enjoy guided **tours**. ___

🔑 Oxford 3000™

a   I don't like to walk around a new city alone.

b   Every year, I go to a different country for vacation.

c   I always go to the beach for vacation.

d   I want to see the ocean or the mountains outside my window.

e   I travel by bus, and I stay in cheap hotels.

f   I like to do new and exciting things.

3 **WHAT'S YOUR ANGLE?** Which sentences in Exercise 2 are true for you? Tell a partner.

Scanning helps you find specific information quickly. When you scan, don't read every word. Instead, look for numbers or key words related to the information you need. Scan a text when you want to find details, not main ideas.

4 IDENTIFY Scan the travel blog to answer these questions. Share your answers with a partner.

1 How much does a 24-hour subway pass cost in Boston? _____

2 In what city did Ayako go on an elevator tour? _____

3 What languages did Liz hear? _____

Home	About		Search 🔍

Everyday adventures

Are you looking for an adventure but can't afford to travel? Try an "everyday adventure"! If you have a few free hours, you can have an exciting adventure close to home. Here are a few examples:

Ben: In Boston, you can buy a 24-hour subway pass for $12. Last Saturday, I got a pass and rode one subway line. I got off at every stop and walked around the neighborhood. I learned a lot about my city!

Ayako: Last Thursday night, some friends and I went on an elevator tour of Tokyo. We took an elevator to the top of a few hotels and looked out the windows. The views were beautiful!

Liz: Last Sunday, I went to a cafe in a neighborhood with a lot of tourists. I listened to people speaking Spanish and Chinese, and I tried to understand them. You don't have to travel to learn a language! In my city, there are lots of places where you can meet people from other countries.

5 WHAT'S YOUR ANGLE? Discuss these questions with a group.

1 Which of the everyday adventures in the blog do you like most? Why?

2 Can you do these everyday adventures in your town or city? Why or why not?

3 What are some other everyday adventures you can do in your town or city?

We use *can* to talk about ability.

*I **can't** read the menu. I don't have my glasses.*

We also use *can* and *can't* to talk about possibilities.

*You **can** buy a cheap 24-hour subway pass.*
*We **can't** go to that restaurant for lunch. They're only open for dinner.*
***Can** we have a room with a view?   I'm sorry, you **can't**. They're all full.*
*Where **can** we get some good pizza near here?*

See Grammar focus on page 164.

6 **IDENTIFY** Complete the sentences with *can* or *can't*.

1 We _____ use that elevator. We have to use the stairs.

2 You _____ hear many different languages at that cafe. A lot of tourists go there.

3 Jack _____ go out tonight. He has to stay home and study.

4 You _____ get breakfast at the hotel or at the restaurant across the street. They both have good food.

5 You _____ take a guided tour to see a lot of sites in one day.

7 **INTEGRATE** Work with a partner. Complete the questions with *can* and the correct word from the box.

do	find	relax	take	hear

1 Where _____ I _____ a good cup of coffee near here?

2 _____ you _____ a bus to English class from your home?

3 In your neighborhood, what _____ you _____ for fun on the weekend?

4 Where _____ you _____ in your neighborhood?

5 Where in your town or city _____ you _____ many different languages?

8   **EXPAND** Listen. People are answering the questions in Exercise 7. Which question does each person answer? Write the correct question number in the chart.

Person	Question number
1	
2	
3	
4	
5	

9 **WHAT'S YOUR ANGLE?** Work with a partner. Take turns asking and answering the questions in Exercise 7.

6.3 Monaco in May

1 ACTIVATE What do you know about Monaco? Discuss these questions with a group. If you don't know the answers, guess.

1 How big is it?
2 Where is it?
3 What is the weather like?
4 What languages do people speak?
5 What fun things can you do there?

2 IDENTIFY Read the travel article about Monaco. Does it answer any of the questions you talked about in Exercise 1? What are the answers to those questions?

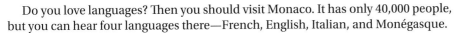

 ## Monaco

Do you love languages? Then you should visit Monaco. It has only 40,000 people, but you can hear four languages there—French, English, Italian, and Monégasque.

Monaco is a great place for car lovers. You should visit in late May, so you can watch the Grand Prix auto race. But you shouldn't drive in Monaco because there's usually a lot of traffic in the city center, and it moves very slowly.

Walking is the best way to see Monaco. You can walk across the country in an hour. It's only two square kilometers!

After your walk, you can relax at Larvotto Beach. It's usually very crowded, so you should get there early to find a place to sit.

Monaco is a wonderful place for a vacation. But it's very expensive, so spend your money carefully!

—adapted from *A Guide to the Countries of the World* by Christopher Riches and Peter Stalker

3 INTEGRATE Discuss the questions with a partner.

1 What kind of person should go to Monaco for vacation?
2 What are three things you can do in Monaco?
3 Do you want to go to Monaco? Why or why not?

VOCABULARY DEVELOPMENT Adverbs of manner

We use adverbs of manner to give more information about verbs. They tell how we do something.

We **quietly** walked / walked **quietly** into the museum.
Spend your money **carefully**.

Most adverbs end with *-ly* or *-ily*.

Common adverbs of manner

carefully	*loudly*
slowly	*safely*
quickly	*happily*
quietly	*easily*

Some adverbs are irregular. *Well* is the adverb form of the adjective *good*. *Fast* is the adverb form of the adjective *fast*. The adverb and adjective forms are the same.

4 **INTERACT** Follow the instructions.

1 Pick five adverbs from the box above.
2 Write a sentence with each adverb.
3 Show your sentences to a partner.
4 Look at your partner's sentences. Identify the verb and the adverb in each sentence, and then replace the adverb with a different adverb.

GRAMMAR IN CONTEXT *Should / Shouldn't*: Advice

We use *should / shouldn't* to ask for advice and give advice.

You **should** visit Monaco if you love languages.
You **shouldn't** visit in the winter. It rains a lot.
Should I bring a jacket?   Yes, you **should**. It's always cool in the evening.

See Grammar focus on page 164.

5 **IDENTIFY** Find the advice in the article about Monaco. Then complete the advice for visiting Miami. Use *should* or *shouldn't*.

1 You _____ visit Miami. It's an exciting city.
2 You _____ go in the summer. It's too hot.
3 You _____ stay in a hotel with an ocean view. They're very expensive.
4 You _____ take a boat tour. They're really fun.

6 **INTEGRATE** Give advice to a visitor to your town or city. Write three sentences with *should* and three sentences with *shouldn't*. You can use verbs from the box or other verbs.

see	go	visit	bring	watch
wear	eat	take	stay	

WRITING SKILL Writing an interesting introduction

The introduction (beginning) of an article should make the reader want to learn more. Starting with a question is one way to do this. Look at the article about Monaco. It begins with the question *Do you love languages?* If a reader does love languages, they will want to read the article.

70

7 **APPLY** Imagine you are going to write articles about three places you know well. Write a question to begin each article. You can start your questions with the phrases in the box.

Do you love…?   Are you interested in…?   Would you like to…?

	Place	Question
1		
2		
3		

8 **PREPARE** You are going to write a travel article for a blog. Think of a place you want to write about. Write notes below.

The place you're going to write about: _____

Why should people visit the place? _____

What can you do there? _____

What should/shouldn't you do when you visit? _____

9 **WRITE** Write a draft of your article. Start with a question. Try to include an adverb of manner in your article. Your article should be about 100 words (two paragraphs).

10 **IMPROVE** Read your article, and correct any spelling or grammar mistakes.

11 **SHARE** Swap profiles with a partner. Give your partner feedback on:

- The question at the beginning: Will it make the reader interested?
- Grammar: Did they use *should / shouldn't* correctly?
- Vocabulary: Did they use an adverb?
- Spelling: Did they spell the names of places correctly?

12 **DEVELOP** Use your partner's feedback to rewrite your article.

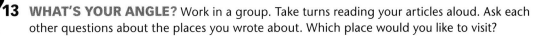

13 **WHAT'S YOUR ANGLE?** Work in a group. Take turns reading your articles aloud. Ask each other questions about the places you wrote about. Which place would you like to visit?

Halong Bay, Vietnam   71

1 ACTIVATE When was the last time someone gave you advice? Was it good advice? Why?

2 ▶ IDENTIFY Read the questions. Then watch the video and answer the questions.

  1 What advice does Max give to Andy?
  2 How does Andy feel about Max's advice?
  3 Does Andy take Max's advice?

3 ▶ NOTICE Watch the video again. How does Andy respond to Max's ideas? Take notes. Then share your notes with a partner.

  1 Max: You should come with me!
  2 Max: No, I mean you should come to London.
  3 Max: Well, flights to the UK are pretty cheap right now. You should think about it.
  4 Max: You know, my uncle has an international law firm in London. You could probably get an internship there.
  5 Max: My uncle has a flat, erm, apartment above the offices. He doesn't live there.

REAL-WORLD ENGLISH Giving, accepting, and rejecting advice

There are various ways to give advice.

If you know a lot about a topic, you can use *should*. It's helpful to say why your advice is good.

A: How should I get downtown?
*B: You **should** take the subway. That's the fastest and cheapest way to get there.*

If your advice is one of several options, it is better not to use *should*. Instead, just give a reason that your idea is good.

A: Where should I go for spring break?
B: Well, Mexico has great beaches.

To accept advice, you can say:

That sounds good.   That's a great idea!   Maybe I'll do that. / go there. / try that.

When you reject advice, give a reason. Don't say directly that you don't like the advice. Use an indirect rejection with a reason.

A: Well, Mexico has great beaches.
B: ~~Going to Mexico is a bad idea.~~   B: Well, I don't speak Spanish very well.
B: ~~I don't like that advice.~~   B: That's a great idea, but I can't afford that right now.

4 **ANALYZE** Look at the examples in Exercise 3 again. Does Andy respond to Max's advice directly or indirectly? Why? Discuss your ideas with a group.

5 **APPLY** Work with a partner. Read the conversations. Revise the last line of each conversation to make it more appropriate.

1 A: What should I do in London?
   B: The guided tours in those big red buses are great!
   A: I don't like that advice.

2 A: Friends are visiting me this weekend. What should we do?
   B: Let's see…I usually take visitors to the art museum.
   A: Good.

3 A: Where should I go camping this summer?
   B: Well, Big Lake Park is really pretty.
   A: No, that's not a good idea.

4 A: Where should I go for vacation this summer?
   B: Well, I went to Japan last year. It was really interesting.
   A: OK.

6 **INTERACT** Work with a partner. Role-play giving advice and saying what you think about the advice. You can ask the questions in the box or use your own ideas. Then switch roles.

| What restaurant should I go to tonight? | Where should I go for my next vacation? |
| What should I do this weekend? | What movie should I watch tonight? |

Student A: Ask your friend for advice.
Student B: Give advice (but don't say *should*).
Student A: Reject B's advice using an indirect rejection.
Student B: Give different advice.
Student A: Accept B's advice.

7 **ANALYZE** Watch another pair's role play. Were they appropriate? Did Student A give good advice?

GO ONLINE
to create your own version
of the English For Real video.

6.5 An Exciting City

1 ACTIVATE When people give advice about visiting a place, what do they often talk about?

2 **IDENTIFY** Listen to the presentation about an exciting vacation. Where does the speaker think you should go? Why?

3 **ASSESS** Listen again. Choose *True* or *False*.

1 You should take a boat ride.	True False
2 The view from the market is beautiful.	True False
3 You should take a lot of pictures.	True False
4 Street markets are expensive.	True False
5 November is a good time to visit.	True False

 PRONUNCIATION SKILL Chunking

In long sentences, speakers often pause between thought groups, or chunks. Listen to the sentences and questions. Notice the pauses between chunks.

It's an exciting city / with many things to see and do.
You should bring an umbrella / because it rains almost every afternoon.

4 **NOTICE** Listen and repeat the sentences. Mark the pauses.

1 You shouldn't go between June and September because it's very hot.
2 There are beautiful views from the boat, so you should take a lot of pictures.
3 They're really fun and not usually very expensive.
4 It has some interesting museums and lots of great restaurants.

 SPEAKING Giving advice in a presentation

You can use *should* and *shouldn't* in a presentation when you want to give your listeners advice. It is a good idea to support your advice with examples or information. Use *because* or a follow-up sentence for this.

You **should** visit Hong Kong. It's such an exciting city.
You **shouldn't** go between June and September **because** the weather is terrible.

5 WHAT'S YOUR ANGLE? Work with a partner. Follow the instructions to make a presentation about a city people should visit.

1 Think of a city you like.
2 Make notes about things visitors should see and do there.
3 Include the best time of year to visit the city.
4 Work with another pair. Share your presentations. Take notes about the advice.

Now go to page 152 for the Unit 6 Review.

7 People

UNIT SNAPSHOT

Whose blog has more than 20 million followers? 76
Who was the father of computers? 80
Why is there a computer language called Ada? 80

What events bring people together?

What skills make people successful?

What people changed your life?

BEHIND THE PHOTO

Work with a partner. Play this game.

1   On one piece of paper, write the names of three famous people who you like.
2   On another piece of paper, write two facts about each person's life. Don't write them in the same order as on the first piece of paper. Don't use the person's name. Start the sentences like this:

    This person…
3   Look at your partner's two papers. Try to guess which person each fact is about.
4   Tell your partner why you like each person.

REAL-WORLD **GOAL**

Contact an old friend you haven't seen for a while

1 ACTIVATE Do you take a lot of photos? Why or why not? What do you like to take photos of?

2 IDENTIFY Read the sentences. Then read the biography, and put the sentences in the correct order (1–6).

___ Brandon Stanton lost his job.   ___ He became a professional photographer.

___ He lived in Georgia.   ___ He worked in Chicago.

___ He started a blog.   ___ He went to college.

Biography of Brandon Stanton

Brandon Stanton is a photographer and blogger. His blog, *Humans of New York*, has more than 20 million followers. He also wrote three books of photos and interviews.

Stanton was born near Atlanta, Georgia. After college, he worked in finance in Chicago. When he was in Chicago, he took photographs of the city in his free time. In 2010, he lost his job and moved to New York City to become a full-time photographer. In November 2010, he started his blog. He photographed and talked to people on the streets of New York and posted the photos and interviews online.

There were some difficult times in the beginning. Stanton worked every day, and he didn't have much money. But his posts were very popular, and Stanton became famous. In December 2013, he was one of *Time* magazine's "30 Under 30 People Changing the World." These days, he interviews people all over the world.

3 EXPAND Discuss the questions with a partner.

1   Do you think Brandon Stanton's job is interesting? Why or why not?

2   What do you think is difficult about Stanton's job? What is easy?

3   Would you like to appear in the *Humans of New York* blog? Why or why not?

VOCABULARY DEVELOPMENT Time expressions

We use time expressions to say when something happened.

When he was in Chicago, *he took photographs of the city in his free time.*

To talk about the past, we can use *last* + noun and noun + *ago*.

last night / week / month / year   *[two / four] days / weeks / months / years ago*

We can use *on* and *in* to talk about a specific date.

on Monday   *on August 15*   *in January*   *in 1989*

We can use *in the* + time to talk about a longer period of time.

in the (early / late) 1800s / 1980s

4 APPLY Choose the correct word(s) to complete the sentences.

1 Brandon Stanton was born *in / on* March 1, 1984.

2 *In / On* the 1980s and 1990s, he lived in Marietta, Georgia.

3 *When / While* Brandon was 26 years old, he moved to New York.

4 I read Brandon Stanton's first book *ago two years / two years ago*.

5 *At / On* Saturday, I bought his second book.

6 *On last / Last* night, I started reading it.

GRAMMAR IN CONTEXT Simple past: *Be*

Was and *wasn't* (*was not*) are the past forms of *is*, *isn't*, *am*, and *am not*.

Brandon Stanton **was** a bond trader.   He **wasn't** happy with his job.

Were and *weren't* (*were not*) are the past forms of *are* and *aren't*.

Brandon's interviews **were** popular.   Some days **weren't** easy for Stanton.

To form questions, we change the order of the subject and *be*.

A: **Was** he famous?   A: **Were** the interviews interesting?

B: Yes, he was. / No, he wasn't.   B: Yes, they were. / No, they weren't.

There was and *There were* are the simple past forms of *There is* and *There are*.

There was a great blog post on Humans of New York *yesterday*.

There were some difficult times in the beginning.

Was there a great blog post yesterday?   Yes, **there was**. / No, **there wasn't**.

Were there difficult times?   Yes, **there were**. / No, **there weren't**.

See Grammar focus on page 165.

5 IDENTIFY Complete the sentences with *was*, *wasn't*, *were*, or *weren't*.

1 In Chicago, most of Stanton's photos _____ of people. He took a lot of photos of buildings.

2 Stanton's first few months in New York _____ difficult because he didn't have much money.

3 Soon after Stanton started his blog, there _____ a lot of followers. People loved it!

4 There _____ a lot of interest in Brandon's photographs and interviews.

5 Many people bought Stanton's first book, *Humans of New York*. It _____ a bestseller.

Ice skating in Bryant Park in New York City, the United States

6 **APPLY** Complete the conversations with *was, wasn't, were,* or *weren't.*

1 A: _____ you at the photography exhibition last night?
   B: Yes, I _____.

2 A: _____ Anna there, too?
   B: No, she _____.

3 A: _____ it good?
   B: Yes, it _____.

4 A: _____ any of the photos black and white?
   B: No, they _____.

5 A: _____ there a lot of people at the exhibition?
   B: No, there _____.

> **WRITING SKILL Writing dates**
>
> In formal writing, we usually write the dates like this: *November 8, 2018.* Write
> the name of the month in full. We don't use abbreviations: ~~11/8/18~~ or ~~2.27.99~~.

7 **INTEGRATE** Write the dates.

1 1/15/1975   *January 15, 1975*   4 10/9/2024   _____
2 7/4/2012   _____   5 3/28/2018   _____
3 12/22/2006   _____   6 5/19/1957   _____

8 **PREPARE** Choose a famous person (alive or dead) to write a biography about. Then do some research about the person, and take notes.

9 **WRITE** Write a draft of your biography. Include some important dates. Try to use *was* and *were.* Your biography should be about 100 words (two paragraphs) long.

10 **IMPROVE** Read your biography, and correct any grammar and spelling mistakes.

11 **SHARE** Swap biographies with a partner. Give your partner feedback on the following.

- Grammar: Did they use the simple past correctly?
- Writing skill: Did they include some dates? Did they write the dates correctly?
- Spelling: Did they spell the months correctly? Did they spell people's names correctly?

12 **DEVELOP** Use your partner's feedback to rewrite your biography.

13 **WHAT'S YOUR ANGLE?** Work in a group. Take turns reading your biography aloud. Write three ways you are like each person your classmates talk about. Then share your ideas with your classmates.

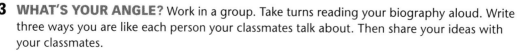

Usain Bolt likes to run. I also like to run.

1 ACTIVATE A biography is the story of someone's life. What questions do biographies often answer? Work with a partner, and make a list of questions. You can use the words in the box for ideas.

| be born | live | family | school | work | die |

Where was she born?

2 VOCABULARY Match the word in bolds with the correct definitions.

1 Ellie **became** a doctor when she was 42 years old. ___

2 Samika's parents always **encouraged** her to do sports. ___

3 Max **failed** the test because he didn't study. ___

4 In 2017, scientists **discovered** seven Earth-sized planets around one star. ___

5 Laura **married** Antonio last spring. ___

6 Daniel **succeeded** in business because he worked very hard. ___

 Oxford 3000™

a did or got what you wanted to do or get
b gave somebody hope or help so that they could do (or continue doing) something
c took somebody as your husband or wife
d found something for the first time
e began to be something
f didn't do something well that you wanted to do

3 WHAT'S YOUR ANGLE? Ask and answer the questions with a partner.

1 A: What did you succeed at doing last year?
   B: I succeeded at _____ing.
2 A: What famous person would you like to become friends with?
   B: I'd like to become friends with _____.
3 A: Who encourages you? What do they encourage you to do?
   B: _____ encourages me to _____.

Main ideas are the most important ideas in a text. You can often (but not always!) find the main idea in the first or second sentence. Finding the main idea will help you decide whether you want to read the whole text.

4 **IDENTIFY** Read the biography, and choose the correct main idea.

a   Ada Lovelace was born in 1815.

b   Ada Lovelace was the first computer programmer.

c   Ada Lovelace was friends with Charles Babbage.

 # Biography of Ada Lovelace

Ada Lovelace was a mathematician and writer. Although she wasn't famous when she was alive, people now know that Ada was the first computer programmer.

Ada was born in London on December 10, 1815. Her father was the famous poet, Lord Byron, and her mother was Anne Isabella Milbanke. When she was 20, she married the Earl of Lovelace, and they had three children.

From a young age, Ada was very good at math and languages. In the 1800s, most girls didn't study math or science. However, Ada's mother encouraged her to study these subjects.

When Ada was 17, she became friends with Charles Babbage, a British mathematician. People often called Babbage "the father of computers." Ada read about Babbage's ideas and improved on them. She developed the idea of using computers for more than calculating.

Lovelace died in 1852, just before she turned 36 years old. In 1980, the U.S. Department of Defense named a computer language *Ada* after Lovelace.

—adapted from "Byron, Augusta Ada, Countess of Lovelace" in *A Dictionary of Scientists*

5 **IDENTIFY** Read the biography again and complete the chart.

Year	What happened?
1815	Ada was born.
1832	
1835	
1852	
1980	

We use the simple past to talk about finished actions and states in the past.

We add *-ed* to form the simple past of most regular verbs.

*She **developed** the idea of using computers for more than calculating.*

With irregular verbs, we do not add *-ed* for the simple past form. There are no rules. They all have different forms.

*She **became** friends with Charles Babbage.*

*She **could** do difficult math problems at a young age. [Could is the past of can.]*

We form the negative in the same way for both regular and irregular verbs.

*Ada **didn't become** famous until after she died.*

*In the 1800s, most girls **didn't study** math or science.*

*Ada **couldn't study** math at a university.*

See Grammar focus on page 165.

6 **INTEGRATE** Complete the sentences with the past tense form of the verb in parentheses.

1   Ada Lovelace _____ (learn) to speak French when she was a child.

2   Ada _____ (live) with her grandmother.

3   Lord Byron and his daughter both _____ (love) poetry.

4   Charles Babbage and Ada Lovelace _____ (meet) when Ada was 17.

5   Babbage _____ (know) a lot about math.

6   Lovelace _____ (write) the first computer program.

7 **ASSESS** The following sentences are false. Correct them and write the true sentences.

1   Ada lived in the United States.

   She didn't live in the United States. She lived in England.

2   Ada married Charles Babbage.

   _____

3   Ada and her husband had four children.

   _____

4   Lord Byron encouraged Ada to study math.

   _____

5   People called Lord Byron *the father of computers*.

   _____

8 **WHAT'S YOUR ANGLE?** Work with a group. Play the game.

Step 1: Write three sentences about things you did last week. Two should be true, and one should be false. You can use verbs from the box and other verbs.

study	eat	work	watch	read	go

Step 2: Read your sentences aloud.

Step 3: Your classmates guess which sentence is false.

Last Monday, I watched a really good movie about a famous scientist.

7.3 Ordinary to Amazing

1 **ACTIVATE** Think of a few amazing people (famous people or people you know). Why is each person amazing?

LISTENING SKILL Understanding contrast linkers

When you listen, notice the words *but*, *however*, and *although*. They show a contrast between two different ideas. Pay attention to the contrasting ideas before and after contrast words. Listen to the examples.

I wanted to be a writer, **but** *I became a lawyer instead.*
I made a lot of money. **However**, *I wasn't completely happy.*
Although *I liked my job, I still always dreamed about writing.*

We usually put the *although* clause first. *However* and *but* can only appear in the second clause or sentence.

2 **APPLY** Listen to the sentences. Do you hear a linker? Which one?

1 ☐ but   ☐ however   ☐ although   ☐ no linker
2 ☐ but   ☐ however   ☐ although   ☐ no linker
3 ☐ but   ☐ however   ☐ although   ☐ no linker
4 ☐ but   ☐ however   ☐ although   ☐ no linker
5 ☐ but   ☐ however   ☐ although   ☐ no linker
6 ☐ but   ☐ however   ☐ although   ☐ no linker

3 **IDENTIFY** Listen to the podcast. Choose the correct answers.

1 The podcast is about…
   a ordinary people who do amazing things.   b amazing people who do ordinary things.
2 When he was young, John wanted to be…
   a an accountant.   b a professional rock climber.
3 What was John's idea?
   a He wanted to become a window washer.   b He wanted to climb buildings for fun.
4 What was the problem with John's idea?
   a It was too dangerous.   b It was too expensive.
5 Now, companies pay John to climb…
   a buildings.   b mountains.

We form simple past *yes/no* questions with *Did* + subject + infinitive without *to*.

A: **Did you like** your job?

B: Yes, I did.

A: **Did you get** a new job?

B: No, I didn't.

We form simple past *wh-* questions with question word + *did* + subject + infinitive without *to*.

A: **Where did you work**?

B: I worked at a bank.

A: **Why did you leave** your job?

B: Because I didn't make enough money.

See Grammar focus on page 165.

4 APPLY Complete the questions and answers in the simple past.

1 A: _____ (you / study) English when you were a child?

B: Yes, _____.

2 A: _____ (they / go) to the movies last night?

B: No, _____.

3 A: _____ (he / call) you this morning?

B: No, _____.

4 A: _____ (we / have) homework last night?

B: Yes, _____.

5 A: _____ (your parents / visit) you on the weekend?

B: Yes, _____.

5 ◀)) INTEGRATE Make *yes/no* or *wh-* questions with the simple past form. Then listen to the podcast again to check your answers.

1 Why / you / become / an accountant?

_____

2 you / talk / to him?

_____

3 What / you / do?

_____

4 you / leave / your accounting job?

_____

6 WHAT'S YOUR ANGLE? Interview a partner. Follow these steps.

1 Ask your partner which topic they want to talk about: their studies, their job, or a hobby.

2 Start the conversation like this:

Tell me about [your studies / your job / one of your hobbies].

3 Ask your partner follow-up questions in the past tense.

A: Tell me about one of your hobbies.

B: Well, I love playing the piano.

A: Really? When did you start playing?

B: When I was…

1 **ACTIVATE** Think of three times when you thanked someone recently. Who did you thank? What did you thank them for?

2 ▶ **IDENTIFY** Watch the video. Who does Max thank? Why does he thank each person? Complete the chart.

Who does Max thank?	Why does he thank the person?

3 ▶ **ANALYZE** Read the Real-World English box. Then watch the video again. Answer the questions.

1 Which expression does Max use for each "thanks" that you listed in Exercise 2?

2 Why do you think he used those expressions? What is different about them?

REAL-WORLD ENGLISH Thanking and responding

To thank someone, we can say:

In any situation
Thanks.
Thank you.

For a big favor/formal situation
That's (That was) very nice / kind of you.
I really appreciate it.
Thank you so much.

We often use *Thanks* followed by another expression.

Thanks. *I really appreciate it.*

To reply, we can say:

In any situation
No problem.
Not a problem.
You're welcome.
Sure.
Anytime.

More formal
It was a pleasure.
My pleasure.

4 ANALYZE Work with a partner. Compare the two situations, A and B. How are they different? What phrases could you use to thank the person in each one? How could the person respond?

1. A After class, a teacher helped you with some math problems for ten minutes.
   B After class, a teacher helped you with some math problems for an hour.
2. A A classmate gave you a ride home from class because it was raining.
   B A classmate picked you up from your house and drove you to class because it was raining.
3. A Friends invited you to their house for dinner.
   B Friends invited you to their house to watch a movie.

5 PREPARE Work with a partner. Choose one of the situations from Exercise 4, and write a short conversation. Use the language from the skill box. Include *thanks* and a response.

6 INTERACT Practice reading the conversations you wrote in Exercise 5 aloud.

7 ANALYZE Work with another pair. Watch their role plays. How did they say thank you in each conversation? How did they reply to the *thanks*?

8 WHAT'S YOUR ANGLE? Do you ever write letters to thank people? In what situations do you think a letter is a good way to thank someone? Think about how the language in a letter could be different from the language in a conversation.

GO ONLINE to create your own version of the English For Real video.

85

7.5 A Childhood Friend

1 ACTIVATE Do you remember any of your friends from childhood? Are you still friends now? Why or why not?

 PRONUNCIATION SKILL *Did you* and *Did he*

🔊 We often pronounce *Did you* like "didja" and *did he* like "diddee."

Listen to these sentences. Notice the pronunciation of *Did you* and *Did he*.

Did you go to the same school?   **Did he** visit you last weekend?

2 🔊 **NOTICE** Listen and draw a line between the linked letters.

1   When did you become friends?
2   Where did you meet?
3   Did you go to the same school?
4   Did he visit your home a lot?

3 🔊 **BUILD** Listen and repeat the questions from Exercise 2.

 SPEAKING Talking about a childhood friend

When you talk about a friend from your childhood (or any other past time), use the past tense. You can use this language:

My best friend from childhood was called…

We became friends when we were ___ years old.
I liked my friend because she was (funny / interesting / good at sports).

4 🔊 **IDENTIFY** Listen to the conversation about a childhood friend. Why were Marco and Manuel friends?

5 🔊 **EXPAND** Listen again and answer the questions from Exercise 2.

 6 WHAT'S YOUR ANGLE? Think about a good friend from your childhood. Why were you friends? What did you do together?

Now go to page 153 for the Unit 7 Review.

8 Stories

UNIT SNAPSHOT

Why can't we see the morning star and
the evening star at the same time?   89
Could you survive a night in the woods?   91
What makes interesting "news"?   93

What kind of story is this?

Why do people enjoy stories?

What kind of stories do you like?

BEHIND THE PHOTO

REAL-WORLD GOAL

Tell a scary story

1 When you read or listen to a story, how important is each thing?

	not important	quite important	very important.
1 It has a happy ending.	☐	☐	☐
2 The characters are interesting.	☐	☐	☐
3 It's exciting.	☐	☐	☐
4 It's true.	☐	☐	☐
5 It teaches me something.	☐	☐	☐
6 The language is beautiful.	☐	☐	☐

2 Compare your answers with a partner. Do you agree?

8.1 The Brothers' Promise

1 ACTIVATE Read the definition of a folk tale. Then discuss the questions below in a small group.

"A folktale is a very old story. We don't know who the author is. Folktales are usually spoken. People tell the stories to their children and grandchildren."
—adapted from *The Oxford Dictionary of Literary Terms* (4th ed.) by Chris Baldick

1 Do you know any folktales? What are they about?
2 Do you like folktales? Why or why not?
3 Why do you think people tell folktales?

2 VOCABULARY Match each bold word or phrase to the correct definition.

1 ___ You can't **force** someone to like you.
2 ___ Don't **hit** your little brother! That's not nice.
3 ___ Please don't **fight**. Someone will get hurt!
4 ___ Will you **make a promise**? While you're away, text me every day.
5 ___ I don't want to **argue** with you. Let's just talk nicely.
6 ___ If you're angry at someone, don't **avoid** the person. Talk to them!

 Oxford 3000™

a to struggle with somebody, physically or with words
b to speak angrily to somebody because you don't agree with them
c to tell somebody that you definitely will or will not do something
d to bring your hand against somebody / something quickly and strongly
e to stay away from somebody/something
f to make somebody do something that they don't want to do

3 BUILD Complete the sentences with the words from Exercise 2. Change the form if necessary.

1 I have a great relationship with my sister now, but when we were kids, we _____ all the time.
2 Richard doesn't like sad stories, so he _____ reading them.
3 In many movies and books, the hero has to _____ the villain.
4 Our teachers_____ us to read Shakespeare, and all the students hated it!
5 In some folk tales, the main character _____ and then breaks it.
6 Julia threw the ball, and it _____ the window. The window broke and she got in trouble.

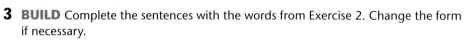

LISTENING SKILL Understanding the speaker's purpose

To help focus your listening, identify a speaker's purpose, or reason for speaking. Three purposes for speaking are:

Inform: To teach or give information to the listener

Persuade: To try to make the listener believe something

Entertain: To make the listener have fun

4 🔊 **IDENTIFY** Listen. What is the speaker's purpose?

___ to persuade   ___ to entertain   ___ to inform

5 🔊 **ASSESS** Listen again. Are the statements true or false? Correct the false statements.

		True	False
1	Tschen and Shen were stars.	☐	☐
2	Tschen was Shen's son.	☐	☐
3	Tschen and Shen were always nice to each other.	☐	☐
4	Shen and Tschen fought.	☐	☐
5	The brothers made a promise to never argue with each other again.	☐	☐
6	People can never see Tschen and Shen in the sky at the same time.	☐	☐

6 **WHAT'S YOUR ANGLE?** Who do you argue with? What do you argue about? How do you usually stop arguing? Tell a partner.

GRAMMAR IN CONTEXT *Must* and *must not / can't*

We use *must* to talk about what is necessary to do (obligation).
*We **must** never look at each other again.*

We use *must not* and *can't* to talk about what it is necessary not to do (what you shouldn't do).
*We are brothers. We **can't** fight!*
*You **must not** talk when you're taking a test.*

We usually form questions with *have to*, not with *must*.
*Do we **have to** take the test?   Yes, you do.*

See Grammar focus on page 166.

7 **INTEGRATE** Read one family's rules. Choose the correct word(s).

1 We *must not / must* be kind to each other.
2 You *can't / must* hit your brothers and sisters.
3 Children younger than ten *must not / must* go to bed later than 9:00.
4 Children older than ten *must not / must* help wash dishes after dinner.
5 You *can't / must* eat your dinner before you can have dessert.
6 You *must not / must* use your phone at the dinner table.

8 **EXPAND** Use the words *must*, *can't*, and *have to* to write statements and questions. Add punctuation.

1 you / pass a test / before you can drive
   You must pass a test before you can drive.

2 the students / go home early
   _____

3 we / show our passports at the airport?
   _____

4 visitors / take photos in the museum
   _____

5 customers / pay before leaving the store
   _____

6 travelers / buy a ticket before they get on the train?
   _____

9 **WHAT'S YOUR ANGLE?** Tell a partner about a folktale that you know.

8.2 A Smart Girl

1 ACTIVATE Look at the photo of people hiking in the woods. Discuss the questions with a small group.

1 Does this look fun to you? Why or why not?
2 What do you think is in the people's backpacks?
3 Do you ever go hiking? Where? What do you bring with you?

2 VOCABULARY Complete the sentences with the correct word from the box.

survive / survived	pretend / pretended	search / searched
save / saved	protect / protected	escape / escaped

🔑 Oxford 3000™

1 Pedro _____ the car accident because he was wearing a seat belt.

2 Children like to _____ that they're adults. They play games like "police" and "firefighter."

3 Everyone _____ from the burning building. Three people had to go to the hospital.

4 Police _____ for three days for the missing hiker, but they couldn't find him.

5 Liz had a bike accident. She was OK because her helmet _____ her head.

6 A lifeguard _____ a child at the beach yesterday.

3 INTERACT Discuss the questions with a small group.

1 When you were a child, what did you like to pretend?
2 When did you last search for something? What was it? Did you find it? Where?
3 If you are lost in the woods, what can help you to survive?

90

Pronouns replace nouns. Writers use subject pronouns (*I, you, we, he, she, it, they*) and object pronouns (*me, us, him, her, it, them*), so they don't repeat the same noun. When you see a pronoun, be sure you understand what noun it refers to.

In this sentence, *her* refers to *Anna*:

*When the dog found **her**, **Anna** was pretending to sleep.*

In this sentence, *They* refers to *searchers*.

***Many searchers** helped to look for Anna. **They** worked in teams of two.*

4   IDENTIFY Read the news story. What noun in the article does each numbered pronoun refer to?

1   she _____   4   they _____

2   her _____   5   them _____

3   they _____   6   it _____

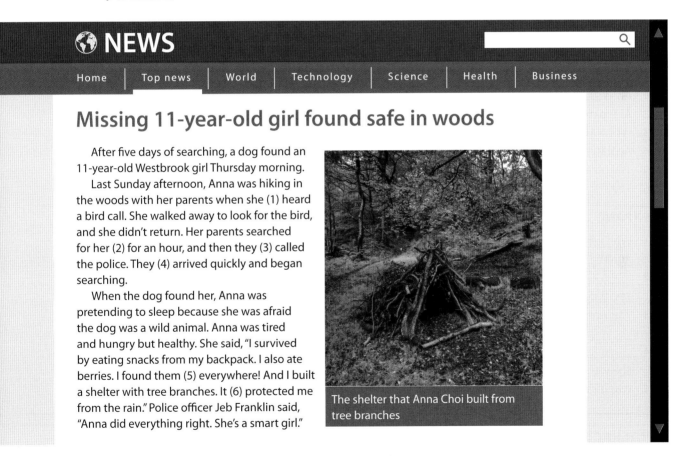

⊕ NEWS

| Home | Top news | World | Technology | Science | Health | Business |

Missing 11-year-old girl found safe in woods

After five days of searching, a dog found an 11-year-old Westbrook girl Thursday morning.

Last Sunday afternoon, Anna was hiking in the woods with her parents when she (1) heard a bird call. She walked away to look for the bird, and she didn't return. Her parents searched for her (2) for an hour, and then they (3) called the police. They (4) arrived quickly and began searching.

When the dog found her, Anna was pretending to sleep because she was afraid the dog was a wild animal. Anna was tired and hungry but healthy. She said, "I survived by eating snacks from my backpack. I also ate berries. I found them (5) everywhere! And I built a shelter with tree branches. It (6) protected me from the rain." Police officer Jeb Franklin said, "Anna did everything right. She's a smart girl."

The shelter that Anna Choi built from tree branches

5   APPLY Read the news story again. Put the events in order (1–6).

____ A dog found Anna.

____ Anna heard a bird.

____ Anna and her parents were hiking in the woods.

____ Anna built a shelter.

____ Anna walked away from her parents.

____ Anna's parents called the police.

6 INTERACT Discuss the questions with a partner.

1 Why did Anna walk away from her parents?
2 Why did Anna pretend she was sleeping?
3 How did Anna survive?
4 Do you agree with Officer Franklin that "Anna did everything right?" Why or why not?

GRAMMAR IN CONTEXT Past continuous

We use the past continuous to talk about being in the middle of an action at a time in the past. We form the past continuous with subject + *was / were* + *-ing*. We form the negative with *wasn't / weren't*.

On Sunday afternoon, Anna **was hiking** *in the woods with her parents.*
When the dog found Anna, she **wasn't sleeping***.*
People **were searching** *for Anna when it started to rain.*
They **weren't carrying** *umbrellas, so they got wet.*

We form *yes/no* questions with *was / were* + subject + *-ing* and *wh-* questions by putting the question word at the start of the question.

Was *Anna* **hiking** *in the woods?*   *Yes, she was.*
Why was *Anna* **pretending** *to sleep?*

See Grammar focus on page 166.

---

7 INTEGRATE Complete the sentences with the past continuous (positive or negative) form of the verb in parentheses.

1 Anna _____ (build) a shelter when it started to get dark.
2 At 9 p.m., it _____ (rain) very hard.
3 When Anna woke up, it _____ (not / rain). It was sunny.
4 At 5:30 in the morning, the birds _____ (sing).
5 The police officers _____ (drink) coffee when Anna's parents called.
6 They _____ (not / drive) in the police car.

8 EXPAND Complete the questions and answers. Use the news story to help you.

1 Who was Anna hiking with?
  Anna _____.
2 _____ the police _____ for her?
  Yes, they were.
3 Was Anna playing in the woods?
  _____
4 _____ when the dog found her?
  She was pretending to sleep.
5 Was it raining in the woods?
  _____

9 INTERACT Complete the sentences with information about you. Use the past continuous. Then read your sentences to a partner. Were any of your sentences similar?

1 One hour ago, I _____.
2 This morning at 7:00, I _____.
3 Last night at 9:00, I _____.
4 Yesterday afternoon at 3:00, I _____.
5 Last Saturday at 1 p.m., I _____.

10 WHAT'S YOUR ANGLE? Do you know any true survival stories? Tell a story to a small group.

8.3 One Stormy Night...

1 ACTIVATE Discuss the questions with a partner.

   1   Do you like scary movies? Scary books? Why or why not?

   2   What kinds of things often happen in scary stories?

2 IDENTIFY Read the story, and answer the questions.

   1   Where was Arturo at the beginning of the story? What was he doing?

   2   What was the weather like?

   3   Why was Arturo afraid?

   4   What did Arturo do?

   5   What was the surprise at the end of the story?

One stormy night, Arturo was at home alone. It was raining and very windy. Arturo was watching a movie when the lights went out. He sat on the sofa and listened to the wind. Suddenly, he heard a strange noise. It sounded like someone was crying. The sound was getting louder, and Arturo was becoming frightened. He was too scared to move. He eventually got up and walked around the house. He looked in every room, but he didn't find anything unusual. Finally, he opened the front door. To his surprise, a tiny kitten ran into the house. Arturo dried off the kitten and gave it some milk. While the cat was drinking the milk, the doorbell rang. It was Arturo's neighbors, Ryan and Diego. They were looking for their new kitten!

 VOCABULARY DEVELOPMENT Time expressions in stories

We often use these words and expressions when we tell a story:

Suddenly	*Recently*
All of a sudden	*Immediately*
To my **surprise**	*Eventually*

All of a sudden and *To my (his / her / our / their) surprise* always go at the beginning of a sentence or clause. A comma follows them.

To his surprise*, a tiny kitten ran into the house.*
All of a sudden*, the lights went out.*

Eventually, suddenly, immediately, and *recently* can go at the beginning of a sentence or just after the subject.

Eventually*, he got up and walked around the house.*
He **eventually** *got up and walked around the house.*

 Oxford 3000™

3 IDENTIFY Find the time expressions in the story. How many are there? How are they used in each sentence?

4 APPLY Match the sentences. Then choose the best word or expression to complete the sentences.

1 ___ I got home from the movies at 11:00.
2 ___ I was working on my laptop.
3 ___ I thought I didn't do well on the test.
4 ___ I drove all morning.
5 ___ I was riding my bike.
6 ___ I *recently / suddenly* read a great book.

a *All of a sudden / Eventually*, the screen went black.
b Then I *recently / immediately* went to bed because I had to get up early the next day.
c It had a surprise ending.
d *To my surprise / Suddenly*, I got an A!
e *Eventually / Recently*, I arrived at the beach.
f *Suddenly / Immediately*, I fell.

 WRITING SKILL Choosing a title

A good title makes people want to read your story. Choose a title that:

- is descriptive (tells what the story is about).

- is interesting (makes the reader want to know more).

- is short (not a full sentence).

- doesn't tell too much about the story (especially not the ending!).

My Summer Vacation is not a good title because it doesn't make the reader curious.

A Summer to Forget is a good title because the reader will think, "Why do you want to forget the summer?"

5 INTERACT Work with a partner. Look at the possible titles for the story in Exercise 2. Answer the questions below.

Arturo's Night at Home	*Arturo Finds a Cat*	*Too Scared to Move*

1 Which title do you think is the best? Why?
2 What is wrong with the other titles?
3 Can you think of another good title for the story?

GRAMMAR IN CONTEXT Simple past and past continuous

We use the past continuous to talk about being in the middle of an action at a time in the past. We use the simple past for finished actions and states.

*He **was watching** a movie when the lights **went** out.*

  [past continuous]   [simple past]

*While they **were eating** dinner, the doorbell **rang**.*

      [past continuous]   [simple past]

See Grammar focus on page 166.

6 IDENTIFY In the story in Exercise 2, find three verbs in the simple past and three verbs in the past continuous.

7 INTEGRATE Complete the sentence with the correct form of the verb (simple past or past continuous) in parentheses.

1 Last night, we _____ (stay) home and _____ (play) video games.
2 My phone _____ (die) while I _____ (talk) to my brother.
3 Daniel _____ (study) when I _____ (text) him.
4 I _____ (take) a test when I _____ (start) to feel sick.
5 They _____ (watch) a movie when a friend _____ (call).

8 EXPAND Read the story. Decide if the underlined words and phrases use the simple past and past continuous correctly or incorrectly.

Lucia's Terrible Day

It ¹was Monday morning. Lucia ²was getting up early and ³was making breakfast. She was feeling nervous because it was the first day of her new job. She ⁴was drinking her coffee when suddenly she ⁵was remembering that it was her sister's birthday. She decided to call her sister, but her phone wasn't on the table, and it wasn't in her bag. She ⁶looked at the clock—she didn't have time to search for her phone because she needed to leave for work.

While she ⁷walked to work, it ⁸started to rain. Lucia ⁹wasn't having an umbrella, so she got wet and cold. When she eventually got to the office, she felt tired and miserable. The receptionist ¹⁰spoke on the phone when she ¹¹arrived. She finished her call and asked Lucia what she was doing there. "Your job starts next week, not today!" the receptionist ¹²said.

9 PREPARE You are going to write a scary story. It can be true (non-fiction) or imaginary (fiction). Think of a character, a place, and an event. Make notes about what will happen in the story.

10 WRITE Write a draft of your story. Use the simple past and the past continuous and some time expressions. Give the story a good title. Your story should be about 100 words and two paragraphs long.

11 IMPROVE Read your story, and correct any spelling or grammar mistakes.

12 SHARE Swap stories with a partner. Give your partner feedback on:

- The title: Will it make the reader interested?
- Grammar: Did they use the simple past and past continuous correctly?
- Vocabulary: Did they use any time expressions?
- Spelling: Did they spell the verbs correctly?

13 DEVELOP Use your partner's feedback to rewrite your story.

14 WHAT'S YOUR ANGLE? Read your classmates' stories. Take a class vote and decide:

- Which story is the scariest?
- Which story has the biggest surprise?
- Which story is the funniest?

An early morning walk in Vietnam

8.4 Really? Wow!

1 ACTIVATE When you are having a conversation or listening to someone tell a story, how can you show you're interested? What can you do and say?

2 ▶ IDENTIFY Read the questions. Then watch the video, and answer them.

1   Why does Cathy talk to Andy?
2   Do Cathy and Andy know each other?
3   What is Cathy's job?
4   What does Cathy give Andy? Why?

REAL-WORLD ENGLISH Listening and showing interest

When you are having a conversation, it's important to show the other person that you are listening to them and interested in what they are saying. This will make them want to keep talking. Use these expressions:

To show you are listening	To show interest
Right.	*(That's) interesting.*
I see.	*Really?*
Oh?	*(Really?) Wow!*
Cool.	*(Really?) That's amazing!*
Is that right?	

3 ▶ INTEGRATE Read the Real-World English box. Then watch the video again. Complete the conversation excerpts below with the words or expressions of interest that Andy and Cathy use.

1   Andy: Political science…
     Cathy: _____
     Andy: But I'm also on the pre-law track.
     Cathy: _____
2   Cathy: We're having a party for our tenth year on Main Street. That's why I'm here… buying healthy snacks.
     Andy: _____ Ten years? _____

ENGLISH FOR REAL

4 **NOTICE** For each conversation in Exercise 3, is the second speaker showing interest or showing they are listening? How do you know?

5 🔊 **ANALYZE** Read the conversations. Which expression do you use in each situation and why? Then listen to check your answers.

1 A: How did you get started in business, Peter?
   B: Well, I studied economics in college.
   A: Oh, I see. / Really? That's amazing!

2 A: How long have you been working here?
   B: About three years. I started as an assistant. Now I'm the vice president.
   A: Wow! / I see.

3 A: What did you do over the summer, Maria?
   B: I hiked Mount Kilimanjaro.
   A: Right. / Really? That's amazing!

4 A: What exactly do you do at work?
   B: Well, I help people with their computer problems.
   A: Cool. / Wow!

6 **INTERACT** Work with a partner. Create three role plays. Each role play should begin with one of the questions listed. Include phrases that show you are listening and appropriate phrases for showing interest.

1 Do you have a job? What do you do at work?
2 What are your career goals?
3 Are you a student? What's your favorite class?
4 What was your best vacation?
5 What did you do last weekend?
6 What are your plans for this summer?

7 **ANALYZE** Work with another pair. Watch their role plays.
Did they use listening and showing interest phrases appropriately?

GO ONLINE
to create your own version
of the English For Real video.

8.5 The Perfect Coat

1 ACTIVATE Do you like to shop for clothes? Why or why not? When you shop, is it easy to find clothes you like? Discuss your ideas with a partner.

> **SPEAKING Using adjectives in a story**
>
> Use adjectives to describe what kind of story it is.
>
> *This is a **scary** / **funny** / **embarrassing** story.*
>
> When you tell the story, you can use adjectives to say how people felt. Use *be* + adjective or *feel* + adjective.
>
> *I was really **surprised**.   I was so **angry**!   I felt **embarrassed**.*

2 🔊 **ASSESS** Listen to Amy's story about shopping. What kind of story is it?

3 🔊 **IDENTIFY** Listen again. How did Amy feel near the beginning of the story? At the end of the story? Why? Complete the sentences.

In the middle of the story, Amy felt *happy* / *angry* / *surprised* because _____. At the end of the story, she felt *angry* / *surprised* / *embarrassed* because _____.

> **PRONUNCIATION SKILL Silent letters**
>
> 🔊 Many English words have silent letters (letters that we don't pronounce). Common silent letters are *l* (before a consonant), *w* (at the beginning of a word), *k* (at the beginning of a word), *e* (at the end of a word), and *gh*.
>
> Listen to these words. Notice that the bold letters are silent.
>
> **k**nee   **w**rong   **k**now
> cou**l**d   ri**gh**t   gav**e**

4 🔊 **NOTICE** Listen and repeat. Write the words you hear. Which letter(s) are silent in each word?

1 _____	4 _____
2 _____	5 _____
3 _____	6 _____

5 APPLY Work with a partner, and make a list of more words with silent letters. Then read your list to another pair. Listen to their list, and write the words you hear.

6 WHAT'S YOUR ANGLE? Have you or anyone you know had an experience like Amy's?

7 INTERACT Tell your classmates a story about a time when you were happy, angry, surprised, or embarrassed.

1 Make notes about your ideas. Use adjectives to say how you felt.
2 Tell a partner your story. Then ask your partner for feedback. Take notes.
3 Use your partner's feedback to improve your story. Then tell a new partner your story.

Now go to page 154 for the Unit 8 Review.

9 Future

UNIT SNAPSHOT

What is "smart clothing"?   101

When is a good time to think about
your future?   103

Can a robot do your job?   106

How did you imagine the future
when you were young?

Is the future or the past
more interesting?

Do you think about the
future a lot?

BEHIND THE PHOTO

1 **Answer the questions.**

1 How do you feel about the future—positive or negative? Why?

2 Do you make lots of plans? How far ahead do you plan?

3 What are your plans for next month?

2 **Compare your answers with a partner. Do you feel differently about
the future? Why and how?**

REAL-
WORLD
GOAL

Arrange to
go somewhere
interesting with a friend

Welcome to the Year 2050

1 ACTIVATE How do we use these things now? Discuss your ideas.

We use computer chips in lots of things—computers, cell phones, TVs.

Computer chips

Fossil fuels (coal, oil, natural gas)

Solar power

Robots

2 ASSESS Read the title of the article, and look at the pictures. What changes do you think the article talks about?

3 IDENTIFY Read the article, and find the topic of each paragraph.

Paragraph	Topic
1	number of people on the planet
2	
3	
4	

READING SKILL Using context clues

You can often use context clues (the words and sentences before or after a word) to guess the general meaning of a new word. For example, here the second sentence gives examples of the bold words in the first sentence.

*Most experts say we won't be using **fossil fuels** for power in 2050. Oil and coal will become things of the past.*

Using context clues can help you understand a text and learn new words.

---

4 APPLY Find three unfamiliar words in the article. Use context clues to guess the meaning of the words. Then look the words up in a dictionary.

Word	My guess	Dictionary definition
planet	Earth	a large round object in space that moves around the sun or another star

Four predictions for 2050

1. Today there are about 7.4 billion people on Earth. Some experts predict that in 2050 there are going to be about 10 billion people on our planet. It's possible that we aren't going to have enough food for everyone.

2. Some people think that by 2050 a computer chip in your brain will connect you to the Internet. You won't need a computer to send emails or photos. You will be able to send them directly from your brain to a friend's brain.

3. In 2050, "smart clothing" will make it easier to do things. Imagine your pants helping you run faster or your shoes helping you jump higher!

4. Most experts expect we won't use fossil fuels for power in 2050. We won't need oil and coal for power because we will use the sun and wind. There will be "solar farms" in sunny places such as the Sahara Desert. They will collect power for places without a lot of sun.

A solar power plant in Morocco

5 WHAT'S YOUR ANGLE? Do you think the predictions in the article are positive or negative? Why?

GRAMMAR IN CONTEXT *Going to* and *will* for predictions

We can use *be going to* to predict what will happen in the future usually because something in the present makes it seem likely.

There **are going to be** around 10 billion people on Earth in 2050.
We **aren't going to have** enough food for everyone.
Is the planet **going to be** hotter?

We can also use *will* and *won't* (= will not) to make predictions.

Cars **will** be very different in the future.
We **won't** use fossil fuels in 2050.
Will people still eat meat?

See Grammar focus on page 167.

6 USE Complete the predictions with the correct form of *be going to* and the words in parentheses.

1 Solar power _____ (be) very common in 2050.
2 We _____ (not / need) fossil fuels in 2050.
3 Most people _____ (have) robots in their homes.
4 It _____ (be) a lot hotter on Earth in the future.
5 _____ people _____ (live) longer?

101

7 EXPAND What do you predict? Complete the sentences with *will* or *won't* and the correct verbs.

go	be	need	use	be

1 In 2050, people _____ passports when they travel abroad.
2 Cities _____ very different in the future.
3 Children _____ to school in 2050.
4 There _____ more cars on the road.
5 In 2050, people _____ paper money.

8 INTERACT Compare your answers to Exercise 7 with a partner. Do you agree?

9 VOCABULARY Match the verbs in each pair of sentences to a definition below.

1 Many scientists worry that in the future, we won't have enough water. ___
2 Many people expect that scientists will soon find a cure for all cancers. ___

a to feel that something bad will happen
b to think something will happen

3 I guess there will be between 9 and 10 billion people on Earth in 2050. ___
4 Scientists predict that we will find life on another planet. ___

c to say what you think will happen
d to give an answer when you do not know if it is right

5 Scientists believe that sea levels will rise by more than a meter by 2100. ___
6 Imagine traveling to work in a flying car! ___

e make a picture of something in your mind
f to feel sure that something is true

Oxford 3000™

10 BUILD Choose the correct words to complete the sentences.

1 Scientists *expect / guess* that people are going to live longer.
2 I *worry / guess* that I'll fail my driving test.
3 The weather forecast *predicted / guessed* cold weather tomorrow.
4 Many people *imagine / worry* robots will make their lives easier.
5 Experts *believe / imagine* that driverless cars will stop many car accidents.

11 WHAT'S YOUR ANGLE? Work with a partner. Take turns asking and answering questions about the year 2050. Use these topics or your own ideas.

have a robot in your home	still eat meat	have more free time	travel to other planets

A: Will you have a robot in your home?
B: Yes, I predict everyone will have a robot. I want the robot to do all my housework.

What's in Your Future?

1 ACTIVATE Which of these things do you want to do in the future? Did you do any of them already?

write a book	get married	start a business
travel to new places	be on TV	make a movie

make a movie

be on TV

travel to new places

2 IDENTIFY Read Tom's email about his plans for the future. Find five things he wants to do.

To: Kieran212@mailinator.com

From: TomTom@mailinator.com

Hey Kieran,

How are things? Did you know it's my birthday in a week? I'm going to be 20—I feel so OLD! I started to think about my future, and I decided to make some plans. What do you think?

First of all, I'm going to travel around Europe next summer. It will be expensive, so I'm going to get a part-time job to pay for it.

I love music, so after graduation, I'm going to learn to play the guitar. But don't worry, I'm not going to sing. I'm a terrible singer!

The most important thing is I'm going to start a business and be a successful entrepreneur by the time I'm 25. My brother is going to give me some money because he thinks I have a great idea: It's a website for—no, I won't tell you. It's a secret! Anyway, now that I have some plans, I'm feeling better about being 20.

I almost forgot to tell you the most exciting thing—my parents are going to buy me a motorcycle for my birthday! How about I come and visit soon? I'll drive us to the beach!

Tom

 GRAMMAR IN CONTEXT
Be going to and *will* for future plans and decisions

We use *be going to* to talk about future plans and intentions. We often use *be going to* with future time expressions.

He's going to travel around Europe next summer.
Where are you going to travel?

We can use *will* and *won't* (= will not) to make decisions. We use *will / won't* when we make a decision at the moment of speaking.

I'll drive us to the beach.
I won't tell you. It's a secret!

See Grammar focus on page 167.

3 INTEGRATE Read the email again and answer the questions.

1 Why is Tom thinking about his future?
2 Why is he going to get a part-time job?
3 What isn't he going to do?
4 Who is going to give Tom money?
5 What are his parents going to buy him?

4 ◀)) **USE** Choose a response from the box to complete each conversation. Then listen and check your answers.

I'll be careful	I'll go after graduation	we'll take a bus
I'll buy one	we'll go in the evening	

1 A: I'm going to live in Tokyo next year.
 B: But you'll still be in school then.
 A: Well, _____.
2 A: I really want to learn to play the guitar.
 B: But you don't have a guitar.
 A: Well, _____.
3 A: I want to drive a race car someday.
 B: But that's dangerous.
 A: Well, _____.
4 A: My brother and I are going to work in the city this summer.
 B: But how are you going to get there? You don't have a car.
 A: Good point. I guess _____.
5 A: Do you want to go to the movies tomorrow?
 B: But we're going to be in class all day tomorrow.
 A: Well, _____.

VOCABULARY DEVELOPMENT Future time expressions

We often use time expressions when we talk about the future. Common future time expressions include:

tomorrow   the day after tomorrow   later   soon

after	graduation	next	weekend	in	a few hours
	the exams		summer		a month
	class		semester		the next few years
					a while (= soon)

by (= not later than)	next week
	December
	2025
	age 30

---

5 IDENTIFY Find the future time expressions in the email.

6 BUILD Choose a future time word or phrase to complete each question. Then ask a partner your questions. (Many different questions are possible.)

1 Are you going to take a trip _____?
2 Are you going to graduate _____?
3 Do you think you will go someplace interesting _____?
4 Do you think you will become fluent in English _____?
5 Is anyone in your family going to get married _____?

7 PREPARE Write five or more things you want to do during your life. Say when in the future you are planning to do each thing.

Do what?	When?

8 WRITE In 100–150 words, write about your plans. Use Tom's email and your notes from Exercise 6 to help you. Remember to use future forms and future time expressions.

WRITING SKILL Checking your work: Spelling and grammar

Check the words in your writing for correct spelling. Use a dictionary for help if you aren't sure about the spelling of a word.

Look for any grammar errors in your writing. Ask yourself these questions:

- Did I use the correct form of each verb?
- Do I need to add *a* or *the* before a noun?
- Do I need to make any words plural?

Check your work carefully, and correct spelling and grammar errors. This will help you avoid making the same mistakes again.

---

9 INTEGRATE Check the sentences for spelling and grammar. Find and correct seven errors.

I have lots of plan. Im going to pas my exams and get a job. In two years, I am gong to move to new city. I want live by the see.

10 IMPROVE Read your paragraph from Exercise 7. Did you…

- ☐ spell all the words correctly?
- ☐ use the correct form of all verbs?
- ☐ use *will* and *be going to* correctly?
- ☐ use future time expressions?

11 SHARE Exchange paragraphs with a partner. Tell the class about your partner's plans, but don't identify your partner. Ask your classmates to guess who the person is.

My partner has a lot of interesting plans. For example, she is going to…

The Swartberg Mountains near
Prince Albert, South Africa

9.3 Exciting Times

1 ACTIVATE What skills do you think this robot has? What jobs can it do?

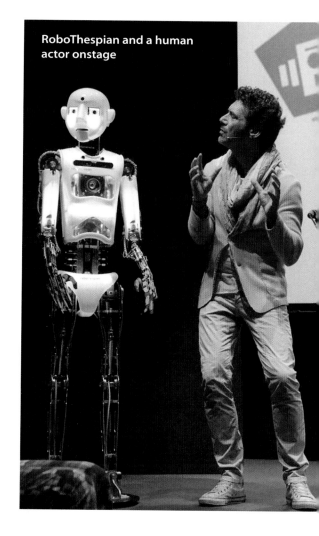
RoboThespian and a human actor onstage

PRONUNCIATION SKILL Contractions with *will*

🔊 We usually contract *will* after pronouns and the word *there*.

*She'**ll** be a great doctor.*
*I'**ll** find a good job soon.*
*There'**ll** be a lot of new jobs.*

2 🔊 **NOTICE** Listen and write the missing words. Then listen again and repeat.

1 I think _____ get a new job.
2 _____ be a great doctor.
3 I think _____ like the job.
4 _____ do the work.
5 _____ help us.
6 _____ be lots of work.

3 INTERACT Work with a partner. Take turns asking and answering the questions. Practice using contractions.

1 Will jobs change in the future?
2 Will we have robot teachers?
3 What jobs will disappear?
4 Will there be new jobs?
5 What job will you have?

A: Will jobs change in the future?
B: Yes, they'll change. People will use more technology.

LISTENING SKILL Focusing on key words

Speakers stress or give extra emphasis to important words. Listening for these "key words" can help you get a general understanding of a text.

Hi, my name is Tom Murphy, and I'm the host of the World of Work *podcast.*

4 🔊 **IDENTIFY** Listen to the first part of a podcast. What is the main topic?

☐ podcasts ☐ technology ☐ changing people's jobs ☐ people wanting new jobs

5 🔊 **APPLY** Listen to the second part of the podcast. Write the key words you hear for each job. Then compare ideas with a partner.

	Key words
Drivers	
Doctors and nurses	
Salespeople	

6 **ASSESS** Listen to the whole podcast, and answer the questions. Then compare your answers with a partner.

According to the speaker:
1   Which jobs will disappear in the future? Why?
2   What new jobs will there be?

> ### GRAMMAR IN CONTEXT *A / an*, *the*, and no article
>
> The first time we talk about one person or thing, we use *a* or *an* + singular noun.
> *My husband is **a** doctor.*
>
> The first time we talk about people or things using a plural noun, we use no article.
> *I think doctors and nurses will always be necessary.*
>
> We use *the* to say "you know which one(s) I mean" when we have already talked about it/them.
> *We have self-driving cars now…we will need people to design and program **the** cars.*

See Grammar focus on page 167.

7 **IDENTIFY** Add an article (*a / the*) where necessary. Some nouns won't need an article. Then ask a partner the questions.

1   Do you want to be ___ doctor?
2   Who is ___ best doctor you know?
3   Do all doctors work in ___ hospitals?
4   Do you think ___ doctors work hard?
5   Will there always be ___ jobs for ___ chefs?
6   What does ___ chef do?
7   Do ___ chefs work hard?
8   Who is ___ chef at your favorite restaurant?

8 **EXPAND** Add an article (*a / the*) where necessary. Some nouns won't need an article.

My uncle is ¹ ___ computer programmer. He works hard, but ² ___ work is interesting. I don't think ³ ___ computer programmers will need to worry about their jobs in ⁴ ___ future. We'll always need ⁵ ___ programmers.

9 **WHAT'S YOUR ANGLE?** Tell your classmates about a friend or relative's job. What is good and bad about their job? Will their job exist in the future?

1 ACTIVATE Look at picture 1. Which word describes Dave?

☐ happy   ☐ calm   ☐ unhappy   ☐ worried

2 ▶ ASSESS Watch the video. What is Dave worrying about?

REAL-WORLD ENGLISH Giving encouragement

In English, we have different ways to give encouragement. For example, when someone is a little worried, we might say:

There's nothing to worry about.   It'll be great.   Don't worry.   Good luck!

When someone is very worried, we might encourage the person by adding something about the person's past experiences. For example, we might say:

You always do well.   You did really well last year.

People respond to encouragement in different ways. They might just say, "Thank you" or "Thanks."

They might also express doubt like this:

Do you really think so?   Are you sure?   Really?

---

3 ▶ IDENTIFY Watch the video again. Who makes each statement?

		Dave	Andy
1	Do you really think so?	☐	☐
2	Don't worry.	☐	☐
3	You did really well last year.	☐	☐
4	Good luck!	☐	☐
5	Really?	☐	☐

4 ANALYZE Which statements in Exercise 3 give encouragement? Which one responds to encouragement? Is this similar to the way you give encouragement in your culture?

5 INTEGRATE Complete the conversations with your own ideas. Then practice with a partner.

1 Friend 1:   Something smells good. What are you cooking?

  Friend 2:   It's spaghetti, but I don't think it's going to be very good.

  Friend 1:   _____. Everything you cook is delicious.

  Friend 2:   _____?

  Friend 1:   I'm positive.

2 Colleague 1: Are you ready for the presentation?

  Colleague 2: I think so, but I'm very nervous.

  Colleague 1: _____.

  Colleague 2: _____.

3 Teacher: You look tired, John. Are you OK?

  Student: I'm just worried about this exam. I don't think I'm going to pass.

  Teacher: Relax. _____.

  Student: _____.

6 INTERACT Work with a partner to write a conversation between two people.

• One person is nervous about something—decide what this person is nervous about.

• The other person gives encouragement—decide how much encouragement this person needs to give.

• Act out your conversation. Remember to include greetings and endings in your conversation.

• Choose a different situation, and switch roles.

7 SHARE Role-play the conversation for your classmates. Get feedback on how well you gave encouragement.

8 IMPROVE Use your classmates' feedback to improve your conversation. Then practice the conversations several times.

GO ONLINE
to create your own version
of the English For Real video.

109

9.5 Great Ideas

1 ACTIVATE Think about your daily routine. What do you usually do?

2 🔊 **IDENTIFY** Listen to the conversation between two friends. Why is Amira happy?

3 🔊 **ASSESS** Listen again. Make notes on her plans.

Yesterday	Today	Tomorrow
	visit the castle	

📱 **SPEAKING Describing plans**

Use *be going to* to talk about your plans and *will* + verb for plans that you make while you're speaking. You can compare your plans with your normal routine by using *instead of* + *-ing*.

I'**m going to** run in the park **instead of going** to the gym.
I'**ll** try your idea.

---

4 PREPARE How can you make your daily routine more interesting? Think about the next two days. Make three plans for each day.

5 INTERACT Work with a partner. Find out about each other's plans.

6 WHAT'S YOUR ANGLE? Share your ideas with the class. Who has the most interesting plans? Who has the most unusual plans? Whose plans sound the most fun?

Now go to page 155 for the Unit 9 Review.

10 Performance

UNIT SNAPSHOT

What can you do to improve your
performance at school? 112
How have sports changed in the last 100 years? 114
What is a performer? 117

**What kind of performance
is going to happen?**

Do you enjoy performing?

**What makes a good
performer?**

BEHIND THE PHOTO

**REAL-
WORLD
GOAL**

Look online for a
performance you want to
see. Ask a friend to come

1 Read the statements, and choose the ones that are true for you.

1 I am an athlete (a person who is good at sports).
2 I like to go to concerts.
3 I enjoy speaking to large groups of people.
4 I saw a great dance performance last year.
5 I am happy with my performance at school.

2 Share your answers with a partner. How similar are you?

10.1 Do Better!

1 ACTIVATE Think of something you want to do better. Tell a partner about it.

I want to write better. What about you?

GRAMMAR IN CONTEXT *-ing* forms

We can use the *-ing* form of the verb like a noun. The *-ing* form can be the subject of a sentence.

Thinking *positively will help you improve your performance.*
Learning *to relax will help you do better.*

We can also use the *-ing* form after certain adjectives + prepositions to talk about likes, abilities, and interests.

*Are you **interested in learning** another language?*
*Many people are **afraid of making** mistakes.*
*Most students want to be **good at taking** tests.*

See Grammar focus on page 168.

2 INTERACT Complete the opinions with the *-ing* form of the verb. Then work with a partner. Decide if you agree or disagree with each opinion.

1 _____ (speak) in front of a group of people isn't easy.
2 _____ (believe) you will do well on a test will help you do better on a test.
3 _____ (learn) to swim is harder than _____ (learn) to sail.
4 It takes hard work to become good at _____ (write).
5 Very few people are afraid of _____ (fly).
6 More men are interested in _____ (play) golf than women.
7 More women than men are good at _____ (sing).

LISTENING SKILL Listening for gist

When you listen for gist, you listen for the big picture (the topic and main idea). Listening especially for the content words will help you find the topic and main idea. After you understand the topic and main idea, you can listen again for the details.

Listening for gist helps you get a general understanding of something.

3 ◀⬤ INTEGRATE Listen to two speakers, and write the content words you hear. Then compare words with your classmates. Based on these words, can you guess each speaker's topic and main idea?

Speaker	Important content words
1	*people, nervous,*
2	

4 ◀⬤ APPLY Listen again for each speaker's topic and main idea. Then compare ideas with a partner.

Speaker 1   Speaker 2
Topic: _____   Topic: _____
Main idea: _____   Main idea: _____

5 🔊 **IDENTIFY** Listen to the complete podcast. Which of these things do the speakers talk about?

☐ eating   ☐ having a good coach   ☐ practicing

☐ exercising   ☐ listening carefully   ☐ taking care of yourself

6 🔊 **EXPAND** What can you do to improve your performances? Listen again, and take notes. Then compare notes with your classmates.

7 **INTERACT** Discuss the questions with a partner.

1 Which of the things from the podcast do you already do?

2 What do you think are the three best ideas from the podcast?

3 What are some other things you can do to improve your performance?

VOCABULARY DEVELOPMENT Adjective + preposition

We use some adjectives together with a preposition. It's helpful to learn the two words together. Some common adjective + preposition combinations are:

afraid	
proud	*of*
tired	
scared	

important	
responsible	*for*
necessary	
useful	

good	
great	*at*
successful	

nervous	*about*
worried	

interested   *in*

different   *from*

You can use a noun or *-ing* form of a verb after an adjective + preposition.

*Parents **are responsible for** their children.*

*Parents **are responsible for taking** care of their children.*

🔑 Oxford 3000™

---

8 **APPLY** Complete each question with a preposition. Then ask a partner the questions.

1 Are you scared _____ snakes?

2 Do you ever get nervous _____ speaking in public?

3 Are you tired _____ going to school?

4 How is riding a bicycle different _____ riding a motorcycle?

5 Are you worried _____ finding a job in the future?

6 Are you proud _____ your grades in school?

7 What are teachers responsible _____?

8 Do you want to be great _____ a sport?

9 **EXPAND** Rewrite each question in Exercise 8 with your own ideas. Then share your questions with your classmates.

Are you scared of flying? Are you scared of failing? Are you scared of spiders?

10 **WHAT'S YOUR ANGLE?** Think of something you want to do well. Then think of four things you can do to improve your performance. Report your ideas to the class.

1 ACTIVATE What was different about sports 100 years ago? Identify the true statements. Then add two more true statements.

- ☐ Sports equipment was much better.
- ☐ People didn't watch sports on TV.
- ☐ There were fewer professional athletes.
- ☐ The Olympic Games didn't exist.

READING SKILL Previewing

The word *preview* means "to look before." When you preview an article, you look over the whole reading before you start to read.

- Look at the title, and predict the topic of the article.

- Look at the pictures, and ask yourself what the article is about.

- Read the first sentence in each paragraph. What do you think the article is about now?

- Think about what you already know about the topic.

- What do you want to know about the topic? Ask yourself questions. Then read the article to find answers to your questions.

Previewing an article can help you understand a text better.

2 APPLY Follow these steps to preview the article. Then share ideas with your classmates.

1 Read the title of the article. What do you think it is about?
2 Look at the pictures. What do you think the article is about?
3 Read the first sentence in each paragraph. Predict the topic and main idea.
4 What do you already know about the topic? Think of three things.
5 What do you want to know about the topic? Write three questions.

3 IDENTIFY Read the article, and look for answers to your questions from step 5 in Exercise 2.

Forty-seven minutes faster

The winner of the 1908 men's Olympic marathon ran 26.219 miles (42.195 km) in two hours and fifty-five minutes. At the 2016 Olympics, the winner of the marathon ran the same distance in just two hours and eight minutes, or forty-seven minutes faster. How is that possible? Why can runners go so much faster today?

The performance of athletes in many sports is much better now than it was 100 years ago. Today's basketball players can jump a lot higher. Cyclists can race much faster. Tennis players can hit the ball farther and faster. Some people say that professional athletes are better today because they are taller, stronger, and healthier. That is true, but there is another important reason for this change in performance. Sports equipment today is very different from the sports equipment 100 years ago. Bicycles are lighter and faster. Running shoes are more comfortable. Even the design of swimming pools allows swimmers to swim faster today. In almost every sport, modern equipment helps athletes perform better.

Johnny Hayes, winner of the Olympic Marathon in 1908

4 INTEGRATE Work with a partner to answer these questions.

1 According to the writer, athletes perform better today than 100 years ago. What examples does the writer give to support this idea?

2 According to the writer, why do athletes perform better today? What other reasons can you think of?

3 Choose one sport. How was the equipment for this sport different 100 years ago?

GRAMMAR IN CONTEXT
Review of comparative and superlative adjectives; comparative adverbs

We use comparative adjectives to describe how one thing or person is different from another thing or person. We use superlative adjectives to describe how three or more things, animals, or people are different from the group they belong to.

*Sports equipment is **better** today than it was 100 years ago.*
*He's **the fastest** runner in the world today.*

We use comparative adverbs + *than* to say that a person or a group does things in a different way from another person or group.

*Athletes today can run **faster than** athletes 100 years ago.*

Spelling rules for comparative adverbs

For most adverbs ending in *-ly* or *-ily*, we form the comparative with *more*.

For adverbs with the same form as the adjective, we add *-er*.

quietly	*more quietly*
fast	*faster*

Some adverbs have an irregular comparative form.

well	*better*
badly	*worse*

See Grammar focus on page 168.

Eliud Kipchoge, winner of the Olympic Marathon in 2016

5 INTEGRATE Use the comparative form of the adjectives to complete the sentences.

1 Bicycles today are much _____ (light) than bicycles in 1908.

2 Bicycles in 1908 were _____ (heavy) than bicycles today.

3 The tires on today's bicycles are a lot _____ (thin).

4 The tires on bicycles in 1908 were _____ (fat) than today's bicycle tires.

5 Modern bicycles are _____ (easy) to ride than bicycles in 1908.

6 Bicycles in 1908 were _____ (difficult) to ride than modern bicycles.

7 People today are _____ (interested in) cycling as a sport.

8 Modern bicycles are _____ (expensive) because they work better.

6 APPLY Complete the questions with the comparative form of the adverbs.
Then ask a partner the questions.

1 Who needs to jump _____ (high)—a basketball player or a baseball player?

2 Which can go _____ (fast)—a racing bicycle or a mountain bicycle?

3 Which do you do _____ (regularly)—walk or run?

4 Which do you do _____ (well)—speak English or write English?

5 How can you learn to speak English _____ (correctly)?

6 Do you think you will speak English better or _____ (badly) in five years?

7 Do you get up _____ (early) or later on the weekend?

8 Do you think _____ (clearly) in the morning or in the afternoon?

7 WHAT'S YOUR ANGLE? How do you think the performance of athletes will change in the future? Tell a classmate.

Riders in L'Eroica bicycle rally in Gaiole, Italy

10.3 Great Performances

1 ACTIVATE Think of a good performer you saw or heard last year. Tell a partner about this person.

2 VOCABULARY Match the captions and photos.

1 models in a fashion show   4 dancers in a dance performance

2 musicians in a concert   5 actors on a stage in a theater

3 movie star   6 people at a live performance

♟ Oxford 3000™

 a ___

 b ___

 c ___

 d ___

 e ___

 f ___

3 USE Complete the sentences with the bold words from Exercise 2.

1 A professional _____ has to be a good athlete.

2 When you go to a _____ performance, you need to buy a ticket.

3 Many clothing companies use _____ to help sell their products.

4 Some _____ play rock music, while others play jazz or classical music.

5 A _____ in a theater is very different from a movie set.

6 There are lots of good actors, but only a few become _____.

7 People go to an art _____ to look at an artist's work.

4 IDENTIFY Read the paragraph, and answer the questions.

1 What is the topic of the paragraph?
2 What positive things does the writer say about going to a live performance?
3 What negative things does the writer say?
4 Which do you prefer—going to a live performance or watching something on TV? Why?

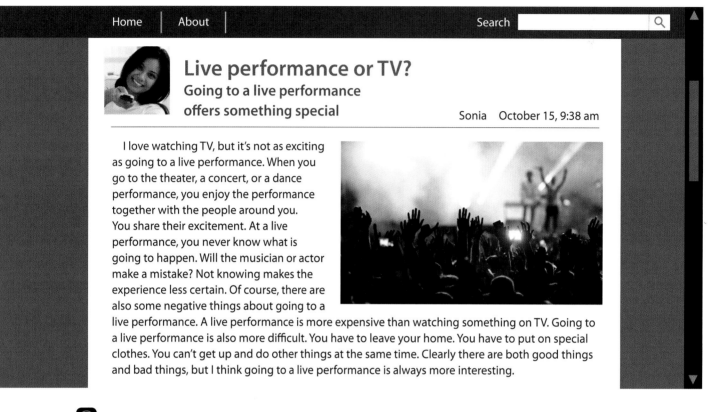

Home | About | Search 🔍

Live performance or TV?
Going to a live performance offers something special

Sonia   October 15, 9:38 am

I love watching TV, but it's not as exciting as going to a live performance. When you go to the theater, a concert, or a dance performance, you enjoy the performance together with the people around you. You share their excitement. At a live performance, you never know what is going to happen. Will the musician or actor make a mistake? Not knowing makes the experience less certain. Of course, there are also some negative things about going to a live performance. A live performance is more expensive than watching something on TV. Going to a live performance is also more difficult. You have to leave your home. You have to put on special clothes. You can't get up and do other things at the same time. Clearly there are both good things and bad things, but I think going to a live performance is always more interesting.

GRAMMAR IN CONTEXT Comparative adjectives:
(*not*) *as...as*; negative comparatives and superlatives: *less* and *least*

We use *as...as* when we want to say that people or things are the same in a particular way.
*Women's basketball is just **as exciting as** men's.*

We use *not as...as* when we want to say that people or things are different in a particular way.
*Watching something on TV is**n't as exciting as** going to a live performance. (= Going to a live performance is more exciting than watching something on TV.)*

We use *less* + adjective + *than...* to talk about how people or things are different.
*Watching a movie on TV is **less interesting than** going to the theater.*

We use *the least* + adjective to talk about how a person or thing is different from a group of people or things.
*I think table tennis is **the least interesting** sport in the Olympics.*

See Grammar focus on page 168.

5 INTEGRATE Rewrite each sentence. Use (*not*) *as...as*.

1 Going to a live performance is more expensive than watching a performance on TV.
2 Theater stages are smaller than movie sets.
3 Models are more attractive than most people.
4 Watching a movie at home is more comfortable than watching a movie in a theater.
5 Actors in a movie are easier to hear than actors in the theater.
6 Watching a live dance performance is more exciting than watching a dance performance on TV.

6 EXPAND Write your own sentence comparing the two things in each item. Use (*not*) *as...as* + adjective or *less* + adjective + *than*. More than one answer is possible.

1 watching a soccer game on TV / going to a soccer game
Watching a soccer game on TV is not as expensive as going to a soccer game.
Watching a soccer game on TV is less expensive than going to a soccer game.

2 reading a book / watching a movie based on the book
3 listening to music on the radio / going to a live concert
4 working as a model / working as an actor
5 reading about a fashion show / going to a fashion show
6 watching the Olympic games on TV / going to the Olympic games
7 watching a sport / playing the sport

7 PREPARE Choose two activities from Exercise 6 to compare, or think of your own. Take notes in a chart like the one shown.

	Watching a dance performance on TV	Going to a live dance performance
Positive things		
Negative things		

8 WRITE Use your notes from Exercise 7 to compare the two activities. You can use the paragraph in Exercise 4 as a model. Write about 120 words.

 WRITING SKILL Checking your work: Spelling rules

Remember to check your writing for spelling errors. Use a dictionary for help when you aren't sure how to spell an *-ing* form. You can also find the spelling of comparative and superlative adjectives in your dictionary.

share verb (shares, sharing, shared)
to have or use something with another person: I share a bedroom with my sister.
fast adjective (faster, fastest)

9 IDENTIFY Find a spelling or grammar error in each sentence. Correct it.

1 Go to the theater is more expensive than watching TV.
2 Playing basketball is less expensive as golf.
3 Swiming is one of the healthiest ways to exercise.
4 Theater actors work more harder than actors in movies.
5 Watching a concert on TV is less espensive than going to a concert.
6 Watching golf is not as interesting watching soccer.

10 IMPROVE Read your paragraph from Exercise 8. Did you...

☐ spell all the words correctly?
☐ use the correct form of all verbs?
☐ use the correct form of all adjectives and adverbs?

11 SHARE Read your paragraph to the class, and ask your classmates how you can improve it. Then rewrite your paragraph, making any necessary changes.

10.4 Are You Busy Tomorrow?

1 **ACTIVATE** Look at the pictures. What do you think Kevin is saying?

2 ▶ **ASSESS** Watch the video. What does Kevin invite Max and Andy to do?

REAL-WORLD ENGLISH Making, accepting, and refusing invitations

When we invite a friend to do something, we often first ask if the person is available.

Are you doing anything tonight?   *Are you busy tomorrow?*

When friends say they are available, they often add *Why?* or *Why do you ask?* Then, you can explain and invite them.

A: *Are you busy tonight?*
B: *No, why?*
A: *I have tickets to a basketball game. Do you want to come?*
B: *Sure. I'd love to.*

When we accept an invitation, we often add a positive comment.

Thanks. That sounds great!
What a great idea! I'll come.

When friends reject an invitation, they often explain why.

A: *Do you want to go for coffee later?*
B: *I'd love to, but I need to go grocery shopping. / Sorry, I can't. I'm meeting my sister.*

3 ▶ **INTEGRATE** Watch the video again, and complete the invitations.

1 Kevin: I was wondering. Uh, _____ tomorrow afternoon?
   Max: Tomorrow? Um, no, I don't think I'm busy. _____?
   Kevin: Well, there's a tennis match tomorrow…and I have three free tickets. And I know you like tennis. So…_____?
   Max: Tennis? _____! That sounds good!

2 Kevin: I have great news. I got these! They're tickets…to the big tennis match tomorrow. So I was wondering… Are you busy tomorrow afternoon? _____?
   Andy: Sorry, Kevin… _____.
   Max: You can't? Hmm.
   Andy: But _____. Max and I have tickets to see Phil in the play.

4 ANALYZE Answer the questions.

1 Kevin asks Max if he is busy tomorrow afternoon. How does Max answer?

2 Kevin asks Andy if he is busy tomorrow afternoon. How does Andy answer?

3 How does Max accept Kevin's invitation? What are some other ways to accept an invitation?

4 How does Andy refuse Kevin's invitation? What are some other ways to refuse an invitation?

5 What do Max and Andy decide to do in the end?

6 How do you accept and refuse invitations in your culture?

5 INTEGRATE Put the lines in the conversations in the correct order. Then practice with a partner.

1
___ I have an extra ticket to a concert. Do you want to come?
___ I don't think so. Why do you ask?
___ I'd love to. Thanks.
___ Are you doing anything next Saturday?

2
___ Thanks for thinking of me.
___ That's too bad. Jack and I are going to the beach. I thought you might want to come.
___ Are you busy Saturday morning?
___ No problem. Another time.
___ Yeah, I have to work.

3
___ Are you busy tomorrow?
___ That would be great!
___ I'm going shopping downtown. Would you like to come?
___ I don't think so. Why?

6 INTERACT Role-play the following conversations with a partner. Remember to include greetings and endings in your role play.

A: You meet your friend at school. You have tickets to a concert on Thursday evening. Invite your friend.

B: You are free on Thursday evening. Respond to the invitation.

A: You meet your friend on the street. You are busy on Saturday.

B: You meet your friend on the street. You have an extra ticket to a dance performance on Saturday. Invite your friend.

7 ANALYZE Get together with another pair, and watch their role plays. Do they...

- use appropriate greetings?
- first ask if the friend is available?
- add why when they say *yes*?
- explain why they aren't available when they say *no*?

GO ONLINE
to create your own version
of the English For Real video.

That's More Interesting

1 ACTIVATE Which of these things do you enjoy doing? Which do you dislike doing?

exercising	going to museums	singing
painting	watching sports	going to concerts

> **PRONUNCIATION SKILL Weak sounds**
>
> 🔊 We can pronounce some very common words (*at, for, can*) in two ways—strongly or weakly. When we want to show that the word is important, we pronounce it strongly. When the word is not important, we pronounce it weakly.
>
>   [weak]   [strong]
>
> What **do** you want to **do** tomorrow?
>
>   [strong]   [weak]
>
> I ate **some** of the cake, not all of it. **Do** you want some?

2 🔊 NOTICE How does the speaker pronounce the bold words? Choose *weakly* or *strongly*. Then listen again and repeat the sentences.

	Weakly	Strongly
1 How well **can** she sing?	☐	☐
2 I really need **some** money.	☐	☐
3 I want **that** book.	☐	☐
4 Who **was** there?	☐	☐
5 What is this made **of**?	☐	☐
6 I want to go, but I **can't**.	☐	☐

3 🔊 APPLY Listen and repeat the sentences you hear.

> **SPEAKING Talking about likes and dislikes; giving preferences**
>
> When we talk about likes, dislikes, and preferences, we often use an *-ing* form after these verbs: *like, dislike, love, hate, enjoy,* and *prefer*.
>
> I **love** going to museums.   He **doesn't like** watching tennis on TV.
>
> We can use comparative and superlative forms when we talk about preferences.
>
> Tennis is **much more interesting** than golf.

4 🔊 IDENTIFY Listen to the conversation between Jack and Ann. What sport does Jack enjoy watching? What sport does Ann enjoy?

5 INTEGRATE Work with a partner to complete the conversation with your own ideas.

A: What do you want to do tomorrow?

B: I don't know. Why don't we _____?

A: You know I hate _____. What about _____ instead? I love _____.

B: _____ is so boring. _____ is much more interesting.

6 EXPAND Work with a partner. Think of six things you can do after class today. Then choose one thing you both want to do.

7 WHAT'S YOUR ANGLE? Share your ideas from Exercise 6 with your classmates. Together choose the most interesting things to do after class today.

Now go to page 156 for the Unit 10 Review.

11 Experiences

UNIT SNAPSHOT

Who built Machu Picchu?   124

How many languages do the "Super Polyglot
Brothers" speak?   128

What is ice swimming? Would you like to do it?   130

▼ **What makes an experience special?**

▼ **How can experience change people?**

▼ **Is experience or knowledge more important?**

BEHIND THE PHOTO

REAL-WORLD GOAL

Tell a friend about something you've always wanted to do

Work with a partner.

1 Think of experiences you've had that are:

   a exciting   d dangerous

   b boring   e interesting

   c funny

2 Write a sentence about each experience. Don't write the adjective in the sentence.
   I flew over the Grand Canyon.

3 Read your partner's sentences and guess which adjective describes each experience.

1 ACTIVATE What do you know about Machu Picchu? Discuss these questions with a group.

1 Where is Machu Picchu?
2 Why is it famous?

3 How old is it?
4 Who lived there?

2 IDENTIFY Read the report about Machu Picchu. Does it mention any of the things you talked about in Exercise 1?

Machu Picchu is the site of an ancient city high in the mountains of southern Peru. The Incas lived in Machu Picchu in the 1400s and 1500s. They made buildings, walls, streets, and steps from stones. They left the city before they completed it, probably because of a war. After that, no one knew about the city for many years.

People have been very interested in Machu Picchu for more than 100 years. Millions of tourists have visited Machu Picchu since 1911. In that year, the American explorer Hiram Bingham "discovered" it. Now, hundreds of thousands of people visit Machu Picchu every year. In 2007, people chose it as one of the New Seven Wonders of the World. The Peruvian government has tried to protect Machu Picchu and prevent damage to the mountainside.

—adapted from "Machu Picchu," in *The Oxford Companion to Archaeology*, 2nd ed., edited by Neil Asher Silberman

GRAMMAR IN CONTEXT Present perfect with *for* and *since*

We use the present perfect with *for* and *since* to talk about present activities or states that started in the past. We use subject + *have / has* + past participle + *for / since*:

*People have been very interested in Machu Picchu **for** more than 100 years.*
*Millions of tourists have visited Machu Picchu **since** 1911.*

Regular verbs have past participles which are the same as their simple past forms, ending in –*ed*.
*visit – visited – **visited***

Irregular verbs have irregular past particples. Sometimes the past participle of an irregular verb is the same as the simple past form and sometimes it is different.
*have – had – **had***
*be – was/were – **been***

See Grammar focus on page 169.

Machu Picchu

3 APPLY Complete the sentences with the present perfect form of the verbs in parentheses.

Home | About | Search 🔍

My uncle ¹ _____ (work) for a Peruvian company for ten years. In 2014, he moved to Peru to work at the company's main office, and I really wanted to visit him. This summer, I finally had enough money to go! I'm in Lima now. I ² _____ (be) here for two months. I'm taking a Spanish class at a private language institute. The class is great. We ³ _____ (learn) a lot of grammar, and we ⁴ _____ (improve) our speaking skills, too. In the class, we ⁵ _____ also _____ (study) the history of Peru. Next weekend, we're going to visit Machu Picchu. I can't wait!

4 EXPAND Complete the sentences with the present perfect form of the verb in parentheses and *for* or *since*.

1 I _____ _____ (want) to visit Peru _____ a long time.
2 Jane _____ _____ (be) interested in designing websites _____ she was in high school.
3 My grandparents _____ _____ (live) in Florida _____ 2010.
4 Bob _____ _____ (not go) grocery shopping _____ two weeks. There's no food in his house!
5 We're going to Hawaii for vacation. We _____ _____ (not take) a vacation _____ last year.
6 Morgan _____ _____ (manage) a team at work _____ three months.

VOCABULARY DEVELOPMENT Collocations with *for* and *since*

We can use the present perfect with *for* and a period of time.

for three years
for five days
for a long time
for a while

We can use the present perfect with *since* and a date, day, time, or event.

since 1998
since I was five
since last year
since November

---

5 INTEGRATE Complete the sentences with *for* or *since*.

1 Machu Picchu has been popular with tourists _____ a long time.
2 They've lived in Peru _____ 2014.
3 I've known Maria _____ a while, but we're not good friends.
4 Francisco has been a tour guide _____ he moved to Peru.
5 Elizabeth has studied Spanish _____ five years.
6 I've spoken Korean _____ I was three.
7 I've worked at this restaurant _____ April.
8 He's been on vacation _____ seven days.
9 Jane hasn't seen her parents _____ last year.

A tour bus in Cusco, Peru

When we write, we use subject pronouns (*I, you, we, he, she, it, they*) and object pronouns (*me, you, us, him, her, it, them*) to avoid repeating the noun.

In this sentence, *it* refers to *Machu Picchu*.

*People have been very interested in **Machu Picchu** since 1911. In that year, the American explorer Hiram Bingham "discovered" **it**.*

6 APPLY Rewrite the second sentence in each set. Replace the repeated nouns with pronouns.

1 My mother called last night. My mother wanted to talk about our trip to Peru.
2 The Incas built a beautiful city. The Incas made the city from stone.
3 My cousins visited last month. I gave my cousins a tour of my city.
4 Henry is leaving for vacation tomorrow. I'm going to give Henry a ride to the airport.
5 Many people visit Machu Picchu. People travel from all over the world to see Machu Picchu.

7 PREPARE You are going to write a report about a historical place. Think of a place you want to write about. Then do some research about the place, and take notes. Answer some of these questions: What does the place look like? How long has it been popular? When did it open? Who discovered it? How many people visit there every year?

8 CREATE Write a draft of your report. Remember to use pronouns to avoid repetition. Your report should be about 100 words and two paragraphs.

9 IMPROVE Read your report, and correct any grammar and spelling mistakes.

10 SHARE Swap reports with a partner. Give your partner feedback on:

• Ideas: Did they tell about the history of the place?
• Grammar: Did they use the present perfect tense correctly?
• Writing skill: Did they use pronouns to avoid repetition?
• Spelling: Did they spell the names of places correctly? Did they capitalize names of places?

11 DEVELOP Use your partner's feedback to rewrite your report.

12 WHAT'S YOUR ANGLE? Work in a group. Take turns reading your reports aloud. Which place sounds most interesting to you? Why? Tell your classmates.

Bayon Temple in Angkor Wat, Cambodia

Super Polyglot Brothers

1 ACTIVATE Discuss the questions with a small group.

1 How many languages do you speak? Which languages?
2 How long does it take to learn a new language well?
3 Do you know someone who speaks a lot of languages? Why did they learn a lot of languages? How did they learn them?

2 VOCABULARY Complete the sentences with words from the box.

method	meaning	translate	progress
memory	communicate	culture	goal

🔑 Oxford 3000™

1 Robert can read Spanish, but he can't _____ in Spanish very well.
2 Lily has an excellent _____. She never forgets a name.
3 Kadir is studying Turkish. His _____ is to speak Turkish to his grandparents when he visits Istanbul next summer.
4 My favorite _____ of learning a language is to listen to songs while reading the lyrics (words).
5 Our Arabic teacher gives us a test every week to measure our _____.
6 I don't speak Portuguese. Can you please _____ this into English for me?
7 I'm really interested in Chinese _____. I like learning about Chinese food, holidays, and beliefs.
8 You can often guess the _____ of a word by looking at the words near it.

3 WHAT'S YOUR ANGLE? Discuss the questions with a partner.

1 Do you have a good memory? What is easy for you to remember? What is difficult for you to remember?
2 What is your favorite method of learning a language?
3 What cultures do you know a lot about? Which cultures would you like to learn more about?
4 Why are you studying English? What are your goals?

READING SKILL Identifying opinions

When you read, it is important to know when someone is giving their opinion (saying what they think). To identify opinions, look for expressions like the following:

I think (that)…
I feel (that)…
I believe (that)…
In my opinion,…

4 IDENTIFY Read the article. Find four opinions.

Super
Polyglot
Brothers

Matthew and Michael Youlden are twin brothers. They're also polyglots—they speak many languages. The brothers have studied languages together since they were eight years old. They've already learned eleven languages, and they plan to learn more! Michael says, "I haven't learned to speak Dutch yet, but I really want to."

The "Super Polyglot Brothers" believe that anyone can learn a lot of languages. It isn't necessary to have an excellent memory or a special study method. Matthew feels that the most important thing is to have a goal. Michael thinks that you should study a language if you are interested in a country's culture. Both brothers believe that having a partner helps them learn languages. Matthew says, "We're lucky. We've always had someone to practice communicating with." But competition between the brothers also helps. They each want to know more languages (and speak them better) than their brother!

Matthew   Michael

5 WHAT'S YOUR ANGLE? Do you agree with Matthew and Michael's opinions? Discuss your opinions with a partner.

Opinion	Do you agree or disagree?	Does your partner agree or disagree?
1		
2		
3		
4		

GRAMMAR IN CONTEXT Present perfect with *just*, *already*, and *yet*

We can use *just*, *already*, and *yet* in present perfect sentences.

We use *just* in positive sentences to talk about very recent events and actions.
*He **has just started** learning Korean.*

We use *yet* in questions and negative sentences to talk about events and actions up to now.
***Have** you **learned** the present perfect tense **yet**?*   *Yes, I have.*   *No, I haven't.*
*I **haven't studied** Dutch yet.*

We use *already* in positive sentences to talk about events that happened before now or earlier than expected.
*They**'ve already learned** eleven languages.*

We usually use the short forms (*I've, you've, we've, he's, she's, it's, they've*) in speaking.

See Grammar focus on page 169.

6 **APPLY** Complete the sentences with *just*, *already*, or *yet*. Sometimes more than one answer is possible.

1   Taylor hasn't cut the grass _____. He'll do it tomorrow.
2   Have you visited Machu Picchu _____?
3   Ben has _____ graduated from college, and he _____ has a job!
4   I've _____ bought his birthday present.
5   They've _____ arrived at the airport.

7 **INTEGRATE** Complete the sentences with the present perfect and *just*, *already*, or *yet*.

1   _____ you _____ (do) the Portuguese homework *just / already / yet*?
2   Sam is only ten years old, and he _____ *just / already / yet* _____ (learn) three languages!
3   Lina _____ *just / already / yet* _____ (start) learning English. She only knows a few words.
4   I don't want to watch that movie. I _____ *just / already / yet* _____ (see) it.
5   They _____ (not study) for the French test *just / already / yet*. They're going to study tonight.

8 **WHAT'S YOUR ANGLE?** Work with a small group. Discuss your experiences learning a language.

1   What helped you the most?
2   What was most difficult for you?
3   How well do you speak the language? Do you want to improve? How do you plan to do that?

white-water rafting

ice swimming

biking down a mountain

doing a parachute jump

1 ACTIVATE Look at the photos. Which "extreme sport" do you think is the...

most dangerous?	most exciting?	easiest?
most fun?	most difficult?	scariest?

> **LISTENING SKILL Listening for specific information**
>
> When you listen, you don't need to understand every word. Before you listen, decide what information you need, and then listen only for that information. This helps you focus and improves your comprehension.

2 ◀)) IDENTIFY Read the questions. Then listen to find the answers.

1 Why is the interviewer talking to Jessica?
2 Why does Jessica ice swim and do other extreme sports?
3 What is the most exciting thing Jessica has done?
4 Does the interviewer want to try ice swimming?

3 ◀)) EXPAND Look at the list of activities. Then listen again. Which things has Jessica done?

☐ been white-water rafting	☐ had a bad accident	☐ been on TV
☐ biked down a mountain	☐ been in the newspaper	☐ swum in icy water

We use *ever* with present perfect *yes/no* questions about life experiences. *Ever* means "at any time before now."

Have* you *ever had an accident?
*Yes, I **have**.*   *No, I **haven't**.*
Has* she *ever been in the newspaper?
*Yes, she **has**.*   *No, she **hasn't**.*

We also use the present perfect with *never*. *Never* means "at no time before now."
*They'**ve never been*** on TV.
*She'**s never had*** an accident.

Irregular verbs have irregular past participles. Sometimes the past participle of an irregular verb is the same as the simple past form, and sometimes it is different.

make, made ⟶ *made*
leave, left ⟶ *left*
know, knew ⟶ *known*

See Grammar focus on page 169.

4 🔊 **APPLY** Unscramble the questions and statements. Then listen to check your answers.

1   you / ever / have / an accident / had / ?
2   done / I've / a parachute jump / never / .
3   Jessica / the newspaper / been / has / ever / in / ?
4   never / I've / down a mountain / biked / .
5   have / ever / they / white-water rafting / been / ?

5   USE Choose *ever* or *never* to complete the sentences.

1   Have you *ever* / *never* visited Turkey?
2   Tina *ever* / *never* eats meat—she's a vegetarian.
3   They've *ever* / *never* made sushi, but they have eaten it a lot.
4   Has she *ever* / *never* given money to charity?
5   Have they *ever* / *never* made their own clothes?
6   Dylan has *ever* / *never* baked a cake before.

6   INTERACT Write questions with *Have you ever* and the present perfect form of the verbs in the box.

1   Ask and answer the questions with a partner. Ask follow-up questions.

be on TV	do something dangerous
bike down a mountain	swim in cold water
have an accident	meet someone famous

A: Have you ever been on TV?
B: Yes, I have.
A: Really? Why?
B: Well,…

2   Tell another student about your partner.

Eduardo has been on TV. When he was
ten years old, he…

1 ACTIVATE Discuss the questions with a partner.

1   When was the last time you offered something to someone? Did the person accept (say yes to) or refuse (say no to) the offer? Why?

2   When was the last time someone offered something to you? Did you accept or refuse the offer? Why?

2 ▶ IDENTIFY Watch the video. What offers does Andy make? Does Max accept or refuse the offers?

What is the offer?	Does Max accept or refuse the offer?

3 ▶ ANALYZE Watch the video again. What words does Max use to accept or refuse the offers? Why do you think he chose those words?

REAL-WORLD ENGLISH Making, accepting, and refusing offers

To make offers, we can say:

You can use my phone.
Would you like a cup of coffee?
Would you like me to open a window?

To accept offers, we can say:

Great, thanks. (for smaller offers)
That's very / really nice of you, thanks. (for bigger offers)
That would be great. (for bigger offers)

To refuse offers, we can say:

That's all right, thanks. (for smaller offers)
That's OK, I can just… (for smaller offers)
That's very / really nice of you, thanks. But… (for bigger offers)

4 ANALYZE Work with a partner, and read the situations. How are they different? What language could you use for offering, refusing, and accepting in each one? Why?

1 Someone forgets their pen in class, and another student offers to lend them one.
2 A group of friends are in a restaurant. One of them realizes they don't have any money with them, and someone offers to buy them dinner.
3 A group of colleagues are having an informal meeting over coffee. Another colleague decides to join them. One of the group offers to get them a cup of coffee.

5 PREPARE Work with a partner. Write a short conversation for each of the situations in Exercise 4. Use the language from the Real-World English box. Include an offer and an acceptance or a refusal.

6 INTERACT Practice reading the conversations from Exercise 5 aloud.

7 ANALYZE Work with another pair. Watch their role plays. How did they make an offer in each conversation? Did they accept or refuse the offer? Was their language appropriate?

GO ONLINE
to create your own version of the
English For Real video.

1 ACTIVATE Do you ever make goals for yourself? What are some goals that you have achieved? What are some goals that you want to achieve?

2   IDENTIFY Listen to two people talking about their goals. What is each person's goal? What have they already done to achieve the goal? Take notes.

3 EXPAND Listen again. What do the people need to do next? Take notes.

> **PRONUNCIATION SKILL Contractions of *have* / *has***
>
> In speaking, we usually contract the subject pronoun and *have* or *has*.
>
> Listen to the pronunciation of these contractions. Notice that the s sounds like /s/ in *it's*, but it sounds like /z/ in *he's* and *she's*.
>
> | | | |
> |---|---|---|
> | *you've* | *we've* | *she's* |
> | *they've* | *he's* | *it's* |

4 NOTICE Listen to the sentences. What sound do you hear at the end of the contractions?

1 /s/   /z/   /v/   4 /s/   /z/   /v/
2 /s/   /z/   /v/   5 /s/   /z/   /v/
3 /s/   /z/   /v/

5 APPLY Work with a partner. Take turns reading the sentences aloud. Give your partner feedback on their pronunciation of the contractions.

1 I've never developed an app.
2 He's always wanted to write a book.
3 She's never seen a whale.
4 They've never been white-water rafting.
5 We've always wanted to visit China.
6 It's never been this warm in January.

> **SPEAKING Talk about goals**
>
> To talk about goals, you can use these expressions:
>
> *My goal is to…*   *I plan / intend / hope to…*
> *I'd like / love to…*

6 WHAT'S YOUR ANGLE? Work in a group. Follow the instructions to tell your classmates about your goals.

1 Think of two goals.
2 List the things you've already done to achieve each goal.
3 What do you need to do next?
4 Work in a small group, and talk about your goals. Ask your classmates follow-up questions about their goals.

A: I'd like to visit China. I've already started studying Chinese.
    I need to save money so I can travel.

12 Change

UNIT SNAPSHOT

What are two effects of population growth?   136

What did Maria Montessori believe that the
goal of education should be?   140

How can we improve air travel?   142

How can changes in the environment
affect your life?

What has changed most in your lifetime?

BEHIND THE PHOTO

Think of some changes that have happened in the past minute, week,
year, and decade (ten years). Is each change good, bad, or neutral
(not good or bad)? Share your ideas with a small group.

Changes in the last...	minute	week	year	decade
In my life				
In the world				
Good, bad, or neutral?				

REAL-WORLD GOAL

Use infographics to
teach a friend about an
important topic

12.1 More and More and More!

1 **ACTIVATE** The population (number of people) on Earth is growing. What do you think are some of the effects of population growth?

2 **VOCABULARY** Read the sentences. Match the highlighted words with the correct definitions.

1 ___ The climate of Egypt is hot and dry.
2 ___ When the temperature increases, the whole planet is affected.
3 ___ To reduce global warming, we should drive electric cars.
4 ___ It's important to protect the environment.
5 ___ One effect of global warming is more big storms, such as blizzards and hurricanes.
6 ___ Global warming causes the sea level to rise.

a becomes bigger
b the air, water, land, animals, and plants around us
c very bad weather with strong winds and rain
d to make something smaller or less
e the normal weather conditions of a place
f to go higher

ꭆ Oxford 3000™

3 **APPLY** Complete the sentences with the correct vocabulary words. Change the form if necessary.

1 Many famous people are interested in protecting animals and the _____.
2 Island countries like the Maldives and Kiribati are worried about how much sea levels are _____.
3 *An Inconvenient Truth* is a movie that educates people about the problem of _____ change.
4 There were many large _____, or hurricanes, in the Caribbean in 2017.
5 The number of cars in the city _____ traffic downtown.
6 In 2016, many countries agreed to _____ global warming.

> **READING SKILL Using visuals and data**
>
> Infographics give you important information about data (facts and numbers). Before you read, look carefully at graphs and charts, and try to understand their meaning. Then read the text to learn more details.

4 IDENTIFY Look at the infographics and photo. What do they tell you about the effects of population growth?

Effects of population growth

Baby orangutan in Indonesia

The world's population is growing quickly. Population growth has many negative effects, such as:

1. Extinction of species: Humans are causing the extinction of other animal species at rates 1,000 to 10,000 times faster than normal. There are several reasons for this. First, humans use many of the world's resources (land, water, etc.). Second, overpopulation increases climate change, and climate change causes loss of animal habitats, such as rainforests. When animals don't have a place to live, they die.

2. Loss of fresh water: There is not enough fresh water for all the people in the world. When the population grows, the shortage of water becomes worse.

3. Increase in crime: If there are fewer resources, people sometimes fight for them. This causes crime to increase.

If we can slow population growth, it will be easier to solve these problems and many others that are caused by overpopulation.

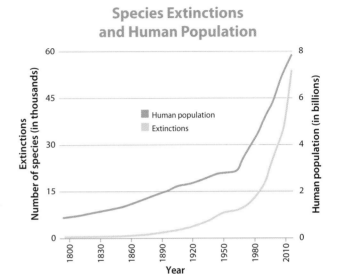

Species Extinctions and Human Population

© Scott, J. Michael, "SLIDES: Threats to Biological Diversity: Global, Continental, Local" (2008). Shifting Baselines and New Meridians: Water, Resources, Landscapes, and the Transformation of the American West (Summer Conference, June 4-6). http://scholar.law.colorado.edu/water-resources-and-transformation-of-American-West/15/

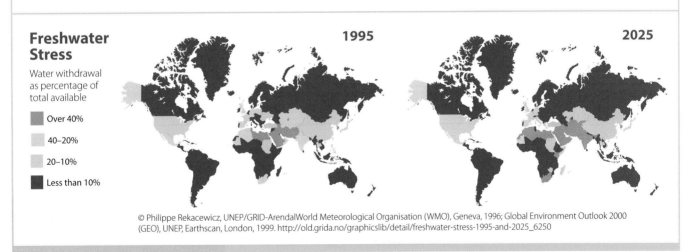

Freshwater Stress

Water withdrawal as percentage of total available

- Over 40%
- 40–20%
- 20–10%
- Less than 10%

1995

2025

© Philippe Rekacewicz, UNEP/GRID-ArendalWorld Meteorological Organisation (WMO), Geneva, 1996; Global Environment Outlook 2000 (GEO), UNEP, Earthscan, London, 1999. http://old.grida.no/graphicslib/detail/freshwater-stress-1995-and-2025_6250

5 ASSESS Read the article, and answer the questions.

1. Was your analysis of the infographics in Exercise 4 correct?
2. What are three effects of population growth?

6 WHAT'S YOUR ANGLE? What do you think people should do to help solve the problems described in the article? Work in a small group, and make a list of ideas. Then share your ideas with the class.

GRAMMAR IN CONTEXT Zero conditional

We use the zero conditional to talk about events and the results that always follow. We usually put the *if* clause before the result clause with a comma after the *if* clause.

We form the *if* clause with:
If + subject + simple present

We form the result clause with the simple present.
If there **are** fewer resources, people **fight** for them.

We can sometimes use *when* instead of *if* with the same meaning.
When the population **grows**, the shortage of water **becomes** worse.

See Grammar focus on page 170.

7 APPLY Match the causes with the effects. Then write zero conditional sentences beginning with *if* or *when*.

Causes

1 _____ there are big storms
2 _____ temperatures increase
3 _____ rainforests disappear
4 _____ animals lose their habitat

Effects

a many animals lose their habitat
b they become extinct
c buildings get damaged and people get hurt
d sea levels rise

1 _____
2 _____
3 _____
4 _____

8 EXPAND Use the facts to complete the sentences with the zero conditional.

1 Plants need water and sunlight to grow.
 When they don't *have water and sunlight, they don't grow.*

2 People who work to protect the environment are called *environmentalists*.
 If you work to _____.

3 People need clean water to stay healthy.
 When people don't _____.

4 Bad storms cause damage to buildings.
 When there is a bad storm, _____.

5 An increase in temperature causes sea levels to rise.
 If there is an _____.

6 Environmentalists want people to drive electric cars.
 If you are an _____.

9 INTERACT Complete the sentences with your own ideas. Then read your sentences to a partner. Ask your partner follow-up questions to learn more about their sentences.

1 When I can't fall asleep, I _____
 _____.

2 If I have a headache, I _____
 _____.

3 When it rains on the weekend, I _____
 _____.

4 If there's a problem with my computer, I _____
 _____.

5 If I'm angry at someone, I _____
 _____.

1 ACTIVATE Think of an important decision you made. What were your options? What did you decide? Why?

2 IDENTIFY Read the blog post. What is the writer thinking about doing next year? What are the advantages and disadvantages of each option?

| Home | About | | Search |

Big changes are coming my way! I'm graduating from college next year, so I need to make some plans. I've already been offered a job at the government organization where I worked last summer. I really liked my co-workers. But I'm not sure I want that job because the work isn't very interesting. Also, the pay isn't great.

I might look for a more interesting job that pays better. But I don't know if I'll find one because I don't have much experience. And if I don't find another job, it will be too late to take the job I've been offered.

Another option is to get a master's degree in early childhood education. I love little kids, and I've always thought about becoming a teacher. However, going back to school would be expensive, and I'm kind of tired of studying.

What do you all think I should do? Help!

3 WHAT'S YOUR ANGLE? What do you think the blog writer should do? Why?

VOCABULARY DEVELOPMENT Noun suffixes: *-tion*, *-ment*

Suffixes are word endings. They help you identify a word's part of speech; *-tion* and *-ment* are common noun suffixes.

Nouns with *-tion* suffix	Nouns with *-ment* suffix
option	*excitement*
organization	*government*
correction	*management*
instruction	*measurement*
direction	*agreement*

These nouns are often formed from verbs. If the verb ends in *-e*, the *-e* is dropped before adding the suffix *-tion*.

| *organize* | *organization* |
| *celebrate* | *celebration* |

This is not true with *-ment*.

| *advertise* | *advertisement* |

---

4 ASSESS How many nouns with *-tion* can you find in the blog post? How many nouns with *-ment* can you find? What do you notice about the spelling?

5 🔲 **APPLY** Complete the paragraph with the noun form (with the suffix *-ment* or *-tion*) of the word in parentheses.

Maria Montessori (1870–1952) was an Italian educator. Her ideas about ¹ _____ (educate) changed the way that many schools around the world teach young children. She believed that the goal of school should be "the ² _____ (develop) of a complete human being." She felt that young children should have ³ _____ (opt) about what to do in the classroom without a lot of ⁴ _____ (direct) from a teacher. Not all educators are in ⁵ _____ (agree) about Montessori ⁶ _____ (instruct), however. Some people feel that it makes classroom ⁷ _____ (manage) too difficult. They also think that there is not enough ⁸ _____ (measure) of students' progress through tests.

—adapted from "Montessori, Maria" in *Who's Who in the Twentieth Century*

🎯 **WRITING SKILL Using *because* and *so* to talk about reasons and results**

We use the word *because* to give a reason. *Because* can be used at the beginning or in the middle of a sentence.

*I'm not sure I want that job **because** the work isn't very interesting.*
***Because** the work isn't very interesting, I'm not sure I want that job.*

We use the word *so* to show an effect or a result. *So* can be used in the middle of a sentence to link two ideas.

*I'm graduating from college next year, **so** I need to make some plans.*

6 **INTEGRATE** Choose *so* or *because* to complete each sentence.

1 I didn't take the job *because* / *so* it didn't pay very well.
2 Madiha wants to become a doctor, *because* / *so* she's taking a lot of science classes.
3 I want to make some extra money, *because* / *so* I'm working two nights a week at a restaurant.
4 *Because* / *So* Franco was late to work today, he missed an important meeting.
5 It's difficult to decide *because* / *so* both jobs are interesting.

7 **EXPAND** Complete the sentences with *so* or *because*.

1 Leslie is moving to Seattle _____ she has a new job.
2 _____ he wants to be a teacher, Deray is studying history and education.
3 Zaheer is saving money, _____ he can buy a car.
4 Our home was damaged by the storm, _____ now we're repairing it.
5 Many people die every year _____ they don't have clean water to drink.
6 _____ the climate is getting hotter, sea levels are rising.

We use the first conditional to talk about possible events and their results. We usually put the *if* clause before the result clause, and we use a comma after the *if* clause.

We form the *if* clause with:
If + subject + simple present

We form the result clause with:
subject + *will* / *won't* + infinitive without *to*

*If I **get** my master's degree, I'll **become** a teacher.*
*If I **don't find** another job, it **will be** too late to take the job I've been offered.*
*If I **take** that job, I **won't make** a lot of money.*

See Grammar focus on page 170.

8 APPLY Complete the sentences with the first conditional.

1 If we study hard, we _____ (do) well on the test.
2 If you don't get your master's degree, you _____ (not get) a teaching job.
3 If I go to college in the U.S., my English _____ (improve) a lot.
4 If he _____ (take) that job, he'll move to Seoul.
5 If they _____ (sell) their car, they'll have to take the subway to work.

9 EXPAND Zero or first conditional? Choose the correct form of the verb to complete each sentence.

1 When the sea level rises, it *causes* / *will cause* the loss of animal habitats.
2 If Mila does well on the test, she *passes* / *will pass* the class.
3 If Maria works late, she always *takes* / *will take* a taxi home.
4 If Costa moves to Chicago, he *has* / *will have* to find a new apartment.
5 If we don't slow global warming, many animals *become* / *will become* extinct.

10 PREPARE You are going to write a blog post about a decision you need to make. Make a list of your options and the advantages and disadvantages of each option.

11 WRITE Write a draft of your blog post. Use some sentences in the first conditional, some reason and result statements with *so* and *because*, and some nouns with *-ment* or *-tion* suffixes. Your blog post should be about 100 words and two paragraphs long.

12 IMPROVE Read your blog post, and correct any spelling or grammar mistakes.

13 SHARE Swap blog posts with a partner. Give your partner feedback on:

• Writing skill: Did they include some reason and result statements with *so* and *because*?
• Grammar: Did they use the first conditional correctly?
• Vocabulary: Did they use any nouns with *-tion* and *-ment* suffixes?
• Spelling: Did they spell the nouns with suffixes correctly?

14 DEVELOP Use your partner's feedback to rewrite your blog post.

15 WHAT'S YOUR ANGLE? Work in a small group. Read your blog posts aloud. Discuss what you think each person should do. Give reasons.

1 ACTIVATE What are some common problems with air travel? Have you ever had any of these problems?

2 VOCABULARY Match the words or phrases to the pictures.

| pilot (n) | take off (v) | gate (n) | luggage (n) | passenger (n) | book a flight (v) |

🔑 Oxford 3000™

3 🔊 **INTEGRATE** Complete the airline announcements. Use the words and phrases from Exercise 2. Then listen to check your answers.

1 Please **stow** your carry-on _____ under the seat in front of you or in an overhead bin.

2 There are three planes **ahead of** us on the runway. We should _____ in about five minutes.

3 Flight 917 will **depart** from _____ 7 at 8:15 p.m.

4 Please **remain** seated until the _____ has turned off the fasten seatbelt sign.

5 Flight 1562 to Tokyo is now boarding all rows. All _____ may board **at this time**.

6 You can _____ using our website. Frequent flyers get special discounts.

We use different levels of formality when we speak. The level of formality depends on who is speaking and who they are speaking to. Identifying the level of formality helps you to focus your listening.

Listen to the formal and informal language. What are some differences?

Announcement in an airport: Attention passengers on flight 734 to New York. There has been a gate change. Flight 734 will now depart from Gate 9. Please proceed to Gate 9 immediately.
Conversation between passengers in an airport: Hey, our gate changed. We have to go to Gate 9. Come on, we need to hurry!

4 EXPAND The boldfaced words in Exercise 3 are formal. Can you think of an informal synonym for each word?

5 ◆) **NOTICE** Listen to four announcements or conversations in an airport. Which ones have informal language? Which have formal language?

1 ☐ formal   ☐ informal
2 ☐ formal   ☐ informal
3 ☐ formal   ☐ informal
4 ☐ formal   ☐ informal

6 ◆) **ASSESS** Listen again. Are the statements true or false?

			True	False
1	a	The flight might be canceled because it's snowing.	☐	☐
	b	The flight has been canceled because it's snowing.	☐	☐
2	a	If the flight is canceled, the speakers will take a flight later tonight.	☐	☐
	b	The speakers want to stay in a hotel tonight.	☐	☐
3	a	There aren't enough seats on the plane for all the passengers.	☐	☐
	b	If a passenger takes a later flight, the airline will give them a free round-trip ticket.	☐	☐
4	a	The speakers want to take a later flight.	☐	☐
	b	The speakers are in line at the gate.	☐	☐

7 INTERACT Discuss these statements with a partner. Decide if you agree or disagree and why.

1 People should only take one piece of luggage when they travel.
2 Being a pilot is a great job.
3 Passengers should not bother the people around them.
4 I like to book my flight online.

8 WHAT'S YOUR ANGLE? What would you like to change about air travel? Make a list of three to four ideas. Share your ideas with a small group.

Yes, but…

1 **ACTIVATE** When was the last time you disagreed with someone? What did you say and do? How did the person respond?

2 ▶ **IDENTIFY** Watch the video. What do the people agree and disagree (not agree) about?

Agreement

Who agreed?	What do they agree about?

Disagreement

Who disagreed?	What do they disagree about?

3 ▶ **INTEGRATE** Watch the video again, and complete the excerpts.

1   Andy: Oh…right, but I said I'd come to London. Sorry, Max…

      Max: Why don't you just ask Cathy for the time off?…I'm pretty sure interns get vacations.

      Andy: _____. But…

      Max: Come on, Andy, you've got nothing to lose!

      Andy: _____. I'll ask her.

2   Cathy: Absolutely! It's very important to have time off before you go back to school.

      Andy: Well, _____!

Agreeing with opinions

You can use these phrases to show you agree with someone.

Yeah, I know.
Yes, I think so, too.
I totally agree.

Politely disagreeing with opinions

To politely disagree with an opinion, you can do one or more of the following:

• Show you are unsure about the other person's opinion.

• Show you understand the other person's point of view.

• Say why you disagree.

Hmm, I'm not sure about that. (It might be too expensive.)
Uh, I don't know. (I might not have enough time.)
I see your point, but...

4 **ANALYZE** In the conversations, do you think Speaker B's responses are appropriate or inappropriate? Why? Rewrite B's responses if they are inappropriate.

1 A: I thought that movie was really boring.
  B: Yes.

2 A: I think we should stay home and study tonight. If we go out, we won't do well on the test tomorrow.
  B: I disagree.

3 A: I think you should quit your job and go back to school.
  B: I'm not sure. My job pays pretty well.

4 A: I think we should fly to San Francisco for vacation. Driving will take too long.
  B: No.

5 **INTERACT** Work with a partner. Read the two situations, and discuss how they are different. Then role-play the conversations.

1 Speaker A is talking to a friend, Speaker B, about a TV show. Speaker A thinks the show is interesting, but the acting isn't very good. Speaker B agrees.

2 Speaker A is talking about a new job. Speaker A thinks they should leave their current job because the new job is better paid, but the hours are longer. Speaker B, a close family member, disagrees and thinks they shouldn't take the new job.

6 **ANALYZE** Work with another pair, and watch their role play. Did they agree and disagree politely?

GO ONLINE
to create your own version of the
English For Real video.

12.5 A Difficult Change

1 ACTIVATE What are some changes that often happen in people's lives? What kinds of changes are usually easy for people? What kinds of changes are difficult?

2 **IDENTIFY** Listen to Jack talk about a difficult change in his life. What was the change? Why was it difficult?

3 **INTEGRATE** Listen again, and answer the questions.

1 Why didn't Jack go out with people from work?
2 Why didn't he meet people from other parts of the company?
3 What did he do on weekends?
4 What did Jack do to meet more people?
5 What does he get now?

 PRONUNCIATION SKILL Suffixes and syllable stress

The syllable stress sometimes changes when we add *-tion* suffix to a word. Stressing the correct syllable helps people understand you.

Listen to these examples:

organize ⟶ organ**i**zation   **op**erate ⟶ oper**a**tion
educate ⟶ edu**ca**tion   **cel**ebrate ⟶ cele**bra**tion

4 **NOTICE** Listen. Which syllable is stressed in each boldfaced word? Then read the sentences to a partner. Did your partner stress the correct syllable?

1 My **communication** skills aren't great.
2 It was a difficult **situation** for me.
3 Now I get lots of **invitations** to do things with friends on the weekend.
4 Tomorrow I have to give a big **presentation** at work.

 SPEAKING Describe a change

Use *because* and *so* to describe why the change happened and what the consequences were.

*I moved to Miami **because** I got a new job.*   *I didn't have any friends, **so** I felt lonely.*

To talk about changes, you can use comparisons and superlatives.

It was the biggest change of my life.   *Eventually, things got better.*

Use *more / less* + noun to compare things before and after the change.

*I spent **more time** on social media.*   *I have **less time** to see friends.*

5 WHAT'S YOUR ANGLE? Tell your classmates about a difficult change that you made.

1 Think of a difficult change you or someone you know made. (You can use your answers from Exercise 1 to help.)
2 Make notes about your ideas.
3 What did you do to make the change?
4 What was the result of the change?
5 Tell a partner about the change. Then ask a partner for feedback. Take notes.
6 Use your partner's feedback to improve your story. Then tell the story to another partner.

Now go to page 158 for the Unit 12 Review.

Unit Reviews

Unit 1

VOCABULARY

1 Choose the correct answer.

1 Rob's a good roommate. He's quiet and *calm* / *noisy*.
2 I'm rather *busy* / *shy* today. I have a lot of work to do.
3 You're very outgoing and *fun* / *serious* to be around.
4 My teacher is not very *honest* / *serious*. She's really funny!
5 I'm relaxed around my friends, but I'm kind of *shy* / *fun* around new people.
6 It's a little *noisy* / *fun* out here. Let's talk inside.

2 Unscramble the words to write sentences. Use contractions and add punctuation.

1 quiet / kind / of / am / I _____
2 it / pretty / today / is / cold _____
3 a little / my best friend / shy / is _____
4 is / she / early / a bit _____
5 of / sort / he / boring / is _____
6 busy / they / fairly / are _____

 GO ONLINE for the vocabulary game.

GRAMMAR

3 Complete the conversation with the correct form of *be* or *have*. Use contractions where possible. Then practice the conversation with a partner.

Takeshi: Excuse me. _____ you here for the meetup group?

Zaid: Yes, I _____. You too?

Takeshi: Yeah. I guess we _____ a little early, huh?

Zaid: Yeah. I _____ Zaid, by the way. What _____ your name?

Takeshi: I _____ Takeshi. Nice to meet you.

Zaid: It _____ nice to meet you, too.

Takeshi: So, where _____ you from?

Zaid: I _____ from Jordan, but I _____ a student here. What about you?

Takeshi: I work for a computer company. They _____ new offices here in Hong Kong.

Zaid: So, you _____ not from Hong Kong?

Takeshi: No, I _____ from Tokyo. But I like it here. The people _____ nice.

Zaid: Yeah, I really like the people, too. Do you _____ friends here?

Takeshi: Yeah, but I want to meet more people.

Zaid: Me too. That _____ why I'm here.

4 Correct the errors.

1 Is your sister have a fun personality?
2 I no have a lot of games on my phone.
3 When you have time to study?
4 Richard doesnt has an online profile.
5 What you have for lunch?

 GO ONLINE for the grammar game.

DISCUSSION POINT

5 Read the quote. Do you have one identity at school or work? Is it different from your identity with friends and family?

 "You have one identity…The days of you having a different image for your work friends or co-workers and for the other people you know are probably coming to an end pretty quickly."

—Mark Zuckerberg, from *Oxford Essential Quotations*, 5th ed., edited by Susan Ratcliffe

 GO ONLINE and listen to a podcast. Then add your comments to the discussion board.

ZOOM IN

6 What about you?

Task 1 Talk about a neighbor or friend who is very different from you.

Task 2 Write about a family member who has an outgoing personality.

Task 3 Find a photo of a friend or family member. Describe the person's personality to your partner.

7 Complete the chart.

	I did this well	I need more practice
Task 1		
Task 2		
Task 3		

Unit 2

VOCABULARY

1 Label the photo with the words from the box.

grandmother	grandfather	aunt	uncle
cousin	niece	nephew	

2 Complete each sentence using *to*, *with*, *for*, *about*, or *on*.

1 I like to spend time _____ my grandparents.

2 I have to work _____ my paper tonight.

3 If you don't understand something, you can ask _____ help.

4 I talk _____ my best friend on the phone every day.

5 Let's talk _____ our plans for this weekend. What do you want to do?

6 I don't agree _____ you that using social media is a problem.

 GO ONLINE for the vocabulary game.

GRAMMAR

3 Choose the correct word to complete the sentences.

1 Oh, is *your / yours* phone not working? You can use *my / mine*.

2 I think *your / yours* grandparents are really cool. *Their / Her* stories are so interesting!

3 Pablo can't go to the party, but *his / he* wife is going.

4 I have *our / ours* concert tickets, but Ron and Jared don't know where *their / theirs* are.

5 I always cleaned *my / mine* room when I was a kid, but my sister never cleaned *her / hers*.

4 Read the information in the social media post. Write *C* for countable or *U* for uncountable under the underlined nouns.

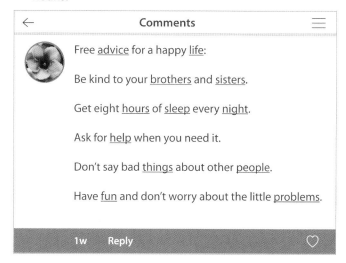

Comments
Free <u>advice</u> for a happy <u>life</u>:
Be kind to your <u>brothers</u> and <u>sisters</u>.
Get eight <u>hours</u> of <u>sleep</u> every <u>night</u>.
Ask for <u>help</u> when you need it.
Don't say bad <u>things</u> about other <u>people</u>.
Have <u>fun</u> and don't worry about the little <u>problems</u>.

1w   Reply

 GO ONLINE for the grammar game.

DISCUSSION POINT

5 Read the quote. Do you agree? Why or why not?

 "To like and dislike the same things, that is indeed true friendship."

—Sallust (86–35 BC), Roman historian, selected from *Oxford Essential Quotations*, 5th ed., edited by Susan Ratcliffe

 GO ONLINE and listen to a podcast. Then add your comments to the discussion board.

ZOOM IN

6 What about you?

Task 1 Talk about the family member who is most like you.

Task 2 Write four sentences about one way that your friends or family members make your life better.

Task 3 Find photos of two of your friends. Describe them to your partner.

7 Complete the chart.

	I did this well	I need more practice
Task 1		
Task 2		
Task 3		

Unit 3

VOCABULARY

1 Complete the sentences with words from the box.

bills	cut	garbage	sheets	fold
carpets	empties	grass	clean	pays

1 Please change the _____ on your bed.
2 Every month, I get several _____ in the mail. I need more money!
3 We have _____ on the floor in the living room.
4 After you wash the clothes, please _____ them.
5 My brother _____ the garbage on Fridays.
6 In the summer, we cut the _____ every weekend.

2 Unscramble the words to complete the sentences.

1 I'm a teacher with 50 years of _____ (cernepxiee).
2 My sister works for a large company. She _____ (agemsna) a team of 55 workers and _____ (dasela) important meetings.
3 Doctors have big _____ (birsepisnosileti). They make _____ (sidesconi) about people's health.
4 I _____ (vodlepe) computer systems for offices. I also teach people to use new computer _____ (gorpsmar).
5 I'm an art history student. I do _____ (caresher) and write reports about not-so-famous art. I'm working on an interesting _____ (jorptec) now!
6 My younger brother has a summer job at an ice cream shop. He _____ (vesser) _____ (muscerots) at the window.

3 Complete the sentences with words from the box.

Sundays	while	week	twice
a week	years	several	

1 I brush my teeth _____ a day.
2 Once _____, I wash my clothes.
3 I clean my bedroom every _____.
4 I cook _____ times a week.
5 Every two _____, I go on a big trip.
6 I visit my friends on _____.
7 I wash my car once in a _____.

 GO ONLINE for the vocabulary game.

GRAMMAR

4 Choose the correct words.

1 In my job, I *have / has* many responsibilities.
2 My sister *don't / doesn't* work. She's a stay-at-home mom.

3 *Do / Does* you write computer programs?
4 Where *do / does* your husband work?
5 He *manage / manages* a theater in the city.
6 I *don't / doesn't* like working in an office.

5 Read each question. Decide if it's a subject or an object question. Write *subject* or *object*.

1 Who teaches your English class? _____
2 Who do you usually have lunch with? _____
3 What do you usually do on Saturdays? _____
4 What makes you happy? _____
5 Who do you call when you have a problem? _____

6 Work with a partner. Take turns asking and answering the questions from Exercise 6.

 GO ONLINE for the grammar game.

DISCUSSION POINT

7 Read the quote. Why do people with power have more responsibility than most people?

"Where there's great power, there must also be great responsibility."
—Lyndon B. Johnson, selected from *The Oxford Dictionary of American Quotations*, 2nd ed., edited by Hugh Rawson and Margaret Miner

 GO ONLINE and listen to a podcast. Then add your comments to the discussion board.

ZOOM IN

8 What about you?

Task 1: Talk about a community you are a part of. What do you and other community members do together? How often?

Task 2: Write five sentences about chores you have to do. Say how often you do them.

Task 3: Find an image of a job you think is interesting. What experience does a person need for that job? What are the responsibilities?

9 Complete the chart.

	I did this well	I need more practice
Task 1		
Task 2		
Task 3		

Unit 4

VOCABULARY

1 Complete the sentences with words from the box.

perfect	typical	spicy	cream
sugar	energetic	sweet	frozen

¹ _____ candy has a lot of ² _____. For many people, the ³ _____ candy is a piece of chocolate. But not all candy is ⁴ _____! In the 1930s, "extreme candy" became popular. The Ferrara Candy Company started making Red Hots—small, red, ⁵ _____ candies. They made people's mouths burn. Today, there are even hotter candies. Children compete to see who can hold the most candies in their mouths for the longest time. These hot candies can make children even more ⁶ _____ than sugary candies!

—adapted from "Extreme Candy" in *The Oxford Companion to Sugar and Sweets*, edited by Darra Goldstein

2 Complete the sentences with the correct preposition (*on top of*, *beside*, *behind*, *under*, *over*).

1 I sat _____ a tall man at the movie theater. I couldn't see the movie.
2 I sat _____ an extremely interesting woman on the plane. We talked for hours.
3 Look at the moon _____ the ocean. It's so beautiful!
4 There's a great little restaurant _____ that mountain.
5 Some whales can stay _____ water for two hours.

 GO ONLINE to play the vocabulary game.

GRAMMAR

3 Complete the sentences with *How much* or *How many*. Then choose the correct words.

A: I'm going shopping for the picnic. ¹ _____ tomatoes do we need?
B: Just *a few* / *a little*. We already have some in the refrigerator.
A: OK. And ² _____ lemonade should I buy?
B: Please get *a lot* / *a little*. It's going to be really hot on Saturday.
A: And…let's see… ³ _____ plates should I get?
B: *Lots of* / *A few* people are coming to the picnic, so get about 50.

4 Work with a partner. Draw a room. Don't show the drawing to your partner. Your partner will ask questions with *Is there…* and *Are there…* and try to draw the room.

A: Is there a table?
B: Yes, there is.
A: Are there any books on the table?
B: No, there aren't.

 GO ONLINE to play the grammar game.

DISCUSSION POINT

5 Read the quote. Do you agree that variety is important? Why or why not?

"Variety's the very spice of life, That gives it all its flavour."

—William Cowper (British poet), selected from *Oxford Dictionary of Quotations*, 8ᵗʰ ed., edited by Elizabeth Knowles

 **GO ONLINE and listen to a podcast. Then add your comments to the discussion board.**

ZOOM IN

6 What about you?

Task 1 Talk about your favorite experience eating a meal.
Task 2 Write about your favorite meal.
Task 3 Find a photo of an extreme room. Describe it to your classmates.

7 Complete the chart.

	I did this well	I need more practice
Task 1		
Task 2		
Task 3		

Unit 5

VOCABULARY

1 Complete the sentences.

build	sell	make	grow	bake

1 Your store is far from where I live. Do you _____ your art online, too?
2 We can't _____ our own vegetables because we live in an apartment building.
3 My roommate loves to _____. We always have fresh cakes, cookies, and bread to eat!
4 I'm learning how to _____ my own clothes.
5 My brother plans to _____ a new house. Right now, he's buying the wood and other materials.

2 Choose the best time expression for each sentence.

1 I'm eating lunch *sometimes / these days / at the moment*. Can I call you back in an hour?
2 My sister *right now / today / often* goes to art museums and galleries.
3 *These days / Never / Today* I live with a roommate.
4 My friend and I are working on a creative project *always / right now / never*.
5 *Today / These days / Sometimes* I'm baking a big cake for my friend's birthday.

3 Match the words to the definitions.

develop	design	organize	event
program	decorate	improve	

1 grow slowly, increase, or change into something else _____
2 make something look more attractive by adding things to it _____
3 become better or make something better _____
4 give a set of instructions to a computer _____
5 put or arrange things into a system or order _____
6 something important that happens _____
7 a way of dressing or doing something that people like and try to copy for a time _____

 GO ONLINE to play the vocabulary game.

GRAMMAR

4 Choose the correct form of the verb.

1 Today we're *study / studying / to study* for a big test.
2 I'd like *learn / learning / to learn* how to build and program a robot.

3 What do you *do / doing / to do* for fun?
4 My friend often *bakes / baking / to bake* cakes.
5 We decided not *took / taking / to take* the class.
6 My phone isn't *work / working / to work* at the moment.

5 Complete the paragraph with the correct verb forms.

Sarah is not a professional artist, but she
[1] _____ (enjoy) DIY projects. She [2] _____ (make) beautiful things like handmade birdhouses, jewelry, and clothes. She'd [3] _____ (like/decorate) cakes, too, but sadly, Sarah [4] _____ (not be) very good at baking. Right now, she [5] _____ (take) a drawing and painting class because she [6] _____ (want/improve) her art skills. Also, she [7] _____ (painting) her living room walls, and she [8] _____ (plan / add) some of her own special designs.

 GO ONLINE to play the grammar game.

DISCUSSION POINT

6 Read the quote. What do you think it means? Do you think it's true? Discuss with a partner.

 "You can't use up creativity. The more you use, the more you have."
—Maya Angelou, selected from *Oxford Essential Quotations*, 5th ed., edited by Susan Ratcliffe

 GO ONLINE and listen to a podcast. Then add your comments to the discussion board.

ZOOM IN

7 What about you?

Task 1 Talk about a skill you'd like to learn. Why do you want to learn it?

Task 2 Write three sentences about something creative that you do. How often do you do it? Are you good at it?

Task 3 Find an image of an interesting event from your life. Describe what's happening in the picture.

8 Complete the chart.

	I did this well	I need more practice
Task 1		
Task 2		
Task 3		

Unit 6

VOCABULARY

1 Where should each person go? Write the correct place next to each sentence.

department store   grocery store   ATM   gym
bakery   farmer's market

1   I need some milk, cereal, and meat. _____
2   I want to buy fresh fruits and vegetables. _____
3   I want to buy some bread. _____
4   I need to get some money. _____
5   I want to exercise. _____
6   I need some new shoes. _____

2 Complete the paragraph with the correct words from the box.

afford   view   go abroad   adventure
guided tour   relax

This summer, I'm going to _____ for the first time! I'm taking a vacation to Gyeongju, South Korea. I can't _____ a hotel, so I'm going to stay with some friends. Their apartment has a beautiful _____ of the city. One day, I'm going to take a(n) _____ of the old part of the city. Another day, I'm going to _____ in a park. My vacation will be an exciting _____!

3 Complete the sentences with the adverb form of the adjective in parentheses.

1   Read your article _____ (careful). Correct any grammar mistakes.
2   The cars in the Grand Prix drive very _____ (fast).
3   The elevator got to the top floor of the hotel _____ (quick).
4   Harriet speaks Spanish really _____ (good).
5   Please speak more _____ (slow). I can't understand you.

 GO ONLINE to play the vocabulary game.

GRAMMAR

4 Choose the correct word or phrase to complete each sentence.

1   I *have to / can* clean my apartment today. My parents are visiting tomorrow.
2   You *don't have to / can't* buy milk. We already have some.
3   We *can't / shouldn't* go to that restaurant tonight. It's closed on Mondays.

4   *Do I have to / Should I* visit that museum? Is it interesting?
5   You *can / should* have a room with a water view or a garden view.

5 Correct the errors.

1   You should to go to that bakery. It has great bread.
2   He doesn't has to get up early tomorrow. It's Saturday.
3   You can taking the bus or the subway.
4   Has Anna to work tomorrow?
5   Carla should studies for the test tonight.

 GO ONLINE to play the grammar game.

DISCUSSION POINT

6 Read the quote. Do you agree or disagree with it? Have you visited a country without knowing the language? Share your ideas with the class.

 "No man should travel until he has learned the language of the country he visits."
—Ralph Waldo Emerson (American writer), selected from *Oxford Dictionary of American Quotations*, 2nd ed., edited by Hugh Rawson and Margaret Miner

 GO ONLINE and listen to a podcast. Then add your comments to the discussion board.

 **ZOOM IN**

7 What about you?

Task 1 Talk about your neighborhood. What can you do there? What do you like and dislike about it?

Task 2 Write about a place you want to visit. What can you do there?

Task 3 Find a photo of a place you know well. Tell your partner about it. What should your partner do if they visit?

8 Complete the chart.

	I did this well	I need more practice
Task 1		
Task 2		
Task 3		

Unit 7

VOCABULARY

1 Complete the sentences with the word from the box.

became	married	encouraged
failed	discovered	succeeded

1 My cousin _____ my best friend last weekend.
2 In 2015, scientists _____ water on the planet Mars.
3 John Jackson's friends _____ him to become a professional climber.
4 Ada Lovelace _____ at writing the first computer program.
5 Brandon Stanton _____ interested in photography when he was in his 20s.
6 I started a software company, but it _____ after only a year. Now I work at a big company.

2 Choose the correct word(s).

1 *When / While* my friend Elena was a child, she loved to play soccer.
2 *In / On* 2005, she started taking private soccer lessons.
3 *Ago two weeks / Two weeks ago*, she became a professional soccer player!
4 *Last / The last* week, I went to her first soccer game.
5 *In / On* Saturday, we went out to dinner to celebrate.

 GO ONLINE to play the vocabulary game.

GRAMMAR

3 Complete the paragraph with *was, wasn't, were,* or *weren't*.

When I ¹_____ a child, my best friend ²_____ my neighbor Sam. He ³_____ in my class at school because I ⁴_____ a year older, but we ⁵_____ always together after school and on weekends. There ⁶_____ a pool in our neighborhood, and we went there together almost every day in the summers. And our parents ⁷_____ friends, so we usually went on vacations together. I didn't see him as much in high school because we ⁸_____ interested in the same things. But we still talk on the phone about once a year.

4 Correct the errors.

1 Where they went rock climbing last weekend?
2 She canned read when she was only three years old.
3 Did he wrote that biography?
4 There were an interesting show on TV last night about the first computer programmers.
5 A: Did you study math in college?
   B: Yes, I studied.

 GO ONLINE to play the grammar game.

DISCUSSION POINT

5 Read the quote. What kind of person can change the world?

 "The people who are crazy enough to think they can change the world are the ones who do."
—Apple Computer Inc. TV ad, 1997, selected from *Oxford Dictionary of American Quotations*, 2ⁿᵈ ed., edited by Hugh Rawson and Margaret Miner

 GO ONLINE and listen to a podcast. Then add your comments to the discussion board.

ZOOM IN

Task 1 Talk about the life of a family member (alive or dead).
Task 2 Write a short biography of a family member.
Task 3 Find a photo of a famous person that you know a lot about. Tell the class about the person's life.

6 Complete the chart.

	I did this well	I need more practice
Task 1		
Task 2		
Task 3		

Unit 8

VOCABULARY

1 Complete the sentences with words from the box.

escaped	survive	save
searched	protect	pretend

1 People can't _____ without water.

2 My daughter likes to _____ she's a bird.

3 I _____ everywhere for my glasses but couldn't find them.

4 Maybe you should put your laptop in a bag to _____ it.

5 Some animals _____ from the zoo last night. They're walking around the city!

6 Police officers _____ three people after the accident. The officers pulled them out of their car.

2 Choose the correct word(s).

1 You shouldn't *fight with / make a promise to* your friends.

2 My kids *argue / hit each other* all the time. Why can't they use words to fix their problems?

3 Do you think he's *avoiding / forcing* me? He doesn't talk to me very much.

3 Write a sentence with each of the words and expressions in the box. Read the sentences to a partner, but say "beep" instead of the word or expression. Your partner guesses the word or expression.

suddenly	recently	immediately	to my surprise

_____

_____

_____

_____

 GO ONLINE to play the vocabulary game.

GRAMMAR

4 Complete the punctuation and capitalization rules. Then write one more rule with *must* and one with *must not* or *can't*.

1 Every statement *can't / must* end with a period.

2 You *must not / must* capitalize the names of countries.

3 You *can't / must* write a sentence without a verb.

4 Questions *must not / must* end with a period.

5 Complete the story with the simple past or past continuous form of the verb in parentheses.

Last night, I ¹ _____ (walk) home from work when I ² _____ (hear) two people talking loudly on the sidewalk. I ³ _____ (stop) and pretended to look in a store window. They ⁴ _____ (argue) about a movie. One person ⁵ _____ (like) it, and the other person ⁶ _____ (hate) it. They ⁷ _____ (be) very angry. Finally, one of them ⁸ _____ (walk) away. I would never argue on the street like that. I only argue at home!

 GO ONLINE to play the grammar game.

DISCUSSION POINT

6 Read the quote. What kind of news do you think is interesting?

"When a dog bites a man, that is not news. But when a man bites a dog, that is news."
—Charles A. Dana, selected from *The Oxford Dictionary Of American Quotations*, 2nd ed., edited by Hugh Rawson and Margaret Miner

 GO ONLINE and listen to a podcast. Then add your comments to the discussion board.

ZOOM IN

7 What about you?

Task 1 Talk about something surprising that happened to you.

Task 2 Write a list of rules for your family.

Task 3 Find a photo of yourself doing something interesting. What were you doing in the photo? Tell the class.

8 Complete the chart.

	I did this well	I need more practice
Task 1		
Task 2		
Task 3		

Unit 9

VOCABULARY

1 Complete the sentences by unscrambling the letters to make verbs.

1 What do you _____ about? (rywor)
2 Why do people try to _____ the future? (dtrepci)
3 Who do you _____ will be leader of your country in ten years? (ginamie)
4 What weather do you _____ tomorrow? (texpec)
5 Do you _____ robots will help people? (livebee)
6 Can you _____ how many questions you will answer correctly? (sgesu)

2 Choose the correct word.

1 We are going to go on vacation *by / in* a month.
2 A lot of my friends will look for jobs *after / next* their exams.
3 I hope to finish college *in / by* age 22.
4 What do you want to do *after / next* lunch?
5 We aren't going to be here *by / next* weekend.
6 I'm going to go out *after / in* a while.
7 *By / In* the future, most people will live in big cities.

 GO ONLINE to play the vocabulary game.

GRAMMAR

3 Put the words in the correct order to make sentences.

1 home / now. / I / I'll / think / go
2 a new phone? / to / you / going / buy / are
3 lots / lose / of / will / jobs. / people / their
4 tomorrow? / rain / it / will
5 become / going / robots / common. / are / to / more

4 Correct the error in each sentence.

1 I'm going buy a new computer next year.
2 I think food will going to become more expensive.
3 I don't think a robot will to replace my job.
4 Don't worry. Everything going to be fine.
5 Lots of people going to come here tomorrow.

5 Complete the paragraph with *a / an*, *the*, or no article.

Can ¹ _____ robot play music? *Yes* is
² _____ answer. Scientists at ³ _____ Waseda University created ⁴ _____ robot Wabot-2. It plays the piano with ⁵ _____ two hands and feet. ⁶ _____ robot also has ⁷ _____ mouth and ⁸ _____ ears, so it can have ⁹ _____ conversations with ¹⁰ _____

people. Honda Motor Company created ¹¹ _____ robot called Asimo. Asimo can play the trumpet and the violin. In 2008, Asimo even conducted ¹² _____ Detroit Orchestra! Toyota also has ¹³ _____ musical robots. These robots can play ¹⁴ _____ instruments such as the violin and ¹⁵ _____ drums. What else will ¹⁶ _____ robots do in ¹⁷ _____ future? Who knows?

—adapted from *The Grove Dictionary of Musical Instruments*, 2ⁿᵈ ed., edited by Laurence Libin

 GO ONLINE to play the grammar game.

DISCUSSION POINT

6 Read the quote and discuss this question: Can you think of someone who helped to invent the future? How did they do it?

 "The best way to predict the future is to invent it."
—Alan Kay (American computer scientist) in *Oxford Essential Quotations*, 5ᵗʰ ed., edited by Susan Ratcliffe

 GO ONLINE and listen to a podcast. Then add your comments to the discussion board.

ZOOM IN

7 What about you?

Task 1 Choose one of the topics and tell a partner how it will be different in ten years.

| cars | clothes | universities | computers | phones |

Task 2 Write 5–6 sentences about a place you like. Say how you hope it will and won't change in the future.

Task 3 Find an image that you think shows the future. Why? Describe it to the class.

8 Complete the chart.

	I did this well	I need more practice
Task 1		
Task 2		
Task 3		

155

Unit 10

VOCABULARY

1 Complete the sentences with *about, at, for, from, in,* or *of.*

1 I'm not afraid _____ flying.
2 I rarely feel nervous _____ speaking in public.
3 I would like to be great _____ playing a musical instrument.
4 I will never get tired _____ watching sports.
5 Parents are responsible _____ taking care of their children.
6 Visiting a country is different _____ living there.
7 I am interested _____ learning about everything.

2 Choose a word from the box to complete each sentence.

dancers	models	show	star
live	musician	stage	

1 A _____ is a very famous actor or actress.
2 Actors perform on a _____ in a theater.
3 A guitar player is one kind of _____.
4 Most _____ wear special shoes when they perform.
5 When you go to the theater, you get to watch a _____ performance.
6 The people in advertisements for clothing and jewelry are usually professional _____.
7 I'd be interested in seeing a magic _____.

 GO ONLINE to play the vocabulary game.

GRAMMAR

3 Complete the paragraph with the comparative form of the adjective or adverb.

Why did bicycles suddenly become popular in the 1890s? For one thing, a new type of tires made bicycles ¹_____ (comfortable) and ²_____ (easy) to pedal. A new type of frame made bicycles ³_____ (strong) and ⁴_____ (light). Mass production of bicycles also made them a lot ⁵_____ (cheap). Almost everyone could now afford a bicycle, and on these new bicycles, they could move ⁶_____ (fast) than almost any animal or machine.

—adapted from *The Oxford Encyclopedia of the Modern World* edited by Peter N. Stearns

4 Rewrite each sentence using the word(s) in parentheses.

1 Going to a fashion show is not as interesting as going to a basketball game. (less)
2 Being a model is easier than being a doctor. (not as...as)
3 Running is more tiring than walking. (less)
4 Dancing is more dangerous than acting. (not as...as)
5 Learning to ride a bicycle is more difficult than learning to swim. (not as...as)

5 Complete the sentences with the *-ing* form of a verb from the box.

breathe	exercise	think	throw	watch

1 _____ positively will help you perform better.
2 _____ correctly can help you relax.
3 I am not very interested in _____ rugby.
4 In basketball, you need to be good at _____ the ball.
5 _____ every day is one way you can improve your performance.

 GO ONLINE to play the grammar game.

DISCUSSION POINT

6 Read the quote. Is it better to promise less ("under promise") and do more than you promise ("over perform")? What example can you give to show this?

"Under promise. Over perform."
—Michael Eisner (chairman and CEO of the Walt Disney Company) in *The Oxford Dictionary of American Quotations,* 2nd ed., edited by Hugh Rawson and Margaret Miner

 GO ONLINE and listen to a podcast. Then add your comments to the discussion board.

ZOOM IN

7 What about you?

Task 1 Make a plan to improve your performance in one area of your life (study, work, sport). Tell a classmate what you are going to do.
Task 2 Write 5–6 sentences about an athlete, actor, or singer you like. What was their best performance?
Task 3 Find an image of someone performing in some way. Say what you like about their performance.

8 Complete the chart.

	I did this well	I need more practice
Task 1		
Task 2		
Task 3		

Unit 11

VOCABULARY

1 Choose *for* or *since* to complete the sentences.

1 People have known about Machu Picchu *for* / *since* a long time.
2 I've been interested in languages *for* / *since* I was in high school.
3 That coffee shop has been there *for* / *since* a while.
4 Chang has worked here *for* / *since* April.
5 They've lived in that apartment *for* / *since* last year.

2 Match the words to the definitions.

1 ___ method
2 ___ translate
3 ___ progress
4 ___ memory
5 ___ communicate
6 ___ culture
7 ___ goal
8 ___ meaning

a the process of improving
b a definition
c the customs, belief, art, and way of life of a country or group
d a way of doing something
e something that you hope to achieve
f your ability to remember things
g to change something from one language to another
h to share information with someone

 GO ONLINE for the vocabulary game.

GRAMMAR

3 Complete the paragraph with the present perfect form of the verbs in parentheses.

Clarissa [1] _____ only _____ (study) English for two years, but she speaks it pretty well. She [2] _____ (take) four English classes already. She [3] _____ just _____ (finish) Level 4, and she's taking Level 5 this semester. She [4] _____ never _____ (be) to the United States, but her goal is to study at an American college someday. However, she [5] _____ (not decide) yet which city she'd like to study in.

4 Correct the errors.

1 Have you ever did a parachute jump?
2 I known Ben for five years.
3 They've worked together for 2015.
4 I haven't never biked down a mountain.
5 Have they learned yet French?

 GO ONLINE for the grammar game.

DISCUSSION POINT

5 Read the quote. Do you think that older people do better work than younger people? Why or why not? Share your ideas with the class.

 "Age is nothing but experience, and some of us are more experienced than others."
—Andy Rooney, selected from *The Oxford Dictionary of American Quotations*, 2nd ed., edited by Hugh Rawson and Margaret Miner

 GO ONLINE and listen to a podcast. Then add your comments to the discussion board.

ZOOM IN

6 What about you?

Task 1 Talk about a place you have never visited but would like to visit. Why do you want to go there? What would you do there?

Task 2 Write about your experience learning a language. What methods worked well for you? What methods do you want to try?

Task 3 Find a photo of an exciting activity. Would you like to do the activity? Why or why not? Tell your classmates.

7 Complete the chart.

	I did this well	I need more practice
Task 1		
Task 2		
Task 3		

Unit 12

VOCABULARY

1 Complete the blog post. Use the words from the box.

storms	reduce	environment
climate	increase	rise

I think overpopulation is a big problem because it makes
¹_____ change worse. This has several negative effects.
First, the ²_____ in temperatures make the ocean level
³_____. This causes terrible ⁴_____ that kill people
and animals. If we want to save the ⁵_____, we must
slow population growth and ⁶_____ environmental
problems.

2 Complete each sentence with the noun form of the word
in parentheses.

1 I work for a big _____ (organize). It has about
1,000 employees.
2 If you want to be a boss, it's important to have good
_____ (manage) skills.
3 The teacher made a lot of _____ (correct) on
my paper.
4 I think we're going in the wrong _____ (direct). We
should be going north.
5 There was a lot of _____ (excite) in our house this
morning because we were packing for vacation.

3 Write the correct words.

luggage	passenger	gate	book a flight
pilot	take off		

1 This person flies a plane. _____
2 This means that the plane starts going into the air.
_____
3 You carry this when you travel. _____
4 You do this before you travel by plane. _____
5 This person rides in an airplane. _____
6 You wait here before you fly on a plane. _____

 GO ONLINE for the vocabulary game.

GRAMMAR

4 Complete the sentences with the correct form of the verb
in parentheses.

1 If it we don't protect the rainforests, many species
_____ (not survive).
2 When there's a bad snowstorm, the airport _____
(close).

3 When children _____ (be) in classrooms with older
children, they learn from them.
4 If I _____ (study) business, I'll get a good job after I
graduate.

5 Match the first and second parts of the sentences.

1 If I take that job,
2 When animals don't have enough water,
3 If the temperature increases,
4 If children have options,
5 When I'm sick,

a the sea level will rise.
b I'll get paid more money.
c I stay home from work.
d they die.
e they learn better.

 GO ONLINE for the grammar game.

DISCUSSION POINT

6 Read the quote. What kinds of things change in life?
Is change always a good thing?

 *"To live is to change, and to be perfect is to have
changed often."*
—John Henry Newman, selected from *Oxford Essential
Quotations*, 5th ed., edited by Susan Ratcliffe

 **GO ONLINE and listen to a podcast. Then add
your comments to the discussion board.**

ZOOM IN

7 What about you?

Task 1 Talk about a travel problem you experienced.
Task 2 Write about a decision you need to make. What are
your options? What do you think you will do?
Task 3 Find a photo that shows an environmental problem.
Describe the problem. What caused it? What are its
effects? How can people solve it?

8 Complete the chart.

	I did this well	I need more practice
Task 1		
Task 2		
Task 3		

 GO ONLINE for your personalized learning path.

Grammar focus

Unit 1

Have and has

FORM

I have a new phone.   *She has brown eyes.*

We form negative sentences with:

Subject + *don't/doesn't* + *have*

You don't have a cold.   *He doesn't have blond hair.*

We form *yes/no* questions with: *Do/Does* + subject + *have*...?

Does he have long hair?   *Do they have a dog?*

If the question is *Do you, Does he,* etc. *have...?*, we form short answers with *do/does*.

"Do you have breakfast every day?"   *"Yes, I do."* (NOT ~~Yes, I have.~~)

USE

We can use *have* to talk about things we own and family, friends, and pets.

I have a new phone.   *She doesn't have a big family.*

We use *have* to talk about habits and routines.

I have coffee every morning.   *Do you have breakfast every day?*

Be

FORM

Positive (+)	Negative (−)
I am / I'm happy.	I am / I'm not sad.
You are hungry.	You are not thirsty.
You're hungry.	You're not thirsty.
He/She/It is early.	He/She/It is not late.
He/She/It's early.	He/She/It isn't late.
We are students.	We are not teachers.
We're students.	We're not teachers.
They are Italian.	They are not Swiss.
They're Italian.	They're not Swiss.

USE

We use the verb *be* when we describe people or things.

He's tall.

We use the verb *be* to talk about age.

I'm eighteen.

Yes/no questions with *be*

FORM

We form *yes/no* questions with *be* with:

Am/Are/Is + subject...?

Are you free tomorrow?

We form short answers with:

Yes + subject + *am/are/is.*   *No* + subject + *am not/aren't/isn't.*

Short answers	
Positive (+)	**Negative (−)**
Yes, I *am*.	No, I'*m not*.
Yes, you *are*.	No, you *aren't*/you'*re not*.
Yes, he/she/it *is*.	No, he/she/it *isn't*/he/she/it'*s not*.
Yes, we *are*.	No, we *aren't*/we'*re not*.
Yes, they *are*.	No, they *aren't*/they'*re not*.

USE

We use the simple present to talk about routines, habits, facts, feelings, and opinions.

"Is it ten o'clock already?"   *"Yes, it is."*   *"No, it isn't."*

Wh- questions with *be*

FORM

We form *wh-* questions with the verb *be* with:

Question word + *be* + subject...?

Question word	*be*	subject	
Where	*are*	you	from?
Why	*is*	she	sad?

USE

We use different question words to ask about different types of information.

Question word	Information
What	things or activities
Who	people
When/What time	time
Where	places
How	way/manner
Why	reasons
How often	frequency

"Who's your teacher?" *"Ed Lewis."* *"Where are they?"* *"At home."*

 GO ONLINE for the complete grammar reference.

159

Unit 2

Possessive adjectives

FORM

Subject pronoun	Possessive adjective
I'm a twin.	*My* twin sister lives in Rio.
You're not in this class.	*Your* class is in room 401.
He's from a big family.	*His* brothers live in Singapore.
She's a good friend.	*Her* name is Jenna.
It's a typical town.	It's famous for *its* food.
We're fluent in Chinese.	*Our* father is from Shanghai.
They're my cousins.	*Their* names are Andy and Kevin.

USE

We use possessive adjectives with a noun to talk about things and people that belong to someone.

My sister lives in Rio.   *Your class is in room 401.*

His brothers lives in Singapore.   *Her name is Jenna.*

This restaurant is famous for its food.

Our father is from Shanghai.   *Their names are Andy and Kevin.*

We use *its* to talk about things and people that belong to a thing.

The city is famous for its universities. (NOT ~~The city is famous for their universities.~~)

Nouns: Countable, uncountable, and plural

FORM

Countable nouns are things that we can count. They can be singular or plural. We can use *a* or *an* with them.

a laptop → two laptops   an insect → lots of insects

Uncountable nouns are things we usually can't count. We don't use *a* or *an* with them and they are never plural.

rice (NOT ~~a rice~~)   *bread* (NOT ~~lots of breads~~)

Some and *any*

USE

We use *some* with plural countable nouns or uncountable nouns in positive sentences.

I'd like some pears and some jam, please.

We use *any* with plural countable nouns or uncountable nouns in negative sentences and questions.

I don't want any bananas.   *Do you have any honey?*

Uncountable nouns are things that we can't count. These include nouns for things, such as *furniture* and *luggage*, and nouns for ideas: *information, advice, news,* and *time.*

Possessive 's

FORM

    Singular *Sam's bicycle*

    Plural *Sam and Emma's house*   *my parents' friends*

             my children's toys

USE

We use possessive *'s* to say that something or someone belongs to a person, place, or thing. The possessive *'s* always comes after a noun.

Sam's bicycle   *the shop's customers*   *New York's nightlife*

When something belongs to more than one person and we give a list of names, we put *'s* on the last name.

Sam and Emma's house (NOT ~~Sam's and Emma's house~~)

With regular plural nouns we use *'* not *'s.*

They're my parents' friends. (NOT ~~They're my parent's friends.~~)

With irregular plural nouns we use *'s.*

They're my children's bicycles. (NOT ~~They're my childrens' bicycles.~~)

Possessive pronouns

FORM

Whose book is this? (**singular**)	
Possessive adjective	**Possessive pronoun**
It's *my* book.	It's *mine.*
It's *your* book.	It's *yours.*
It's *his* book.	It's *his.*
It's *her* book.	It's *hers.*
It's *our* book.	It's *ours.*
It's *your* book.	It's *yours.*
It's *their* book.	It's *theirs.*

Whose books are these? (**plural**)	
Possessive adjective	**Possessive pronoun**
They're *my* books.	They're *mine.*

USE

We use possessive pronouns instead of a possessive adjective + noun to talk about things we possess.

These are my books and those are yours.

Your coat isn't very warm. You can wear mine, if you like.

We use *Whose...?* to ask questions.

"Whose pen is this?"   *"It's mine."*

The form is the same for singular and plural.

"Whose pens are these?"   *"They're mine."* (NOT ~~They're mines.~~)

 GO ONLINE for the complete grammar reference.

Unit 3

Simple present: Positive and negative

FORM

Simple present positive (+)		
Subject	**verb**	
I/You/We/They	*cook*	on the weekend.
He/She/It	*cooks*	

Simple present negative (−)			
Subject	***don't/doesn't***	**infinitive without *to***	
I/You/We/They	*don't*	*like*	tea.
He/She/It	*doesn't*		

USE

We use the simple present to talk about routines and habits.

*I **study** every day.*   *She **plays** tennis on Saturdays.*

We also use the simple present to talk about facts, feelings, and opinions.

*He **doesn't speak** French.*   *Penguins **eat** fish.*

Simple present: *Yes/no* questions

FORM

Do/Does	**subject**	**verb**	
Do	you	*like*	your job?
Does	she	*get up*	early?

Short answers	
Positive (+)	**Negative (−)**
Yes, I *do*.	No, I *don't*.
Yes, he/she/it *does*.	No, he/she/it *doesn't*.

USE

We use the simple present to talk about routines, habits, facts, feelings, and opinions.

*"**Do** you **practice** the violin every day?"   "Yes, I **do**./No, I **don't**."*

Simple present and adverbs of frequency

FORM

*I **always** get up early.   I **don't always** have breakfast.*

We form questions with:

***How often** + do/does* + subject + verb?

How often do you go swimming?

USE

We use adverbs of frequency with the simple present to say how often we do something.

100%					0%
always	usually	often	sometimes	hardly ever	never

We don't use a negative verb with *hardly ever* or with *never*.

*You **hardly ever** write.* (NOT ~~You don't hardly ever write.~~)

*It **never** rains in the summer.* (NOT ~~It doesn't never rain in the summer.~~)

Subject and object questions in the simple present

FORM

In subject questions, the question word is the subject.

Subject + main verb + object?

Subject questions		
Subject	**main verb**	**object**
Who	likes	music?
Who	plays	football?
Answers		

In object questions, the question word is the object.

Object + auxiliary verb + subject + main verb?

Object questions			
Object	**auxiliary verb**	**subject**	**main verb**
Who	*do*	you	know?
What	*does*	she	play?
Answers			

USE

There are two types of *wh*-questions: subject questions and object questions

In object questions, the question word is the object.

We use *do/does* in the simple present.

*"**Who do** you **know** at this party?"   "I **know** Sarah and Kevin."*

*"**What does** Anna **play**?"   "She **plays** tennis."*

In subject questions, the question word is the subject. We don't use *do/does*.

*"**Who likes** music?"   "I **like** music."* (NOT ~~Who does like music?~~)

*"**Who plays** football?"   "Sam **plays** football."* (NOT ~~Who does play football?~~)

 GO ONLINE for the complete grammar reference.

Unit 4

How much/How many with countable and uncountable nouns

USE

We use *How much/How many* to ask about quantities of things or people.

> *How much cake is there?*
>
> *How many apples would you like?*

We use *How many* with countable nouns.

> *How many books does she have?*
>
> *How many cars are there?*

We use *How much* with uncountable nouns.

> *How much money do you need?*
>
> *How much cheese do you eat?*

We can answer with a short answer.

> *"How much money do you have?"   "A little./None."*
>
> *"How many stores are there?"   "A few./ A lot."*

Or we can answer with a full sentence, using a quantifier + noun.

> *"How much money do you have?"   "I don't have any money."*
>
> *"How many stores are there?"   "There are a lot of stores."*

Quantifiers: *A few/a little/a lot/lots*

FORM

Countable	Uncountable
a lot of / lots of books	*a lot of / lots of* homework
a few books	*a little* homework

USE

We use quantifiers before nouns to talk about quantities.

We use *a few* with countable nouns in positive sentences to talk about a small number of people or things.

> *I have a few books.*

We use *a little* with uncountable nouns to talk about a small amount of something.

> *We have a little time.*

There is... / *There are...*

FORM

	Singular	Plural	Uncountable
+	*There's* a gym.	There are two restaurants. There are some tomatoes.	*There's* some cake.
–	*There isn't a* shop.	*There aren't any* towels.	*There isn't* any cake.
?	*Is there a* gym?	*Are there any* towels?	*Is there* any cake?

USE

We use *There is / There are* to talk about things that are in a place.

> *There's a whiteboard in our classroom.*

We use *a/an* with singular countable nouns.

> *There's a movie theater but there isn't a playhouse.*

We use *There are* with plural countable nouns. We can use *some* when we don't want to say exactly how many.

> *There are two farms near us.*

We use *There aren't any* with plural countable nouns in negative sentences.

> *There aren't any good movies playing this week.*

We use *Is there...? / Are there...?* to ask about things in a place. We usually answer *yes/no* questions with short answers. We use *a/an* with singular countable nouns in questions.

> *"Is there a hospital in the town?"   "No, there isn't."*

We use *Is there...? / Are there...?* to ask whether something exists or not. We usually answer *yes/no* questions with short answers. We use *a/an* with singular countable nouns in questions.

> *"Is there a beach near here?"   "No, there isn't."*

We use *any* before plural nouns in questions.

> *"Are there any horses on the farm?"   "No, there aren't."*

We use *Is there + any...?* with uncountable nouns.

> *"Is there any tea?"   "Yes, there is."*

 GO ONLINE for the complete grammar reference.

Unit 5

Present continuous

FORM

We form the present continuous with:

Subject + **be** + **-ing** form.

She's studying.

We form *yes/no* questions with:

Be + subject + *-ing* form?

Are we making a cake?

We form short answers with *be*.

"Are you getting the drinks?" *"Yes, I am."*

"Is he doing the dishes?" *"No, he isn't."*

We form *wh-* questions with:

Question word + *be* + subject + *-ing* form?

Question word	*be*	subject	*-ing* form	
What	*am*	I	doing?	
Where	*are*	you	going?	
Why	*is*	he/she/it	laughing?	
Who	*are*	we/you/they	talking	to?

USE

We use the present continuous to talk about actions happening now.

Andy is getting the dinner. What are you doing?

We're watching a movie.

"Is Lisa doing the dishes?" *"No, she isn't."*

We also use the present continuous to talk about the situation around now (today, this week, etc.).

I'm not going to school today. I don't feel well.

I'm not working today. I'm staying at home.

"Are the students going to college this week?" *"No, they aren't. They're studying in the library."*

Verbs + *to* infinitive

FORM

We sometimes use a second verb after a main verb.

Subject + verb + *to* infinitive...

Subject	verb	*to* infinitive	
I/We/They	*want*	*to play*	tennis.
You	*don't want*		
He	*needs*	*to buy*	a ticket.
She	*doesn't need*		

The first verb changes according to the subject or the tense. The *to* infinitive never changes.

Sarah wants to read her book. (NOT ~~Sarah wants to reads her book.~~)

Sam wanted to play tennis. (NOT ~~Sam wanted to played tennis.~~)

USE

We use a *to* infinitive after these verbs: *want, need, would like,* and *like*.

We use *want* or *would like* + *to* infinitive to talk about our wishes.

Sarah wants to play the piano.

I'd like (= I would like) to visit Venice.

We use *need* + *to* infinitive to talk about actions or results that are necessary.

I need to buy a ticket.

Anna needs to pass her test.

We use *like* + *to* infinitive to talk about activities that we like or don't like when we want to say when (*in the morning/ afternoon*) or how often (*every day/week*).

Sue likes to swim every day.

Andy likes to go to the theater in the evening.

Simple present and present continuous

FORM

Present continuous	Simple present
I*'m wearing* a jacket today.	I *often wear* a jacket.
You *aren't wearing* shoes.	You *never wear* shoes at home.
She *is studying* at home today.	She *doesn't usually study* at home.

USE

We use the present continuous to talk about something happening now or around now (today, this week).

We're watching a movie. We aren't waiting for Kevin.

"What is he wearing today?" *"Jeans."*

We use the simple present to talk about habits or routines, and things that happen all the time.

In the evenings I study or go out with my friends. I don't often watch TV.

"What does he usually wear in the office?" *"A business suit."*

 GO ONLINE for the complete grammar reference.

Unit 6

Have to and *don't have to*

FORM

We use *have/has to* with an infinitive.

Subject + **have/has to** + infintiive.

Positive (+)

I/You/We/They *have to* go home now.

He/She/It *has to* make dinner.

In negative sentences, we use *don't/doesn't have to*.

Negative (-)

I/You/We/They *don't have to* pay for this course.

He/She/It *doesn't have to* get up early.

We use *do/does* with *have to* to form questions.

Do/Does + subject + *have to* + infinitive?

Questions (?)

Do I/you/we/they *have to* do this exercise?

Does he/she/it *have to* do this exercise?

We often give short answers to questions with *have to*.

"**Do I have to wait for them?**" "*Yes, you do.*" (NOT ~~Yes, you do have.~~)

"**Does he have to go to Boston tomorrow?**" "*No, he doesn't.*" (NOT ~~No, he doesn't have.~~)

USE

We use *have to* to talk about rules. (It is necessary.)

All students **have to take** one foreign language.

He **has to** call his sister.

"**Do I have to read this book?**" "*Yes, you do.*"

We use *don't/doesn't have to* when there is a choice. (It is not necessary.)

I **don't have to get up** early tomorrow.

"**Does she have to come with us?**" "*No, she doesn't.*"

Can for possibility

FORM

We use an infinitive without *to* after *can* and *can't*.

Subject + **can/can't** + infinitive without *to*.

+ I/You/He/She/It/We/They *can* go to the museum.

- I/You/He/She/It/We/They *can't* see the doctor now.

Can't is the short form of *cannot*. We usually use the short form, but we sometimes use the full form in formal writing.

To form questions, we change the order of *can* and the subject.

Can + subject + infinitive without *to*?

Questions (?)

Can I/you/he/she/it/we/they take a train to New York?

Can I/you/he/she/it/we/they hear the traffic outside?

We usually answer *yes/no* questions with short answers.

"**Can you hear the traffic outside?**" "*Yes, I can.*"

"**Can we take a train to New York?**" "*No, you can't.*"

USE

We use *can* and *can't* to talk about abilities and possibilities. A possibility is a thing that you can do at a particular time because of the situation you are in.

*We **can take** the 6 o'clock train.* (= It is possible for us to take the 6 o'clock train – we have enough time to get to the station before it leaves.)

We use *can* to ask *yes/no* about possibilities.

"**Can we stay one more night?**" "*No, I'm sorry – you can't.*"

Should/Shouldn't: Advice

FORM

We use *should/shouldn't* with an infinitive without *to*. The form of *should/shouldn't* is the same for every subject.

Subject + **should/shouldn't** + infinitive without *to*.

*You **should** wear a coat.*   *He **shouldn't** stay up late.*

To form questions, we change the order of *should* and the subject.

Should + subject + infinitive without *to*?

***Should** we exercise more?*

We often use short answers with questions that begin with *should*.

"**Should I buy this T-shirt?**" "*No, you shouldn't.*"

"**Should I exercise more?**" "*Yes, you should.*"

What/When/Where/Who (object)/*Why/How* + *should* + subject + infinitive without *to*?

Who (subject) + *should* + infinitive without *to*?

*What **should** I wear to the party?*

USE

We use *should/shouldn't* to give advice and ask for advice.

*Your cough sounds bad – you **should** see a doctor.*

*You **shouldn't** drive so fast in the rain.*

"**Should I invite Tom to the party?**" "*Yes, you should./No, you shouldn't.*"

 GO ONLINE for the complete grammar reference.

Unit 7

Simple past: *Be*

FORM

Was and *wasn't* (*was not*) are the past forms of *is, isn't, am,* and *am not.*

Were and *weren't* (*were not*) are the past forms of *are* and *aren't.*

Positive (+) and negative (-)

+ I/He/She/It *was* at home.
- I/He/She/It *wasn't* at home.
+ You/We/They *were* in class.
- You/We/They *weren't* in class.

To form questions, we change the order of the subject and *be.*

Yes/no questions

"Were they in class yesterday?" *"Yes, they were."*

"Was it cold in Norway?" *"No, it wasn't."*

Wh- questions

"What was your last job?" *"I was a teacher."*

"When were they born?" *"In 1998."*

USE

We often use *was/were* with past time expressions, e.g., *last week, in 2003, 500 years ago, yesterday.*

They were at school two hours ago. *It **wasn't** very hot yesterday.*

There was... / There were...

FORM

There was and *There were* are the simple past forms of *There is* and *There are.*

USE

We use *There was/wasn't* to talk about things in a place in the past.

We use *Was there / Were there* to ask about things in a place in the past.

Simple past: Positive

FORM

We add *-ed* to form the simple past of most regular verbs. The form of the simple past is the same for every subject.

I/You/We/They/He/She/It *lived* in Vietnam.

FORM

With irregular verbs, we do not add *-ed* for the simple past form. There are no rules. They all have different forms.

The simple past is the same for every subject (*I, you, he,* etc.) for both regular and irregular verbs, except for the verb *be.*

I/You/We/They/He/She/It *came* home.

USE

We use the simple past to talk about finished actions and states in the past.

*She **finished** all her homework.*

When we use the simple past, we often say when the action happened, e.g., *last winter, in 1999, ten minutes ago.*

*I **made** dinner last night.*

Simple past: Negative

FORM

We form the simple past negative with:

Subject (*I, you, he,* etc.) + ***didn't*** + infinitive without ***to.***

+ I **felt** sad when I left home.
– I **didn't feel** sad when I left home.
+ She **walked** to school on Monday.
– I **didn't walk** to school on Monday.

We usually use the short form (*didn't*), but we sometimes use the full form (*did not*) in formal writing.

USE

We use the simple past to talk about finished actions and states in the past.

*He **didn't leave** the house in the evening.*

Simple past questions

FORM

We form simple past *yes/no* questions with:

Did + subject + infinitive without ***to?***

Did I/he/she/it/you/we/they *visit* London?

Did I/he/she/it/you/we/they *read* about Egypt?

The form is the same for every subject (*I, you, he,* etc.).

Notice that the main part of the verb is the infinitive without to (*visit*), not the simple past form (*visited*).

Did you visit the Grand Canyon? (NOT ~~Did you visited the Grand Canyon?~~)

We form simple past *wh-* questions with:

Question word + ***did*** + subject + infinitive without ***to?***

What did you do there? *When did* he leave?

The form is the same for every subject (*I, you, he,* etc.).

USE

We use the simple past to talk about actions in the past.

"Did you go on vacation last summer?" *"Yes, I did."*

We use the simple past to talk about finished actions and states in the past.

"Why did they take the train?" *"Because it was cheaper."*

 GO ONLINE for the complete grammar reference.

Unit 8

Must and *must not/can't*

FORM

We use *must* with an infinitive without *to*. The form of *must* is the same for every subject.

Subject + **must** + infinitive without **to**.

> We **must** finish all the homework.

To form the negative, we use *must not/can't*.

Subject + *must not/can't* + infinitive without *to*.

> You **must not/can't** use cell phones in class.

USE

We use *must* to talk about what it is necessary to do (obligation).

> I **must** go to bed earlier.

We use *must not* or *can't* to talk about what it is necessary not to do.

> You **can't** tell Sarah—it's a secret.

Be careful! In this meaning, *can't* is not the opposite of *must*. If you want to say that it is not necessary to do something, use *don't/doesn't have to*. Compare these sentences.

> You **must** pay Jack for the work he's done.
> You **don't have to** pay Jack—I've already paid him.
> You **can't** pay Jack—he hasn't done any work yet.

We usually form questions with *have to*, not with *must*.

> "**Do we have to** do all the exercises?" "Yes, you do." (NOT ~~Must we do all the exercises?~~)

Past continuous: Positive and negative

FORM

We form the past continuous with:

Subject + **was/were** + **-ing** form.

> I **was** running. We **were** talking.

We form the negative with *wasn't/weren't*.

Subject + **wasn't/weren't** + **-ing** form.

> You **weren't** hiding. She **wasn't** shouting.

We usually use the short forms *wasn't* and *weren't* but we use the full forms in formal writing.

USE

We use the past continuous to talk about being in the middle of an action at a time in the past.

> At 8 o'clock last night I **was** watching TV.
> You **weren't** listening to the teacher when she asked the question.

We often use the past continuous to describe a scene, especially at the start of a story.

> The sun **was** shining and the birds **were** singing.

Past continuous: Questions

FORM

We form *yes/no* questions with the past continuous with:

Was/Were + subject + **-ing** form?

> **Was** I arguing? **Were** we talking?

We form *wh*-questions with the past continuous with:

Question word + **was/were** + subject + **-ing** form?

> **What were** you doing in the mountains?
> **Why was** she climbing a tree?

USE

We use the past continuous to talk about being in the middle of an action at a time in the past.

> "**Was** it raining when you left?" "Yes, it was."
> "**What were** you doing at 3 p.m. on Wednesday?" "I **was** watching TV."

Simple past and past continuous

FORM

Past continuous	Simple past
Action in progress	*Completed action*
He **was riding** his bike.	He **fell off** and **broke** his arm.
They **were arguing**.	They **didn't go out** together last night.

USE

We use the past continuous to talk about being in the middle of an action at a time in the past.

> She **was playing** volleyball when she fell and broke her leg.
> When I got home, they **were talking** in the kitchen.

We use the simple past for finished actions and states.

> I **made** a cake this morning.
> J.K. Rowling **wrote** the Harry Potter books.

We often use the simple past and the past continuous together for actions that happened at the same time. We use the past continuous for the longer action and the simple past for the shorter action.

> It **was raining** so I **called** a taxi.
> While I **was waiting** for you, I **made** a few phone calls.

 GO ONLINE for the complete grammar reference.

Unit 9

Going to and *will* for predictions

FORM

We can use *be going to* to make predictions.
Subject + *be* + *going to* + infinitive.

    We aren't going to have enough food for everyone.

    Is the planet going to be hotter?

We can use *will* and *won't* to make predictions:
Subject + *will/won't* + infinitive without *to*.

    Kevin will win the competition.   *Sarah won't be late.*

The form of *will* or *won't* is the same for every subject. In spoken English we usually use the short form of *will* with personal pronouns (*I'll, you'll, he'll*, etc.).

To form *yes/no* questions, we change the order of the subject and *will*.

    Will we be late?

We usually answer with a short answer.

    "Will there be cars without drivers?"   *"Yes, there will."*

USE

We use *be going to* to predict what will happen in the future, usually because something in the present makes it seem likely.

    Look at that black cloud! It's going to rain.

    She's going to have a baby.

We use *will* and *won't* to make predictions about the future.

    She'll win the tennis match tomorrow.

We often use *I think…* or *I don't think…* to introduce a prediction.

    I think you'll get a good job.

    I don't think he'll remember your birthday.

Going to and *will* for future plans and decisions

FORM

We use the form:
Subject + *be* + *going to* + infinitive.

    You're going to drive.

To form *yes/no* questions, we change the order of *be* and the subject:

Be + subject + *going to* + infinitive?

    Are we going to go out?

We usually answer with a short answer.

    "Are you going to walk to work tomorrow?"   *"Yes, I am."*

We form *wh*-questions with:

Question word + *be* + subject + *going to* + infinitive?

    What are you going to do this summer?

We can use *will* and *won't* to make decisions:

Subject + *will/won't* + infinitive without *to*.

    +   *I'll call* Mom.

    -   *I won't go* shopping.

The form of *will* or *won't* is the same for every subject. In spoken English we usually use the short form of *will* with personal pronouns (*I'll, you'll, he'll*, etc.).

USE

We use *be going to* to talk about future plans and intentions.

    I'm going to visit my aunt in the hospital.

    "How are we going to celebrate your birthday?"   *"We're going to have a party."*

We often use *be going to* with future time expressions, e.g., *tomorrow, next week, tonight, next year,* etc.

    "Are you going to bicycle to work tomorrow?"   *"Yes, I am."*

We use *will/won't* when we make a decision at the moment of speaking.

    "We're going to be late."   *"OK. I'll text Mom."*

    "Jenna will be here in a few minutes"   *"OK. I won't go shopping now."*

A/an, the, and no article

FORM

	article	adjective (optional)	noun	
I'm	a		student.	
She's	an	English	teacher.	
Lima is	the		capital	of Peru.
Kate has		two	children.	

USE

The first time we talk about one person or thing, we use *a* or *an* + singular noun.

    I'm a student.   *She's an English teacher*

The first time we talk about people or things using a plural noun, we use no article.

    Kate has two children.   *I like cats.*

We use *the* to say "you know which one(s) I mean"…

…when we have already talked about it/them.

    Sam lives in an apartment in a large city. The apartment has three rooms

…when we make it clear in the sentence.

    The stores on my street are expensive.

…when there is only one.

    Lima is the capital of Peru.

We use no article for names, cities, streets, and most countries.

    Lisa is going to Germany next week.

We use no article for meals, times, and days.

    We had dinner at eight on Friday.

 GO ONLINE for the complete grammar reference.

Unit 10

-ing forms

FORM

The *-ing* form can be the subject of the verb.

> *Having dinner with friends is fun.*

USE

We can use the *-ing* form of the verb like a noun.

> *Running is my favorite sport.*

We can also use the *-ing* form after some adjectives + prepositions to talk about likes, abilities, and interests.

> *Sarah's **afraid of failing***
>
> *Sam's **good at playing** football.*

We can use the *-ing* form as the subject. The *-ing* form on its own can be the subject…

> *Running Is good for you.*

…or the *-ing* form + phrase can be the subject.

> *Eating junk food is bad for you.*

Comparative adverbs

FORM

For most adverbs ending in *–ly* or *–ily*, we form the comparative with *more*.

For adverbs with the same form as the adjective, we add *-er*.

Comparative adverbs		
adverbs that end in *-ly* or *-ily*	*more* + adverb	quietly → *more quietly* easily → *more easily*
adverbs with the same form as the adjective	add *-er*	fast → *faster* hard → *harder*

Some adverbs have two different forms: one like a regular adverb (e.g. *quickly*); and one that is the same as the adjective (e.g. *quick*). These adverbs also have two different comparative forms.

> *My sister eats ice cream **more quickly / quicker** than me.*

Some adverbs are irregular and have an irregular comparative form.

Adjective	Adverb	Comparative adverb
good	well	better
bad	badly	worse

USE

We use comparative adverbs with *than* to say that a person or a group does things in a different way from another person or group.

> *The girls play **more quietly than** the boys.*

Negative comparatives and superlatives: *Less* and *least*

FORM

We form negative comparative adjectives with *less*.
We form negative superlative adjectives with *the least*.

Adjective	Comparative	Superlative
expensive	less expensive	the least expensive
interesting	less interesting	the least interesting

USE

We use *less* + adjective + *than…* to say that a person or thing is different from another person or thing because it has less of a particular quality.

> *Computers are **less expensive than** cars.*

We can also use *less* without *than* when it is clear what we are comparing.

> *I prefer tennis to baseball. Baseball is **less exciting.***

We use *the least* + adjective to say that a person or thing is different from the group it belongs to because it has less of a particular quality.

> *Water and milk are **the least expensive** drinks.*

Comparative adjectives: *As…as*

FORM

We can form positive comparatives with *as…as….* We can form negative comparatives with *not as…as….*

Positive and negative					
	Subject + *be*	*as/not as*	adjective	*as*	
+	I'm	*as*	tall	*as*	Jack.
–	You're He's/She's/It's We're You're They're	*not as*	happy interesting		

USE

We use *as…as* when we want to say that people or things are same in a particular way.

> *Maya's **as tall as** Jack.*

We use *not as…as* when we want to say that people or things are different in a particular way.

> *My sister's **not as noisy as** my brother.*

 GO ONLINE for the complete grammar reference.

Unit 11

Present perfect with *for* and *since*

FORM

We can use the present perfect with *for* and a period of time.
We can use the present perfect with *since* and a date, day, time, or event.

> *I have been here for ten minutes.*

USE

We use the present perfect with *for/since* to talk about present activities that started in the past.

We use *for* to talk about the period of time up to the present, e.g., *for four years, for two days*.

> *The company has been in business for four years.*

We use *since* to talk about the time when an activity started, e.g., *since 2013, since yesterday, since I was ten years old*.

> *I've been here since 8 a.m.*
> *I've known Cathy since I was ten.*

Present perfect with *just*, *already*, and *yet*

FORM

We can use the present perfect positive with *just* or *already*:
Subject + *have/has* + *just/already* + past participle.

> *I have just arrived.*

We usually use short forms (*I've, You've, He's,* etc.) when we're speaking.

We can use the present perfect negative with *yet*:
Subject + *haven't/hasn't* + past participle + *yet*.

> *We haven't left yet.*

We can form present perfect questions with *yet*:
Have/Has + subject + past participle + *yet*?

> *Have you arrived yet?*

USE

We use the present perfect to talk about recent events or actions. We can use *just, already,* and *yet* in present perfect sentences.

We use *just* in positive sentences to talk about very recent events or actions.

> *I've just arrived.*

We use *yet* in questions and negative sentences to talk about events and actions up to now.

> *Have you called Mom yet?*

We use *already* in positive sentences to talk about events and actions that happened before now or earlier than expected.

> *The party has already finished.*

Present perfect: Negative and *never*

FORM

We form the present perfect negative with:
Subject + *haven't/hasn't* + past participle.

> *She hasn't had swimming lessons.*
> *They haven't sent the email.*

We can also form the present perfect negative with *never*:
Subject + *have/has* + *never* + past participle.

> *I have never eaten Japanese food.*

We usually use short forms (*I've never, You've never, He's never, She's never, We've never, They've never*) when we are speaking.

USE

We use the present perfect negative to talk about life experiences that did not happen.

> *I haven't had swimming lessons.*

We can also use *never* to emphasize that something did not happen. It means "at no time in your life."

> *Mike has never visited New York.*

We also use the present perfect negative to talk about recent events or actions that didn't happen.

> *They haven't done their homework.*

Present perfect: *Yes/no* questions and *ever*

FORM

We form present perfect *yes/no* questions with:
Have/has + subject + (*ever*) + past participle?

> *Have you ever played in a band?*

We form short answers with:
Yes + subject + *have/has*.
No + subject + *haven't/hasn't*.

USE

We use present perfect questions to ask about life experiences.

> *Have you seen that movie?*

We often use *ever* with present perfect *yes/no* questions about life experiences. *Ever* means "at any time in your life."

> *Have you ever played in a band?*

We also use present perfect questions to ask about recent events or actions.

> *Has she passed her test?*

We usually answer with a short answer.

> *"Have you ever taken guitar lessons?"   "Yes, I have."*

 GO ONLINE for the complete grammar reference.

Unit 12

Zero conditional

FORM

We form the zero conditional with *if* clause + result clause.

We form the *if* clause with *If* + simple present.

We form the result clause with the simple present.

if clause		result clause
If	**simple present**	**simple present**
If	you *heat* water,	it *boils*.

USE

We use the zero conditional to talk about events and the results that always follow.

If you heat water, it boils.

We usually put the *if* clause before the result clause, with a comma after the *if* clause.

If you press that button, the alarm rings.

We can put the result clause before the *if* clause. We don't use a comma after the result clause.

Water boils if you heat it.

We can sometimes use *when* instead of *if* with the same meaning.

When you heat water, it boils.

First conditional

FORM

We form the first conditional with:

if clause + result clause. (OR result clause + *if* clause.)

We form the *if* clause with:

If + subject + simple present.

We form the result clause with:

subject + *will/won't* + infinitive without *to*.

	if clause		result clause	
	If	**simple present**	**will/ won't**	**infinitive without to**
+	If	we *plant* trees,	we *'ll*	*help* the environment.
–	If	we *use* clean energy,	we *won't*	*harm* the environment.

USE

We use the first conditional to talk about possible events and their results.

If we save energy, we'll reduce global warming.

We usually put the *if* clause before the result clause, and we use a comma after the *if* clause.

If we plant trees, we'll reduce carbon dioxide.

We can put the result clause before the *if* clause when the result is important. We don't use a comma after the result clause.

We'll reduce global warming if we save energy.

GO ONLINE for the complete grammar reference.